The
Newspaper

A Reference Book for Teachers and Librarians

The
Newspaper

A Reference Book for Teachers and Librarians

Edward F. DeRoche

ABC-CLIO

Library of Congress Cataloging-in-Publication Data

DeRoche, Edward F.
  The newspaper : a reference book for teachers and librarians /
Edward F. DeRoche.
    p.   cm.
  Includes bibliographical references (p.) and index.
  1. Newspapers in education—United States.   I. Title.
  LB1044.9.N4D38   1991   371.3′2—dc20   91-633

ISBN 0-87436-584-8 (alk. paper)

98 97 96 95 94 93 92 91   10 9 8 7 6 5 4 3 2 1

ABC-CLIO, Inc.
130 Cremona Drive, P.O. Box 1911
Santa Barbara, California 93116-1911

This book is printed on acid-free paper ∞ .
Manufactured in the United States of America

CONTENTS

5 Newspaper Curriculum Resources for Teachers and Librarians, 69

6 Newspaper Strategies for Teachers and Librarians, 127

7 Newspaper Names and Addresses, 167

PREFACE

For the past 20 years, the American Newspaper Publishers Association Foundation has promoted a nationwide program called Newspapers in Education (NIE).

There are about 500 newspapers in the United States and Canada participating in NIE programs that involve approximately 3,000,000 students, 90,000 teachers, and 16,000 schools each year.

This book is about NIE programs focusing on teaching-learning strategies, research, and resources. As such, it is a one-volume reference book for teachers, librarians, administrators, media specialists, and NIE coordinators.

This book is a time-saver. One of its values is the time it saves you from plowing through a plethora of materials about the newspaper as an instructional resource. It is a compendium of resources about newspapers in education that has yet to be found in one volume. What you will find in this reference book are answers to your questions about newspaper in education research, strategies for using newspapers to teach subject matter and other content, and information about the resources available to teachers and librarians.

Like most reference books, you don't have to read this book chapter by chapter. As the table of contents shows, most chapters are independent of one another. As a reader, you can refer to a specific chapter to answer your questions. However, chapter 1 should be read first because the content offers a rationale for using newspapers in education.

So, for the first time, there is a reference book that provides in one volume newspaper in education research, resources, and references. As such, it is a reference book that should be on your bookshelf.

This book is dedicated to my colleagues who over the years were responsible for enhancing the quality and popularity of newspaper in education programs. To name a few—Harold Schwartz, Stu Kendall, and Bob Tottingham; Sallie Whalen and Shirley Foutz; John Haefner and Merrill Hartshorn; Judy Hines, Marvin Maskovsky, Linda Skover, and Betty Sullivan; King Durkee and Kitty Rawlings.

Special recognition and thanks to the teachers at William B. Sweeney School, Willimantic, Connecticut, who in the late 1960s showed me the value of using newspapers to teach subject matter and to motivate students to read.

The Newspaper

A Reference Book for Teachers and Librarians

CHAPTER 1

Why Newspapers Should Be Used for Educating Children, Youth, and Adults

This chapter explores three reasons for using newspapers in education:

1. As a supplement to teaching and learning a variety of subject matter in schools.
2. As a text for improving reading and writing literacy.
3. As a resource for civic and global literacy.

Teaching and Learning Subject Matter

Let's begin with the first reason, newspapers as a supplement to teaching and learning subject matter, and look at five ways newspapers help teachers and learners.

Motivation. Why does newspaper use motivate students to learn subject matter? Teacher testimony has presented a variety of reasons.

First, newspapers contain interesting things to read. School-age learners enjoy reading the comics, the entertainment pages, and the sports pages. With some encouragement from teachers, they come to value the news and editorial pages.

Second, children and teenagers perceive newspapers as a medium that adults read and use. Thus, such modeling suggests to them that there is value in reading a newspaper.

Third, newspaper use in classrooms is a good bridge between home and school. Creative teachers have used the newspaper as a means of getting parents involved in the learning that their children are pursuing at school. Parents feel more comfortable with a newspaper than with a textbook. Many teachers send home newspaper activities for parents to share with their children as a supplement to school work. When one sixth-grade teacher asked students what they liked about using newspapers, one responded, "It gave me and my Dad a reason to talk to one another."

Fourth, teachers report that students become far more interested in newspaper content than in traditional school texts. That is, the newspaper is a text of real-life problems that motivates students to learn the skills and content taught at each grade level.

Fifth, newspapers are a thinking person's medium. One reads the newspaper for a purpose—pleasure, information, problem solving, decision making. Its content contributes not only to learning the basic skills of reading, writing, and computing, but, when properly used by the teacher, it can be a major resource for helping learners with the higher-order thinking skills of comprehension, analysis, synthesis, evaluation, and application. Thus, motivating students to learn subject matter and the basic and higher-order thinking skills is a major reason for using newspapers as a useful supplement to teaching and learning.

Information. A second way newspapers help teachers and learners as a major instructional resource is through the information newspapers publish. First and foremost, the daily newspaper is a news medium that answers two basic information questions:

¶ What's going on? (News)
¶ What does it all mean? (Editorials/columns)

Of course, the newspaper provides other kinds of information through its columns, advertisements, special feature stories, and entertainment features. It is a medium that includes social, emotional, political, economic, and personal information. In other words, it has subject-matter content useful in mathematics, social studies, language arts, English, economics, geography, and science. In addition, the information is presented in words, sentences, paragraphs, pictures, cartoons, comics, graphs, charts, and maps, all of which are useful to a teacher and a classroom of learners.

Articulation. Articulation is a third way newspapers are useful in classrooms. Articulation means that newspaper content cuts across and brings together several subject matters and many skills.

Let's explain articulation by example. If a teacher uses a newspaper to teach reading skills, he or she also automatically teaches content. For example, should a teacher use political cartoons to teach the skills of comprehension and maybe the subskills of symbolism, satire, and hyperbole, the students will not be able to comprehend (get the main idea of the cartoon) without background information about the event or person in the cartoon. Thus, the teacher brings to the lesson and to the learner the articulation of content and skill development.

The example of the weather map may make the point even more strongly. Using the weather section of the newspaper, a teacher can articulate (bring together) geography, science, social studies, and mathematics. For example, in geography a teacher might teach map reading, location, longitude, and latitude, and relate these to the science concepts of fronts, pressure, symbols, and weather patterns. The teacher could also introduce mathematical concepts and the use of numbers, decimals, and the like.

As you can see, a teacher who carefully identifies the skills to be taught and subject matter to be learned can use this valuable instructional resource to help learners see the relationships between information and thinking, and between learning "school stuff" and real-world problem solving. That's articulation.

Appreciation. This is the fourth of the five ways newspapers help teachers and learners. When students come to appreciate the newspaper as a source of information and service, they will appreciate the importance of daily newspaper reading. When you as a teacher explore the many ways newspaper content can be a supplement to what you teach; when you learn to use this medium as a way to motivate and stimulate students, as a way to inform students, and as a means of articulating thinking skills and subject matter, then you will come to appreciate this powerful instructional resource.

To appreciate what the newspaper, as a service, can do for the reader both in problem solving and decision making, let's examine a problem. As we do this, you can think about the problem in terms of what your students could be learning as they attempt to solve similar problems.

Suppose you want to sell your piano. Your first problem is: What do you do? You might list many options. One choice is to place an ad in the classified ad section of your local newspaper. So, you've solved your first problem. But that decision leads to another problem: What do you say in the ad? Once you solve that problem you have to determine how long you want to run the ad and what the cost will be. Then, of course, you have the problem of deciding whether to stick to the asking price or negotiate with the potential buyer.

Do you see the point of this example? Using situations like this for learners helps you create multiple-step problems. Newspaper content helps your students learn multiple-level problem solving and decision making.

You and your students will come to appreciate the newspaper more and more as you use it on a daily basis. If you look at it as a 200–250-page textbook placed on your classroom doorstep each day, with varying content, then you come to realize its potential for teaching and learning content and skills.

Cooperation. The fifth way the newspaper is useful to teachers and learners is that it seems to change one's teaching style. Teachers say that, when using the newspaper, they tend to assign more project type work. They also group students to work in pairs or in small groups. Newspaper strategies seem to get students to discuss problems and issues more among themselves. Teachers say that newspaper strategies seem to lead students to work together to solve problems and complete projects. In other words, using teacher strategies based on newspaper content seems to cause students to cooperate with one another, to work together to get things done, to take responsibility for monitoring each other's work, and to contribute to a climate of cooperative learning in the classroom.

Summary. So far we have looked at five ways that newspapers help teachers and learners: motivation, information, articulation, appreciation, and cooperation. You should consider daily newspapers as an instructional supplement to the textbook. They can also be used as the main text that brings the real world into your classroom.

Now, let's briefly examine the other two reasons for using newspapers in education—reading and writing literacy, and civic and global literacy.

Reading/Writing Literacy

There is no need to restate here the statistics about the illiteracy rate in this country. The topic has been in the headlines ever since Jonathan Kozol published *Illiterate America* in 1985. An estimated 27 million people are labeled as functional illiterates, lacking reading, writing, and computational skills. One could add to these figures the number of nonreaders currently enrolled in elementary and secondary schools (the word "illiterate" usually refers to a nonreading adult). These nonreaders (a term I prefer to "illiterates") lack skills necessary to enhance their personal lives (reading for pleasure), solve their personal problems (reading for information), and contribute to their community (applying the skills of reading, writing, and computing).

Newspaper businesses serve two roles in helping reduce the number of nonreaders. First, they can promote public awareness of the problem in their communities by publishing human interest stories that depict nonreaders' problems in coping with day-to-day problems at home, on the job, and in the community. Secondly, through newspaper in education (NIE) managers, the newspaper business can mobilize, coordinate, and expand current NIE programs to include literacy education services. Some newspapers are doing this now, and their efforts are described in a booklet published by the American Newspaper Publishers Association (ANPA) Foundation, *Showcase of Newspaper Adult Literacy Projects* (1989).

Most, if not all, literacy programs should use the daily newspaper as the main text primarily for the reasons already stated. But there are other reasons as well. Newspapers, unlike most texts and workbooks used in literacy programs, do not stigmatize the nonreader and thus contribute to poor self-esteem. Rather, nonreaders can look to the newspaper as a resource used by other adults. Further, the variety of content found in newspapers is a major contributor to reading for a purpose as one learns how to read.

Many literacy programs use materials that lack relevant adult content and thus teach reading as if it were some abstraction divorced from thinking and from real-world problems and events. We need to teach nonreaders to learn to read, write, and compute in relation to the way they think. A newspaper has content worth thinking about. Most literacy training texts do not.

Also, a nonreader of any age needs instructional materials that raise his or her self-esteem, rather than materials that say, "You are a nonreader, so here are simple books with few words and large print that may help you."

Finally, it might be best if most agencies would use one instructional resource, the newspaper, and then train their tutors to use it with small groups of nonreaders. We don't have adequate resources to solve the problem through one-to-one tutoring. A single instructional resource, for the most part, would enable administrators, researchers, teachers, and tutors to establish some standards for instruction, monitor nonreader progress, and create some sense of accountability. These aspects are currently missing from the plethora of literacy programs operating in communities throughout the country.

Civic/Global Literacy

Study after study reports students' lack of geographical and historical knowledge. Our students do not know what's going on in today's world. In some studies, most students report that what they do know about the day's issues and events is gleaned from watching television news.

Another aspect of this dilemma is the need for young people and adults to better understand the ethnic and cultural diversity in this country, particularly as it reflects our cultural heritage and strengths.

How do daily newspapers play a role in civic and global literacy? First and foremost, understanding the events in this world requires more than television watching. One needs, at minimum, to read daily newspapers regularly to understand and respect the freedoms in the United States.

Using newspaper content to teach about the freedoms upon which our daily lives are based should be an essential part of social studies and literature classes throughout our schools. The daily newspaper is filled with information about people seeking these freedoms. Thus, we can use the newspaper to teach students about government, freedom, and what is required of citizens in a democracy.

Second, many civic issues should be studied using newspaper content. Five major issues that appear frequently in daily newspapers are those related to economics, politics, ecology, technology, and the quality of life.

Newspapers are only one of many resources that will enhance students' civic and global literacy. The newspaper's major advantage in this area is the fact that it updates content each day. It becomes a vehicle for providing current information on issues also found in textbooks, trade books, and reference books.

Chapter Summary

It has been said that the daily newspaper is an intergenerational instructional resource usable from preschools to prisons. As this chapter has illustrated, the newspaper is an excellent resource for supplementing the teaching and learning of subject matter. The content found in newspapers is valuable for developing younger and older learners' skills of reading and writing. Newspapers are also a good resource for those who wish to be literate regarding civic and global events and issues.

Let's underscore one important point before we examine the research in some detail. It is clear, as will be shown in the next two chapters, that young people who get in the habit of regular newspaper reading are likely to enhance their civic awareness and thus become better informed citizens. There are other benefits as well, but this fact alone makes newspaper in education programs worthy of our attention.

CHAPTER 2

Newspapers in Education Research: Surveys, Attitude Studies, Dissertations, and Theses

The story is told of four blind men having their first experience with an elephant.

The first one put his arm around the elephant's leg and reported, "An elephant is shaped like a large tree."

"No," said the second blind man. "It's like a snake with very coarse skin and a strange soft mouth." He felt the trunk.

The third swore, after feeling its ear, that an elephant was shaped like the sail of a boat.

Finally, the fourth insisted it was simply like an old piece of rope; he had grabbed the tail.

And so it is for newspaper in education research. What one perceives it to be, it is. Some say it is sparse and irrelevant. Others say that it tells an interesting story. Still others call for more comprehensive research with greater control of variables. Each reader will have to be the judge.

Surveys

Over the past 20 years, the progress and growth of newspaper in education programs have been gratifying. Those readers who were around in the 1960s will recall how many of us struggled to get the newspaper industry and school districts to view the newspaper as a valuable instructional resource.

What follows is a summary of two surveys about NIE programs, focusing on information about purpose, budget, circulation, services, and staffing.

The ANPA Foundation and the International Newspaper Promotion Association reported in June 1981 that more than one-half (907) of the newspapers in the United States had NIE programs. Among other findings:

¶ The major purposes of NIE programs were to build future readership, to serve the community, and to help promote awareness of freedom of the press.

¶ The greater the circulation, the greater the likelihood that a newspaper had an NIE program.

¶ The average NIE program was five years old, had a budget of more than $13,000, and involved 50 schools, 70 teachers, and 2,300 students.
¶ The average NIE program distributed about 39,000 newspapers annually to schools, with 68 percent charging schools one-half the normal newsstand price.
¶ Almost 75 percent of the NIE programs offered curriculum materials, about one-half offered filmstrips, and about 25 percent provided no instructional materials.
¶ Almost 40 percent of the programs had systematic methods of evaluating curriculum materials.
¶ About 66 percent conducted workshops for teachers and/or parents, with about half of the teacher workshops offered for college or in-service credit.

In 1989, Media General Research surveyed daily newspapers in North America to assess the level of sponsorship of newspaper in education programs. Of the completed questionnaires 97 percent were from newspapers in the United States. A summary of some of the major findings follows.

¶ There was a 6 percent increase in the percentage of newspapers reporting NIE programs since 1986. Most newspapers without NIE programs lack budget and staff to support such a program.
¶ In addition to distributing newspapers to schools, most NIE programs also provide instructional materials, newspaper tours, and guest speakers. Some newspapers offer free curriculum materials; others offer additional materials with a subscription.
¶ Two major reasons for NIE programs are cultivating future readers and providing a community service.
¶ Almost half of the respondents charge the schools one-half the newsstand price of a single copy of the newspaper while 20 percent charge one-half of the basic carrier price.
¶ About 75 percent of the newspapers offer college credit or district in-service credit through teacher workshops.
¶ More than one-third of the responding newspapers say they have adult literacy programs.
¶ There is a decline in both full-time and part-time staffing of NIE programs.
¶ The average NIE program budget, excluding salaries and newspapers, is $10,390. The median salary for the chief NIE staffer is $23,283, and the median annual salary outlay for the entire NIE staff is $25,361.

These highlights provide a picture of newspaper in education programs during the 1980s. But this picture is incomplete without the results of studies of the value of NIE programs to their participants.

The Newspaper Advertising Bureau (NAB) in 1977 surveyed 3,000 adults and queried half of them about their childhood exposure to newspapers. Forty-three percent of the sample reported that one or more of their teachers had regularly used a daily or Sunday newspaper in school as part of the classroom work or for assignments. Among those who had used the newspaper in school, two out of three are current subscribers. This positive influence showed up among blacks as well as whites, but it was more marked among blacks who had not had a newspaper at home.

The NAB, in a 1980 report titled *Daily Newspapers in American Classrooms* offered these highlights:

¶ Children start using newspapers in the early grades in school as part of learning how to read.

¶ By the time teenagers finish high school almost all of them have used newspapers for some assignments, and more than half used them in the current year, especially in social studies.

¶ The use of newspapers in school is more common among middle-class youngsters in higher-income, better educated families who have a newspaper at home.

¶ Parents and children of all ages have positive attitudes about newspaper use at school.

¶ Using newspapers in school has positive effects on the child's involvement with newspapers. That is, many more children like using newspapers in school than dislike it. Those who use it have less trouble reading the newspaper, have more positive attitudes toward newspapers, and are more likely to read it on their own.

¶ There is a positive relationship between the use of newspapers in school and children's social and political awareness.

¶ School use of newspapers reinforces the effects of living in a family with a daily newspaper. It also has been found to compensate to some degree for the irregular presence of a newspaper in the home.

A report in *Update NIE* (1980) regarding a survey by the Oklahoma Newspaper Advertising Bureau shows that people who read newspapers regularly are more likely to be active voters. The survey found that voters read more national, state, and local news than nonvoters. Editorials were read by 84.1 percent of the voters and 70.8 percent of the nonvoters. Voters were found to read newspapers more often than nonvoters, and women read newspapers more than do men and vote more than men.

Windhauser and Stone (1981) designed a study to determine whether students' exposure to newspapers in grade school or high school was related to increased use of newspapers in college. A total of 788 college students were asked about a wide range of newspaper reading habits with one specific question relating to childhood use: "Do you remember being in a program in high school or earlier where the newspaper was actually brought into class for pupils to read and made part of the regular classroom program?"

These researchers found, among other things, that early exposure to newspapers had more of an influence on the later readership of males than of females; that self-declared daily newspaper reading was higher for those exposed to newspaper in education programs; and that parental interaction with children about the newspaper is a strong influence on later readership by children.

Rhoades (1982) studied news media use by newspaper in education (NIE) and non–newspaper in education (non-NIE) students. The author used a sample of college students, a little over half of whom recalled using newspapers in their high school or earlier classes. It was found that, compared to the non-NIE group, the NIE group spent more time reading the newspaper; spent more time on the average each day reading news from all major news media; spent more time acquiring news; and had greater interest in news, and thus became more conscious of current events. Rhoades concludes that newspaper in education programs serve two of their major goals—increasing awareness of current events and promoting reading of newspapers.

The Dubuque *Telegraph Herald*'s 1983 newspaper in education coordinator surveyed fourth and fifth graders in two elementary schools to determine newspaper usage, awareness, and attitudes toward the local newspaper. The survey was taken after an experiment in which one school had served as the experimental newspaper-use group, using newspapers each week throughout the school year, and the other school served as the control group, not using newspapers. A few of the major findings showed that

¶ Three-fourths of the students in the experimental group read the Sunday newspaper nearly every week, while only two-thirds of the control group did so.

¶ Seventy-five percent of the experimental group students read the newspaper once per week or more.

¶ The students in the experimental group were more likely to read news about their town and other parts of the United States, and showed significantly greater interest in local government, neighborhood events, current issues, and foreign affairs.

¶ Sixty-seven percent of the control group was constant in reporting that they never read business news. The percentage of those in the experimental group who never read business news changed from 72.5 percent before the project to 59.4 percent after the project.

¶ While both groups reported difficulty reading the newspaper on the pretest, twice as many control-group students as experimental-group students reported having trouble on the posttest.

Stone (1988) provides an interesting analysis of the problem of trying to measure adult readership and offers a valuable summary of the research, given the few studies on this topic and the methodological problems of current research. Stone summarizes the influence of using newspapers in the classroom as follows.

¶ In some respects NIE use makes up for young people not having a newspaper in their homes.

¶ NIE students report enjoying reading newspapers more than those who haven't had the NIE experience.

¶ NIE students say they have less trouble reading newspapers.

¶ NIE students are more likely to be newspaper readers than non-NIE students.

¶ NIE students more habitually keep up with "hard" news.

¶ NIE students are more aware of political and public issues.

The highlights of all these studies could lead one to conclude that students who use newspapers in their classes are socially and politically aware of what's going on in the world, are more likely to have positive attitudes toward newspapers, read newspapers out of school, and interact with their parents about newspaper content.

These findings will be substantiated as we examine other studies. Next, let's look at two national studies of newspaper readership as they relate to newspaper in education programs.

Readership Surveys

The Newspaper Advertising Bureau issued a report, *Children and Newspapers* (1980), based on a nationwide study of 817 households with 1,156 children ages 6 to 17. It used personal interviews conducted by the Child Research Service, Inc., Center for Family Research. The summary that follows addresses children's media habits, especially changes in their newspaper-reading habits, but does not include all of the findings reported in the study.

¶ Newspapers are part of a child's home environment. Older children and those from more favored economic and social circumstances have greater accessibility to the newspaper.

¶ Parents highly approve of their children reading newspapers. However, children don't find newspaper reading very entertaining compared with other media services.

¶ Newspaper reading seems to follow developmental lines including reading skills and habits, with older children having less difficulty with newspaper content than younger children.

¶ Newspaper readership goes hand in hand with the reading of other print media, opportunities for access, and parental role models.

¶ Children's television watching does not affect their reading of newspapers.

¶ Children who frequently read newspapers are more likely than nonreaders to be reading other things in daily life. This suggests that it is the reading habit that conditions the appeal of newspapers to children.

¶ The effects of newspaper reading on children's citizenship education are profound. Only age and the cumulative effects of school play more significant roles in the level of children's political awareness.

¶ Only 43 percent of the children believe that the press should be free to criticize an important government official, but support for a free press is consistently stronger at every age among children who read a newspaper regularly.

¶ The newspaper emerges as a significant educational force shaping children's knowledge, beliefs, and attitudes about our political system, current events, and issues.

Another 1980 NAB survey titled *Mass Media in the Family Setting* offers some interesting information about children's exposure to the mass media in their homes and the influence of the family on how children use the media. One highlight for those interested in newspaper in education programs is a conclusion that "the crucial mediating role that parents play in making media available to children, providing them with models of adult behavior, and stimulating or regulating their use for the children, needs to be kept in mind in devising strategies for increasing newspaper reading among children" (p. xv).

Another interesting finding is that mothers are aware of their children's newspaper reading and have positive attitudes about their reading newspapers both in and out of school.

Next is a review of some studies that report findings about the attitudes of teachers, students, and parents toward newspapers and newspaper in education programs.

Attitude Studies

Teachers' Attitudes toward Newspapers. Plawin (1975) examined English teachers' attitudes toward newspaper use in secondary schools. Most teachers who used newspapers in their classes were positive about the program, a few were negative about it, and several expressed the need for more teacher training, particularly in understanding the purposes and use of newspaper in education programs.

A study commissioned by the Canadian Daily Newspaper Publishers Association (1976) examined whether the attitudes of elementary and secondary teachers toward the use of newspapers in the classroom were improved by participation in workshops. Three groups of teachers were sent questionnaires—teachers with strong background in NIE training, teachers with limited NIE training, and teachers who had no familiarity with NIE. The findings revealed that teachers who participated in NIE workshops had more favorable attitudes toward newspapers, the use of newspapers as a teaching tool, and the quality of news coverage. This group also had greater agreement with editorial views of their local newspaper and more acceptance of all mass media in education.

Geyer (1977) sent 400 questionnaires to teachers in 92 schools involved in the *San Francisco Examiner*'s NIE program. Some 92 percent of the teachers surveyed felt that the newspaper was an effective teaching tool and an aid for increasing student motivation to learn, and 96 percent said it was an effective resource for achieving their teaching objectives. Eight out of ten teachers reported that newspaper use promoted positive changes in classroom attitudes of their students and that it increased student interest in government, the economy, and world and local civic affairs.

The NIE project in the Volusia County, Florida, school district (1980) included a sample of students in grades four, five, and six. After a three-year period only sixth graders were evaluated. Although the researchers described a variety of problems with the project, the following results were reported.

¶ The newspaper in education groups exhibited significantly superior gains in spelling and vocabulary and had more positive attitudes toward the newspaper and its continuance in their classes.

¶ School principals supported the project and reported that it improved educational opportunities for the students.

¶ Parents supported the project as well. They also reported instances of positive pupil response in their homes.

¶ Most teachers who participated in the project saw it as worthwhile and of benefit to students in their classes.

It is clear from these studies that teachers who use newspapers in their classes have very positive attitudes toward this instructional resource. Of importance to teachers who will use newspapers are teacher-training workshops. As described in the next section, the workshops, usually conducted by NIE managers, are the teachers' best introduction to the idea that the newspaper can be used to help teach subject matter or as a unit in itself.

Attitudes toward Teacher-Training Workshops. As early as 1953, Schoenoff, a school superintendent, conducted a series of three teacher workshops on using newspapers in classrooms. At the end of these workshops and after the use of newspapers through the year, approximately 175 elementary teachers were asked to evaluate the program, using eight general questions. There was agreement on the value of newspapers as a resource for making learning more meaningful, for updating the textbook, for material that meets the needs and interests of students, for enriching background for oral and written expression, for developing study skills, and for developing natural situations that promote sharing and good sportsmanship.

The effect of teacher-training workshops was also investigated by DeRoche (1968). This study compared the attitudes of teachers who attended summer newspaper in education workshops and teachers who did not attend such workshops. Attitudes were examined in four categories: (1) the newspaper as an instructional tool, (2) the newspaper's publishers and product, (3) attitudes toward the use of newspapers in the curriculum, and (4) problems in having newspapers in the classroom. The results showed that teachers who participated in NIE workshops had significantly more favorable attitudes toward newspapers as an instructional tool, the goals of NIE programs, and the newspaper as a product than did nonworkshop teachers.

Daniel's dissertation study (1972) examined the quality and effects of the Iowa Newspaper in the Classroom workshops from 1963 to 1969 and explored the impact of newspaper use on teaching. The researcher found that more than three-fourths of the teachers used newspapers in their teaching after the workshops. Workshop participants also reported that they influenced other teachers to use newspapers, appreciated the support from publishers, and judged the quality of instruction in the workshops to be superior to other university instruction. Some of the participants reported that their use of newspapers was impeded by lack of support from school administrators, lack of funds, and a rigid curriculum.

Berger and Kleiman (1987) surveyed coordinators of state NIE weeks. The overwhelming response to the question of the usefulness of workshops was very positive. The researchers found that a workshop's presenters are the key to its success; participants appreciate enthusiastic, well-organized presentations of practical ideas for their teaching areas.

One can conclude from these four studies that teacher-training workshops are worthwhile and help develop positive attitudes among the teacher attendees. In fact, one should be hesitant about allowing teachers to use newspapers in their classes without preparation. It could do more harm than good.

If teachers have positive attitudes toward newspaper in education programs, what about student attitudes? We already have some clues from the surveys and readership studies, but let's examine some specific studies on the topic.

Students' Attitudes toward Newspapers. In 1964, Scantlen reported on a study by Copley Newspapers built around a program whereby a kit containing a two-week teaching unit, a packet of suggestions for using the newspaper, and a handbook of teaching aids was distributed to 5,000 teachers. A local public school used the program for two weeks, distributing one newspaper daily to every first through sixth grader.

A before-and-after experiment was designed to measure attitudes toward newspapers, media usage, and knowledge of current events and facts about newspapers among the school's entire enrollment of fourth, fifth, and sixth graders. All grades demonstrated statistically significant increases in the use of the newspaper at home, in knowledge of current events, and in knowledge of facts about newspapers. Initial attitudes toward newspapers were positive. While there was an increase in favorable attitudes it was not statistically significant.

Whitaker (1969) examined the use of newspapers and a unit on "teaching laws affecting our youth" in two sixth-grade classes in three schools. After a month of instruction and posttesting, the researcher concluded that a unit on the newspaper and the law can bring about an improvement in attitudes toward the law.

Verner and Murphy (1977) examined the effects of the use of newspapers in classes on the attitudes of students toward school, community, nation, self, and newspapers. The local daily newspaper was used as an instructional resource for four weeks in six inner-city high schools involving 148 students. The results showed slight but important increases in positive attitudes. The greatest positive change was in students' attitudes toward their city. The smallest change was in attitudes toward self.

East Baton Rouge Schools (1978) selected three middle schools for evaluating its NIE project. The findings showed that students had positive attitudes toward newspaper use and that they viewed newspapers as a way to increase their awareness of world and local events. In evaluating reading skills, the study also found that vocabulary skills appeared to be the most substantial area of growth.

West (1979) examined the use of newspapers in language arts classes and the effect on word-recognition skills, basic skills, and attitudes toward newspapers and television. The sample included 102 sixth-grade students divided into experimental (using the newspaper) and control (textbooks only) groups. Results on the Slosson Oral Reading Test for word recognition favored the experimental group. There were no differences between the two groups on the Comprehensive Test of Basic Skills. The experimental group was more likely to believe that newspapers are fair, truthful, responsible, fresh, unbiased, exciting, colorful, and valuable. West reported that exposure to newspapers in the classroom may establish in students a daily newspaper-reading habit and that students learned the benefits of all media.

A study sponsored by the *Milwaukee Journal/Milwaukee Sentinel* (1980) involved 200 eighth graders who used newspapers over a nine-week period in a middle school. Newspaper-use classes were compared to non–newspaper-use classes on verbal skills, newspaper reading, current events, and attitudes toward newspapers. The newspaper-use group performed as well as the non–newspaper-use group on verbal skills but scored 10 percent higher on newspaper reading, 15 percent higher on newspaper knowledge, and 13 percent higher on current events tests. Students who used newspapers were found more likely to think that a student's knowledge of current events came mostly from reading the newspaper, that newspapers informed better than radio and television, and that a free press is essential if the country is to survive.

Hanna (1980) reported on a survey that showed that exposure to newspapers at home may be at least as important as exposure to newspapers at school. The researcher found that frequent newspaper in education users had better attitudes than nonusers toward the newspaper. There were significant differences between users and nonusers on these statements— Reading the newspaper: helps me form opinions, helps me feel up-to-date, is fun, and helps me sort out what is most important.

Dewell (1980) designed a study to find out if students who use the newspaper in their classrooms showed a more positive attitude toward reading than students who had not used newspapers. The total sample included 3,021 students in six elementary schools, two junior high schools, and two senior high schools. Using statistical procedures, the researcher found that the newspaper was a motivational tool that produced positive attitudes toward reading when used as a supplement to classroom texts. Dewell also found that use of the newspaper is most effective in low-middle-class communities for improving both elementary and secondary girls' attitudes toward reading.

We have already seen that the newspaper in education program in Volusia County, Florida, (1980) reported that students had very favorable attitudes toward newspaper use in their classrooms and favored its continued use. In addition, the NAB's 1980 report, *Daily Newspapers in American Classrooms,* supported many of the findings of the previous studies, particularly the facts that many more children liked using newspapers in school than disliked it and that those who use it have more positive attitudes toward newspapers and are more likely to read it on their own.

Chattman (1982) reported on a study conducted under the auspices of the NAB that found that "students who used newspapers more consistently showed more positive changes in newspaper reading behavior, in their attitudes toward newspapers and in their interest and knowledge of current events."

Parents' Attitudes toward Newspapers. Three studies reviewed earlier in this chapter assessed the attitudes of parents toward newspaper in education programs and the use of newspapers in their children's classrooms. It is informative to highlight some of the findings again.

The NAB's 1980 report, *Daily Newspapers in American Classrooms,* indicated that parents have positive attitudes about newspaper use at school and that school use of newspapers reinforces the effects of living in a household with a daily newspaper. (Another 1980 NAB report, *Children and Newspapers,* also showed that parents highly approve of their children reading newspapers.)

NAB's *Mass Media in the Family Setting* (1980) supports the role of parents as models for newspaper reading and reports that mothers have positive attitudes about their children's reading newspapers in and out of school.

Finally, the newspaper in education project conducted by the Volusia County, Florida, school district (1980) reported parent support for the project.

The efforts of the ANPA Foundation and individual newspapers to develop parent interest in daily newspapers through workshops, awareness programs, and special projects are on the right track because parents can become effective newspaper-reading models for the next generation.

Dissertations

Wardell (1973) created a workbook containing ten exercises, a mastery skills sheet, and six supplementary exercises for each of the skills designed to ensure students' ability to locate specific information, distinguish fact from opinion, discern major ideas and minor details, and select favorable and unfavorable statements while reading a newspaper. Some 300 ninth graders used newspapers and the exercises and then were given three standardized tests.

The conclusions and implications based on the findings showed that students' proficiency in distinguishing fact from opinion, discerning major ideas from minor details, and total newspaper-reading ability were increased through classroom use of materials based on actual newspaper articles. These students also exhibited greater proficiency in locating information. Wardell also reported that students with high intelligence from low socioeconomic levels and students with low intelligence from high economic levels seemed to benefit most from instruction in newspaper-reading skills.

Cowan (1978) studied three communication problems faced when a newspaper industry and a few educators worked to develop an educational program to be used in school systems statewide. The problems analyzed were: (1) the communication campaign used to obtain teacher enrollments in workshops and in-service courses; (2) the instructional strategies utilized in training the enrollees; and (3) the relationship between definable obstacles to the success of NIE programs and the communication campaign or the instructional strategies used.

The analysis revealed that the communication campaign was a success and newspaper advertisements were the most effective means of communication. Analysis of the instructional strategies revealed that 67 percent of the enrollees were currently using or had recently used newspapers in their classes. School administrators supported the instructional strategies and results from the ANPA Newspaper Reading Test.

Sutro's dissertation (1979) was a historical study of newspapers in education, a description of the present state of the field, and a series of recommendations for improving contemporary-affairs programs in the schools. Interviews were conducted with key people in the field. A review of the literature and an extensive bibliography about the historical development of newspaper in education programs are included.

Durawall (1979) studied the impact of newspaper use in learning the seventh-grade mathematics concepts of fractions, decimals, currency, and averages. Over a six-week period, teachers of six classes in two schools used the local newspaper as a supplement to the textbook, and another class used the textbook only. Using the Iowa Test of Basic Skills, the researcher found that the overall performances of the newspaper groups were considerably higher than the achievements of those in the textbook-only groups.

Flynt (1980) developed and evaluated newspaper-based materials to supplement a local reading program. The lesson plans, which focused on four skill areas—vocabulary, word recognition, comprehension, and study skills, were evaluated by 45 professional educators. The lesson plans were rated good to excellent, and teachers who used them with small groups of students indicated positive interest by these students.

Can use of newspapers as a supplemental reading source influence students' attitudes toward reading? Leblanc (1980) sought answers to this question by randomly selecting 270 seventh-grade students and arranging them into experimental and control groups. The experimental group used newspapers for four weeks at a minimum of 75 minutes a week. The researcher found no significant differences between the two groups in attitudes toward reading, although a degree of positive change in attitude occurred in the newspaper-use group.

Subgroup analysis showed measurable improvement in attitudes toward reading. Students in the newspaper-use group who were reading below grade level experienced the least positive change, while students reading above grade level experienced the greatest positive change. Students in the experimental group thought of reading as significantly more relaxing than did control-group students. Students in the newspaper-use group who were reading below grade level had a better attendance record than did those in the control group who were reading below grade level.

Hsieh (1981) studied the newspaper-reading habits of selected high school students in southern Illinois. The researcher reported a range of findings regarding reading habits relative to variables such as grade level, parents' education, family size, sex, academic grade point average, and course work related to newspaper reading, writing, and editing. Of all the findings two are reported here. Students who had taken courses in which newspapers had been used as a teaching tool read more newspapers than those who did not take such courses. Parents' education, particularly that of the father, related to children's newspaper reading habits.

Olson (1984) studied teachers' use of free newspapers in one circulation area in Oregon. Findings indicated that elementary teachers, in rural and urban districts, used newspapers more than secondary teachers. Half of the teachers who ordered free newspapers did so only once for short units rather than for regular use throughout the school year. Only 10 percent of the sample who ordered newspapers during the last year had placed an order in the previous three years.

Teachers reported their aim to be teaching about the newspaper, but study of assignments indicated that newspapers were used as text for learning content. Teachers reported that the main goal for using newspapers was skill development, but they identified the most positive outcomes of newspaper use to be improvement in knowledge and attitudes. Although they valued newspapers, 83 percent of the teachers were not sure they would order the newspaper if it were not free.

King (1984) developed a newspaper-based supplemental reading program for fifth-grade students to be used for 30 minutes, three times per week, for 12 weeks. Using the pretest and posttest on a standardized achievement test to measure vocabulary and comprehension, the researcher found no significant test score differences between fifth graders who used newspapers as a supplement and those who did not. King reports that teachers and students using the newspaper-based supplemental reading program felt positively about it and that students preferred it to the basal reading text and workbook activities.

Gillis (1984) selected 93 seventh graders and randomly arranged them into two experimental groups that used newspapers and a control group that did not. A standardized reading test was administered after completion of the project in two successive 12-week periods. The researcher found significant differences between the two groups in reading comprehension and thus concluded that participation in the newspaper activity enabled students to increase their reading comprehension test scores significantly.

On the language arts subtests, the control group scored significantly higher than either of the two experimental groups in usage, spelling, and study skills. It was concluded that participation in basal test instruction was more successful in increasing scores in language arts.

Hussey (1985) designed a study to determine the effect of three-, six-, and nine-week periods of instruction using the newspaper with sixth-grade students. The three experimental groups were compared to the control groups (not using newspapers) on a posttest assessing newspaper reading habits, attitudes toward newspapers, and political awareness. No significant differences were found between the two groups. The researcher concluded that the time period was too brief to produce measurable changes and the instruments were not sensitive enough to measure the changes that did occur.

Skidell (1986) used newspapers to begin the literacy process with 20 mentally retarded adults. The adults were assigned to one of two groups, a newspaper nonpicture group and a model developed for the study identified as the newspaper picture group. Among the findings, the researcher reported that both groups benefited from language-based instructional programs using newspapers. The newspaper was found to be an appropriate medium of instruction on the basis of gains in pretest and posttest scores and growth in oral response ability. All adults learned and maintained strategies to use newspapers but did not spontaneously implement them.

Oates (1988) found little support for the hypothesis that newspaper audiences read more of the content that they can read easily than of the material they find more difficult. Using a cloze test with 48 adults, the researcher found that local news was most difficult to read, yet readers placed it first or second in their frequency of reading. Life-style news was easiest to read, but readers read it less frequently. Reported enjoyment of a variety in content was frequently associated with high readership.

Theses

In 1972, Theine completed a master's essay that researched the habits and attitudes of preadolescents regarding the mass media. The survey included 399 sixth- through eighth-grade students. Analyzing results pertaining only to newspaper-reading attitudes and habits of this sample, the researcher found that the students seldom read the newspaper outside of school but newspaper articles were commonly discussed in classes. Preadolescents, the researcher concludes, still look upon the media (television, audio, newspapers, magazines) as a source of entertainment although they realize they can also be a source of learning.

Epple (1975) studied the effects of a two-week newspaper unit on elementary school children's knowledge of newspapers and current events. An experimental group of students in grades one, three, and five used newspapers in their classes. Students in grades two, four, and six were used as the control group. Both groups were given a posttest on knowledge of newspapers and a current events test. On the newspaper knowledge test, students in grades one and three scored significantly higher than the one-year-older children in grades two and four. No differences were found between students in grades five and six. On the current events tests administered only to grades three through six, the researcher found that third graders scored significantly higher than fourth graders but there were no differences between students in grades five and six.

Ross (1977) completed a research report that examined the influence of newspaper use in teaching four specific reading skills to two sixth-grade classes of students with below-average reading ability. The skills were comprehension of facts, interpretation of facts, main ideas, and discovery of meaning through context. The *Weekly Reader* Silent Diagnostic Reading Test was used as a pretest and posttest. After six weeks of instruction with newspapers, the experimental group, using newspapers, had significantly higher gain in scores than the control group in comprehension, interpretation, and vocabulary in context. Although there were no significant differences between the groups on the main idea variable, the mean score of the experimental group was higher than that of the control group.

Sherman (1980) studied the relationship between newspaper reading and vocabulary growth. Comparing 28 sixth graders' vocabulary scores on the Nelson Reading Test, this researcher found that students who used newspapers over a six-week period did not outscore a comparable control group of non–newspaper-use students.

Woodell (1982) examined the effects of the use of the newspaper in teaching critical reading through propaganda techniques. The newspaper-use group, 15 eighth-grade students who used newspapers 20 minutes per day twice a week for six weeks, significantly outscored a control group on a teacher-made critical-reading test using propaganda techniques.

Chapter Summary

This chapter has reviewed a representative sample of the research on newspapers in education, including surveys, dissertations, and thesis work. Much of the research seems to have occurred in the 1970s. A reason may have been the request at that time by the ANPA Foundation's leaders and school administrators for evidence that newspapers in classrooms pay off in terms of student attitudes, reading habits, and reading achievement. With the growth of newspaper in education programs among daily newspapers and the overwhelming evidence of positive teacher testimony, this research thrust dissipated somewhat in the 1980s.

Given that most newspaper in education studies reviewed in chapters 2 and 3 suffer from research methodological design problems, the accumulating data nonetheless may warrant some generalizations.

Newspaper in education programs are growing, both in the newspaper industry and in schools, and in special programs such as those for parents and adult literacy. More and more newspapers are viewing the NIE program as a way of developing future readers and as a service to the community.

This service is being recognized by students, parents, teachers, and some principals who clearly support efforts to bring newspapers into the school's instructional programs.

Teachers in particular have expressed positive attitudes about using newspapers in their classes. They also value teacher-training workshops as a means of learning effective teaching strategies, understanding the newspaper as a business, learning about newspaper personnel, and finding out how newspapers gather and report the news.

Teachers generally report that newspaper use seems to motivate students. For their part, students like using newspapers in their classes. Both teachers and students believe that newspaper use increases students' knowledge of current events, understanding of the newspaper as a business, and appreciation of its usefulness as a learning resource for information and entertainment. There is some evidence that newspaper use may improve students' reading habits, increase vocabulary development, and heighten awareness of public issues and government functions.

In chapter 3, we will take a closer look at the influence of newspaper use in subject-matter areas including math, social studies, and language arts to see if some of the findings reported in this chapter can be supported by other research studies.

References

ANPA Foundation. *Foundation Annual Report, (1986)*. Washington, DC: 2–4.

ANPA Foundation and INPA. (1981). *Newspaper in Education Survey*. Washington, DC.

Berger, A., and I. Kleiman (1987). *How Useful Are Workshops Conducted during National Newspaper in Education Week?* Oxford, OH: Miami University.

Canadian Daily Newspaper Publishers Association. (1976). *Report on a Survey of Teachers' Attitudes toward Use of Mass Media in Education*. Data Laboratories Research Consultants.

Chattman, R. (1982). *The Newspaper in Education: What It Does to Children's Civic Awareness and Attitude toward Newspapers*. Research Summary. Washington, DC: ANPA Foundation. October.

Cowan, M. (1978). *The Newspaper in Education Program in the State of Maryland: A Case Study in the Communication of a Statewide Program to the Educators of the State*. Philadelphia: Temple University. Unpublished dissertation.

Daniel, E. (1972). *An Evaluation of the Iowa Newspapers in the Classrooms of a Free Society Workshops and an Assessment of the Impact of Newspaper Instruction*. Iowa City: University of Iowa. Unpublished dissertation.

DeRoche, E. F. (1968). *A Study of Teacher Attitudes toward the Press in the School Curriculum*. Milwaukee: Marquette University. Unpublished paper.

Dewell, B. (1980). *A Test of an Effective Model of Reading: The Study of the Use of Newspapers in Education*. Tulsa: University of Tulsa. Unpublished dissertation.

Dubuque Telegraph Herald. (1984). NIE Newsletter, "Newspapers in Education Survey."

Durawell, A. (1979). *The Effectiveness of the Newspaper as an Instructional Tool To Teach Seventh-Grade Mathematics Classes*. Memphis: Memphis State University. Unpublished dissertation.

East Baton Rouge Evaluation Project Board. (1978). *Report on Newspapers in Education Program*. Baton Rouge, LA: East Baton Rouge School Board.

Epple, R. (1975). *The Results of a Two Week Newspaper Unit on Children's Knowledge about Newspapers and Current Events*. Milwaukee: Marquette University. Unpublished master's essay.

Flynt, E. (1980). *Development and Evaluation of Newspaper-Based Lesson Plans Designed To Supplement Second Grade Reading Programs*. Athens: University of Georgia. Unpublished dissertation.

Geyer, R. (1977). Student Research Study. San Francisco: *San Francisco Examiner* Newspaper in Education Program.

Gillis, R. (1984). *The Use of Newspapers for Teaching Language Arts and Reading*. Johnson City: East Tennessee State University. Unpublished dissertation.

Hanna, G. (1980). *1979–1980 Research*. Minneapolis: *Minneapolis Star and Tribune*.

Hsieh, M. (1981). *Newspaper Reading Habits of Selected Southern Illinois High School Students*. Carbondale: Southern Illinois University at Carbondale. Unpublished dissertation.

Hussey, C. (1985). *Impact of Newspaper in Education in Selected Variables with Sixth Grade Students in Anchorage, Alaska*. Provo: Brigham Young University. Unpublished dissertation.

King, D. (1984). *The Development of a Newspaper-Based Supplemental Reading Program*. Logan: Utah State University. Unpublished dissertation.

Leblanc, R. (1980). *Affecting Attitudes of Seventh Grade Students toward Reading through Using Newspapers*. Houston: University of Houston. Unpublished dissertation.

Media General Research (1989). *Newspaper in Education Survey*. Washington, DC: ANPA Foundation.

Milwaukee Journal/Sentinel. (1980). "Reading Papers Can Help Students." September.

Newspaper Advertising Bureau. (1977). *The Influence of Childhood Experience with Newspapers on Adult Newspaper Habits*. New York: Newspaper Advertising Bureau, Inc.

Newspaper Advertising Bureau. (1980). *Children and Newspapers*. New York: Newspaper Advertising Bureau, Inc.

Newspaper Advertising Bureau. (1980). *Daily Newspapers in American Classrooms*. New York: Newspaper Advertising Bureau, Inc.

Newspaper Advertising Bureau (1980). *Mass Media in the Family Setting*. New York: Newspaper Advertising Bureau, Inc.

Oates, R. (1988). *Reading Ease as a Factor in Newspaper Readership Research: A New Application of the Procedure*. Bloomington: Indiana University. Unpublished dissertation.

Olson, R. (1984). *A Study of the Uses of the Daily Newspaper in the Curriculum of Elementary and Secondary Schools*. Eugene: University of Oregon. Unpublished dissertation.

Plawin, S. (1975). *Use of Newspapers in the Classroom in Norfolk City Schools*. Norfolk, VA: *Virginian Pilot/Ledger Star*. Unpublished paper.

Rhoades, G. (1982). *Newspaper in Education (NIE) and News Media Use*. A Review from the Southwest Education Council for Journalism/Mass Communications Annual Conference, October 3–4, 1982.

Ross, S. (1977). *The Effect of Using the Newspaper To Teach Reading Skills to a Select Group of Sixth-Grade Students with below Average Reading Ability*. Shippensburg, PA: Shippensburg State College. Unpublished research report.

Scantlen, A. (1964). *Student Attitudes about Newspaper Usage and Knowledge of Current Events and Facts about Newspapers*. La Jolla, CA: Copley Newspapers, Inc.

Schoenoff, K. R. (1953). "How the Teachers of Saulk County Used the Newspaper as a Tool of Learning." *Education*. October: 96–99.

Sherman, C. S. (1980). *The Relationship between Newspaper Reading and Vocabulary Growth*. Long Beach: California State University. Master's thesis.

Skidell, M. (1986). *Using Newspapers To Effect Oral Literacy with Intellectually Impaired Adults*. Hempstead, NY: Hofstra University. Unpublished dissertation.

Stone, G. (1988). "Measuring Adult Readership Potential of the Newspaper in Education Program." *Newspaper Research Journal*. Winter: 77–86.

Sutro, E. (1979). *Newspaper in Education Programs: A Case for Contemporary Affairs in the Social Studies Classroom*. Palo Alto: Stanford University. Unpublished dissertation.

Theine, C. (1972). *A Study of Habits and Attitudes of Pre-Adolescents regarding Mass Media*. Milwaukee: Marquette University. Unpublished master's essay.

Update NIE. (1980). "Study Links Newspaper Reading to Voting Habits." August.

Verner, Z., and Murphy, L. (1977). "Does the Use of Newspapers in the Classroom Affect Attitudes of Students?" *The Clearing House* 50 (no. 8): 350–351.

Volusia County [Florida] Schools (1980). *Final Evaluation Report: NIE Project.* Evaluation Systems, Inc.

Wardell, P. (1973). *The Development and Evaluation of a Reading Program Designed To Improve Specific Skills in Reading a Newspaper.* Boston: Boston University. Unpublished dissertation.

West, J. (1979). *A Study of Using the Newspaper in Teaching Language Arts in Middle School.* Columbia: University of South Carolina. Unpublished master's thesis. Also reported in *Southern Newspaper Publishers Association Bulletin,* February 26, 1979.

Whitaker, V. (1969). *A Study of the Newspaper in Teaching a Greater Respect for the Law.* San Diego: San Diego State University. Unpublished master's thesis.

Windhauser, J., and Stone, G. (1981). "Effects of NIE on Adult Newspaper Use." *Newspaper Research Journal.* October: 22–31.

Woodell, P. (1982). *The Effect of the Use of the Newspaper in Teaching Critical Reading through Propaganda Techniques.* Dayton: University of Dayton. Master's project.

CHAPTER 3

Newspapers in Education Research: Teaching and Learning Subject Matter

The question most often asked about newspapers in education is: What effect does using newspapers have on test scores? In this chapter we'll explore the answers to this question. We already have some clues from chapter 2. Given the caution one must apply to the interpretation of results of studies—cautions that result from research design and methodological problems—certain tendencies, trends, and generalizations may be made. If newspaper use motivates students, develops their interests, enhances newspaper reading skills, improves current events knowledge, and is seen by teachers who use it as a valuable instructional resource, then it may influence achievement test scores.

Before looking at what research is available to answer the question, let's begin by answering another question often asked by teachers: At what grade level is the newspaper written? Most answers suggest a level somewhere between grades four and eight.

Readability Studies

First of all, the question of readability is peculiar to our profession. Reporters and editors don't know what we mean when we ask them to tell us at what grade level their stories are written. They write to inform the reader in the clearest way possible, they will say. However, readability studies have been made of newspaper content.

Bormuth (1974) took a sample of eight articles from news publications and, using a cloze readability test, tested students in grades three through twelve from middle-class homes in a residential suburb of a large midwestern city. Bormuth was able to calculate the grade-level scores of the average student who answered 35 percent or more of the test items correctly, a percentage the researcher found is necessary if the reader is to understand the information. This researcher concluded that a reader with a 10.5 grade-level score was able to understand half of the newspaper articles read.

It may be that even high school graduation is not a certain criterion for literacy. Other researchers have suggested that achievement grade-level scores do not provide any information on what kinds of real-world reading tasks a person can perform competently.

Update NIE (1982) reported on two research projects that studied the readability of a variety of daily newspapers. Both studies reported an overall average reading level to be around the eleventh grade.

Smith (1984) studied three standardized readability formulas to see if these tests agreed when rating selected articles from several newspapers. Using statistical techniques, Smith found that the three formulas rated newspaper articles higher than the reading ability of most Americans. Smith says, "One can conclude from the findings that research needs to be done to determine which, if any, of the readability tests gives the most accurate assessment of the difficulty of newspaper content." (p. 7)

It seems apparent that newspapers are an adult medium that, according to readability formulas, would probably be best used with high school students. But readability formulas were made for text type material. They are based on word difficulty and sentence length. They don't account for content or the background information the reader brings to the text.

Maybe the best that can be said for readability formulas applied to newspaper content is that the findings set a target for teachers who want to raise the reading level of all students. Most newspaper in education programs are found at the middle-school level (grades four through eight). Most teachers and students, at all grade levels, find newspapers to be a useful instructional resource regardless of the readability level of their content.

Secondary School Studies

Studies that deal with the teaching and learning of subject matter (reading, language arts, social studies, mathematics) include studies of adult literacy (very few), those that include elementary and secondary students as a group (grades kindergarten through twelve), and those that sampled students in grades eight through twelve. Excluded from this review section are studies that used the American Newspaper Publishers Association (ANPA) Foundation's Newspaper Reading Test.

Drake (1968) reported on 80 high school students (42 percent on probation or parole) with approximately equal IQ's (average 102.5) who participated in a five-month experimental project designed to test the idea that students having an almost total lack of interest in reading would be motivated more positively by newspapers than by conventional textbooks. Students were divided into two experimental groups and one control group. While the experimental groups used newspapers, the control group was taught using conventional English class textbooks.

In this project, the experimental groups made more than average gains. A general conclusion indicated that Textbook-World, as the project was called, would advance high school students in the fields of reading, comprehension skills, and social sciences at least as rapidly as students under conventional instruction. This conclusion was supported by the results of the evaluation. In fact, the experimental groups' mean scores were more than two months ahead of the control group's on a standardized reading test for vocabulary and comprehension. Side effects of this program indicated improved class attitude and a perceived sense of community involvement by the students. Reading of such a varied amount of materials in the experimental groups caused what appeared to be a willingness to attack new words in context.

As reported in chapter 2, Wardell's 1973 study of 300 ninth graders who used newspapers and specially prepared exercises did show improvements in their skills in distinguishing fact from opinion, locating information, discerning main ideas from minor details, and newspaper-reading ability.

In an article in *Social Education,* Lewellen (1976) reviews several studies that support the thesis that exposure to the news media may influence children's and young people's political knowledge, interest, and participation. The researcher examined the relationship between media exposure and subsequent political participation patterns (but not attitudes and opinions) by surveying students in the Presidential Classroom for Young Americans. This was not a representative group, the researcher admits, and thus the generalizability of the study is limited. Lewellen's statistical analysis concluded that

> the more students are exposed to the news media, the more likely they are to engage in a broad spectrum of political participation activities. . . . Media exposure partially promotes participation in high intensity political activities. . . . These findings indicate a direct relationship between media exposure and significant political participation patterns. (p. 460)

Rowe (1977) found that a group of 40 low-level tenth-grade English class students who used newspapers outperformed a non–newspaper-use group on a diagnostic reading test and a newspaper-reading test.

Norman (1978) studied the effect of newspaper use in promoting student participation in classroom interaction or discussion. Each of 12 classes was assigned to an experimental or a control group. Each sample group was comprised of one reading class, one English class, and one social studies class. One experimental group used newspapers as a supplement to the text. A second experimental group used newspapers as the primary instructional resource. The control group did not use newspapers.

The Flanders Interaction Analysis Scale, a widely used classroom observation system, was used to measure students' verbal responses in all three groups as a pretest and a posttest. In summary, the researcher found that all eight sample classes using newspapers improved or increased in student verbal participation with the largest increases noted for the group that used a combination of newspaper and textbook. Thus, significant changes in the amount and quality of student talk occurred in experimental classes but not in control-group classes. Newspaper use seemed to influence students' verbal participation in class.

Chapter 2 cited a study sponsored by the *Milwaukee Journal/Milwaukee Sentinel* (1980) reporting that students had favorable attitudes toward using newspapers. This study also found that eighth graders who used newspapers outperformed a non–newspaper-use group on verbal skills, newspaper knowledge, and current events tests.

Chapter 2 also described Woodell's study (1982), which examined newspaper use for teaching critical reading through propaganda techniques. The researcher reported that the experimental group of eighth graders significantly outscored a control group on a teacher-made critical-reading test.

An ANPA Foundation publication (1987) describes an adult literacy project called Read-Up, sponsored by the *Tulsa World* in Oklahoma. The newspaper produced a 12-week program for inmates at a local correctional center, using the newspaper as the basic teaching resource. The posttest results showed that the entire group in the program made substantial gains in reading vocabulary, comprehension, and total reading skills.

In a practicum report in 1987, Hoffner investigated whether the directed use of newspapers could ensure the level of content acquisition in a basic-level secondary American government course. Fifteen students received instruction through the combined use of a textbook, a daily newspaper, and curriculum materials that directed students' use of newspapers. Pretests and posttests were given during the 18 weeks of instruction. Results indicated that students answered 48 percent of the posttest items correctly compared to 18.5 percent on the pretest.

The *NIE Information Service* (1987) reported on a study of the effects of newspaper use on students' writing skills. Three groups of students in grades eight through twelve were studied. One group used newspapers and related reading and writing instructions three times a week. A second group used newspapers but received no related instruction. The third group used traditional reading and writing materials without newspapers. Students' writing performance was tested before the project began, three months into the project, and then at the end of the six-month project. The researcher reports that eighth graders who used newspapers with related instruction made the largest gains (12 percent). Students in grades nine through twelve who used the newspapers with related instruction increased writing scores by more than 9 percent; the group that used newspapers with no related instruction improved by 6 percent; the group who didn't use newspapers showed no improvement.

Poindexter-Wilson (1987) reports on a ten-week pilot training program for 70 teachers in grades kindergarten through twelve. The program evaluated students who used the newspapers in these teachers' classes in comparison to those who did not use newspapers. According to teacher testimony, students increased their interest in reading, increased vocabulary, improved skills in following directions, improved critical-reading skills, improved reading comprehension skills, and improved student consumer skills; the program also helped low achievers feel successful. The two groups were compared on reading comprehension, knowledge of people and places in the news, vocabulary in the news, and general vocabulary questions. An analysis across the grade levels showed the pilot program's students in grades five and six scored significantly higher than nonpilot fifth and sixth graders in each category.

Palmer (1989) examined the effects of using daily newspapers to supplement normal classroom instruction with at-risk students in middle and secondary schools. Following a day-long orientation/training seminar, 5 teachers from four middle schools taught 12 classes, and 12 teachers from three secondary schools taught 29 classes. The 41 intact classes of at-risk students were assigned to three conditions of newspaper usage over an 18-week period: one in which students received newspapers three times per week with related instruction using a whole language approach, one in which newspapers were available without related instruction three times per week, and a control group in which no newspapers were used to supplement normal classroom instruction. Analyses of pretest and posttest scores from 627 students revealed consistently higher improvement in reading vocabulary, reading comprehension, and writing performance for both middle and secondary students who had newspapers with instruction. Less improvement was found in the same measures for students who had newspapers without instruction, but even these improvements were generally greater than those of students who had no newspapers. Other analyses indicate that secondary school users benefit most from newspaper usage, that benefits of newspaper usage increase with time, and that one-day training will not produce uniformly effective classroom use of newspapers among all teachers.

In summary, these studies tell us that newspaper use seems to influence to some degree students' achievement in reading, particularly in comprehension; that it may have a positive influence on other reading skills; that it seems to help improve students' verbal interactions; and that it improves students' knowledge of government and their political participation.

It will be interesting to see if these findings are confirmed by the results of studies done at the elementary and middle school levels.

Elementary—Middle School Studies

Most newspaper in education studies have been done in grades one through seven. This section will review those studies that examine the influence of newspapers in teaching and learning subject matter.

Lumley (1965) reports that 743 13-year-old elementary school students participated in a six-week reading-improvement program. The program was designed for pupils whose performance was not up to the junior high level and yet were to be transferred from elementary school when they reached 13.7 years of age. At the start of the session, most of the children read at a second-, third-, or fourth-grade level. At the end, the reading levels of more than two-thirds of the students went up by more than a year. Ten students gained two years, and two children gained more than three years. These significant results, achieved within six weeks, were attributed to the use of newspaper clippings and magazines.

Wilson (1966) asked the question: Can the daily newspaper be as effective, or perhaps more effective, a classroom teaching instrument as the standard textbook? He divided a class of 52 sixth graders into a traditional textbook-use group and a group that used newspapers as the main instructional resource for one school year. A standardized achievement test was used as a pretest and posttest. The newspaper-use group scored significantly higher than the traditional group in social studies, language arts, and arithmetic. There were no differences between the two groups in reading achievement. The traditional group did better in science; this might be due to the use of textbooks that addressed the content of the test better than did newspaper content.

Schuster (1971) describes a pilot summer program in two schools. The teacher used the daily newspaper and supplemental materials for problem-centered, question-centered, activity-centered inductive learning. After 40 hours of instruction using newspapers, students showed a gain of more than one year on a standardized reading achievement test.

Reid (1972) conducted My Classroom Project in her fifth-grade class for four months, using the newspaper to supplement the regular textbooks for language arts. Exposure to the project did not result in perceptible differences in performance on a semantic differential test of seven concepts or on the Gates-MacGinitie Reading Tests, when compared with a control group. However, the results of a newspaper survey before and after the project and the teacher's comments indicated that the project had desirable effects on the students.

Longley (1973) designed a pilot program for 185 students in five classes, grades six through eight, using newspapers daily from September through January. On a standardized reading pretest administered between April and September before the newspaper-reading program began, 31 percent of the students had a vocabulary measure of 0.5 of grade level, and 41 percent had 0.8 of grade level. When tested during the pilot program, 75 percent of the students showed a 1.2 average grade-level increase in vocabulary and 72 percent had a 1.1 average grade-level increase in comprehension.

Peiler (1975) reported on a study supported by the *Chicago Tribune* in a parochial school sixth grade. The students utilized newspapers and other supplemental materials for 11 weeks in their reading classes. Results on a standardized reading test showed that each student gained about one year when pretest results were compared to posttest results.

Chapter 2 described a study by Epple (1975) in which, on a teacher-constructed current events test, students in grade three who used newspapers scored significantly higher than their one-year-older schoolmates in grade four, but no differences were found between fifth and sixth graders.

Schofer (1976) designed a seven-week current events program for second-grade students. The program included learning factual information through a weekly discussion of issues and news items. One morning a week a session was held at which the students were asked to briefly explain news clippings they selected from a newspaper or magazine. The information was discussed, maps used, bulletin boards made, a news summary chart developed, and unusual words or place-names identified. At the end of the project a current events test was administered orally to the project students and a comparable control group. Predictably, the project group outscored the control group on every test item. The greatest difference appeared on items covering international and national news events. The author points out that observable benefits to this current events program include geographical skills, communicative skills, poise and self-assurance, research skills, increased awareness of current events, and awareness of the variety and roles of the news media.

Adams and Cook (1977) designed a study in which seventh graders in a North Carolina school participated in a 12-week language arts program in which each student was given a daily newspaper and a study guide to reading a newspaper. The guide consisted of 26 lessons designed to develop reading skills. While the report included no information about evaluation methods, the authors report that participating students did improve their reading ability.

Update NIE (1977) reports on a study in which first graders participated in an experimental reading and writing project employing newspapers and other reading materials. The core of the program was the two and one-half hours per day the children spent on learning to read and write, with 30 minutes given to phonics and the remaining time spent on writing and reading for information. On the pretest, 85 percent of all 442 students scored below the national reading average, but on the posttest the project group scored at the 74th percentile while a control group scored at the 59th percentile. Students in the project were generally from low-income families.

Ross's thesis (1977) was described in chapter 2. This researcher found no significant differences on a standardized reading test between a newspaper-use group and a control group of sixth graders with below-average reading ability. While the difference on the main variable, finding the main idea, was not significant, the newspaper-use group had a higher mean score than the control group.

As reported in chapter 2, the East Baton Rouge School study (1978) found that of the reading skills evaluated, students' vocabulary skills were the most influenced by newspaper use. Durawall (1979) reported that newspaper-use groups scored higher on the mathematics section of a standardized test than did a textbook-use group of seventh graders. West (1979) found no differences on a test of basic skills between two groups of sixth graders, one group using newspapers, the other group using textbooks. However, an oral reading test showed word-recognition gains favoring the newspaper-use group.

Michalski (1979) designed a research project to determine if there was a significant relationship between newspaper presence in the home and vocabulary development as measured by a standardized achievement test. A random sample of 104 questionnaires given to fifth- and eighth-grade students was categorized into two groups. One group of students received the newspaper in the home on a regular basis, the other group on a minimal basis. The researcher found a significant relationship between vocabulary achievement and presence of newspapers in the home.

Seely (1980) conducted a seven-month study among average and above-average sixth graders in which newspapers and textbooks were used to teach reading comprehension. This group was compared to a textbook-only control group on a standardized reading test. The experimental group scored significantly higher in reading comprehension than did the textbook-only group. Teachers reported greater motivation to read by the group that used the newspaper and textbook and noted a lower absentee rate on days when the newspaper was used.

In 1980, the Memphis *Commercial Appeal* reported that students in a fifth-grade class that used newspapers scored higher than any of the sixth-grade classes on a standardized reading test. The fifth-grade class in a private school had an average score of 8.5 months' gain in reading comprehension, 7.7 months in vocabulary, and 8.2 in total reading. The school's sixth-grade average gain was 7.5 months in reading comprehension, 7.2 in vocabulary, and 7.4 in total reading.

The following additional studies, described in chapter 2, included findings regarding student achievement in subject-matter areas. The Volusia County, Florida, (1980) study reported that sixth-grade newspaper-use groups were significantly superior to control groups in spelling and vocabulary. Sherman (1980) found that sixth-grade students who used newspapers did not outscore non–newspaper-use students in vocabulary growth on a standardized reading test. King (1984) found no significant test score differences on a standardized reading test measuring vocabulary and comprehension between fifth graders who used newspapers and those who did not. Gillis (1984) discovered significant differences between a newspaper-use group and a control group of seventh graders on a reading comprehension test. Hussey (1985) found no differences on a political awareness test among sixth-grade students, some of whom used the newspaper for three weeks, six weeks, and nine weeks, and a control group who did not use it at all.

Edfeldt's report (1990) of NewRead, a three-year project conducted in Stockholm, Sweden, is probably one of the most comprehensive studies on the use of newspapers for the teaching of reading. There were nine experimental classrooms of 300 students in grades one through nine, and 7,515 students in the same grades served as a control group. The experimental group used newspapers as their sole reading text for two years (1985–1987) with 1987–1988 as the evaluating and reporting year.

The teachers in the experimental group coupled the use of newspapers with the analytical method of teaching reading, which treats reading as a process whereby all the communicative effects depend on the students' qualifications to interpret (understand) and use (act upon) the message. This method also assumes that preunderstanding exists before reading and that there is some real interest in the content to be read. The control group used the synthetic method where breaking the code (phonics) is the key ability. Experimental-group teachers attended a one-week training session before the project began. The author called for continuous in-service work to help the teachers implement the reading method and learn how to use newspapers.

Reading development was assessed using Stockholm's 23 qualitative steps on the Reading Development Scale. In the lower grades (one through three), the newspaper group showed better and faster reading development and more general linguistic development than did the control group. For example, in the second year of the project more than half of the newspaper group in grade two had reached step 16 on the reading scale compared to only one-third of the students in the control group. "This developmental gap in reading ability equals a whole school year . . . one of the most significant differences between the newspaper-based and the school-based teaching of reading." (p. 15)

Lower-grade teachers reduced their control over text material the students were allowed to select from newspapers for classroom reading, and by the end of the project students' self-determination of content "became a very strong ingredient in pupils' increasing ability to take an interest in and responsibility for their own reading achievement." (p. 9) It was not until the second semester in grade five that the control-group middle-grade students surpassed the experimental-group students who were then in grade two.

Additional findings indicated good individual and group achievement, an increased capacity for listening and respecting the opinions of others, recognizing and acknowledging good performance of others, and a highly developed metalinguistic understanding and capability. Younger children in the newspaper-use group showed faster reading development than did older children.

In the middle and upper grades, students in the newspaper-use group showed accelerated increases in reading development. While the control-group students seemed to reach a standstill in their reading development, the experimental students experienced a slow but steady increase. This suggests that newspaper reading seems to add the needed momentum to reading development.

Some other results of this study are important to teachers and librarians. For example, students in the experimental group were more motivated to read, thereby increasing knowledge on their own. They seemed to be better in spelling and in their ability to write essays. The project seemed to increase parents' interest in their children's schoolwork.

ANPA Foundation Newspaper Reading Test

In the early 1970s, the Educational Testing Service in Princeton, New Jersey, developed, for the American Newspaper Publishers Association (ANPA) Foundation, the Newspaper Reading Test, which was designed to assess student competency in reading newspapers. It was the foundation's intention to use a measuring instrument that would assess skills in reading and understanding the newspaper and thus more directly assess the effects of newspaper in education programs.

Diederich (1971) of the Educational Testing Service conducted the first research study using the Newspaper Reading Test with 13,000 students in grades seven through twelve. Scores were compiled for two groups— regular classes in which newspapers were not used, and classes in which newspapers were used as the text or as a supplement to regular school work; in other words, newspaper in education programs. The researcher found that 13 percent more students in the newspaper-use group scored above the national norm on the test than in the control group. Diederich concluded that differences this large are not generally found in reading-improvement programs, especially at the junior high and senior high school levels.

The Gannett Rochester Newspapers (1971) developed a program for 300 "disadvantaged" students in grades four through six. The goal of the program was to raise reading scores significantly and to help develop skills in reading newspapers. After 7 months using the newspaper as part of the instructional program, fourth and fifth graders showed a 17-month gain on a standardized reading test, and sixth graders a 20-month gain. Two-thirds of the students showed a significant gain in the ability to read a newspaper as recognized by the ANPA Foundation's Newspaper Reading Test.

Berryman (1972a) designed a project that covered ten weeks of instruction using newspapers with students in grades four through seven who typically were below grade level in reading. About 98 percent of the students were black, with annual family incomes below $3,000. A standardized reading test and the ANPA Foundation's test were used as measuring instruments for the project.

After the 50 days of instruction, it was found that 21 of the 23 classes scored significant gains in newspaper-reading skills and general reading skills. Specifically, fourth graders were better newspaper readers after instruction than seventh graders before instruction. In grades five and seven, gains in general reading ability appeared to have more than tripled those that might have been anticipated with regular non-newspaper instruction. In grades four and six, the gains were approximately double the amount anticipated. In summary, gains during the 50 days of instruction were approximately equal to those ordinarily attained in a full year in that school district.

Berryman (1972b) designed a set of 50 instructional modules to be used by teachers in grades seven, eight, and nine in an experimental project where newspapers were the major module resource. Students were administered the ANPA Foundation test before and after the project. There were significant differences between pretest and posttest scores in each of the three grade levels and in 13 of the 16 class sections. The researcher concluded that the newspaper instructional modules significantly improved the newspaper-reading skills of junior high school students, including those whose general reading skills were two or more years below grade level.

The third of Berryman's studies (1972c) was designed to determine whether the variables of sex, race, prior reading ability, and same or opposite race of teachers and students influenced newspaper-reading skills. The research was conducted in fourth-, fifth-, and sixth-grade social studies classes where newspapers were used over a 50-day period. All classes, with the exception of students who were poor readers in fourth and sixth grades, showed significant gains in newspaper-reading skills on the ANPA Foundation's Newspaper Reading Test. Gain scores were strongly influenced by prior reading ability. There were no differences in newspaper-reading gain scores by sex or race.

Riggs (1972) evaluated a Title I reading project designed to help overcome negative attitudes of students in two junior high schools toward reading through the utilization of newspapers, magazines, paperback books, and other materials. A standardized reading test was used as a pretest and posttest for all students, and the ANPA Foundation's test was given to eighth graders only. At the end of the project, seventh-grade students showed a gain six times greater than the average 0.4 months of instruction while eighth graders showed a gain three times as great as the statewide average of 0.7 months on the standardized test. Greater than average gains were also reported on the newspaper-reading test.

Avery (1973) examined the question of whether integrating the newspaper in 76 ninth-grade American history classes would have any effects on the newspaper-reading skills of students. Teachers in the experimental group were asked to use the newspaper for at least 20 minutes a day over a three-and-one-half-week period. Prior to the study, the ANPA Foundation's Newspaper Reading Test showed no differences between the two groups. At the end of the project, the newspaper-use groups scored significantly higher on the posttest than did the nonuse groups.

How many copies of the newspaper are required to conduct an effective newspaper-in-the-classroom project? Avery (1974) attempted to answer this question by distributing newspapers to 12 junior- and senior-level high school classes. In each of four different schools, one class received one copy of the newspaper for every four students, another class received three copies for every four students, and a third class received one copy for every student. The assumption that posttest scores on the ANPA Foundation's Newspaper Reading Test would increase over pretest scores as the number of students per paper decreased did not stand up. There were no significant differences in the scores comparing the three types of classes. The researcher concluded that when at least one copy of the newspaper for every four students is employed in a classroom, the improvement in scores on this test will be just as substantial as when there is one copy per student.

Fox (1974) designed a five-week summer Upward Bound Reading Program. The purposes were to improve the reading skills of each student by at least six months, to improve by 10 percent the skills used in reading and analyzing daily newspapers, and to develop confidence and positive attitudes toward reading. Instructional methods included individualized and small-group lessons, games, and discussions, all involving newspapers, magazines, and paperback books. A standardized reading test, the ANPA Foundation's test, and an informal reading survey were used to test the achievement of the students in the project. Students gained the projected six months on the standardized test; they learned 2 times more than expected in speed, 16 times more in vocabulary, and 24 times more in comprehension. The Newspaper Reading Test proved too difficult for most students, so the evaluative data were not useful. Students rated the course very highly.

Reynolds (1975) conducted a study whereby a group of seventh-grade students of average or above-average ability in reading were assigned to a newspaper-in-the-classroom language arts class. A standardized reading test and the ANPA Foundation test were used as pretests and posttests for both the project class and a comparable control group. The results from the ANPA test showed that the project class had a 38 percent increase in skills necessary to read newspapers. There were no significant differences on the standardized reading test between the two groups, but the project class did show more positive changes on both reading grade-equivalent scores.

Rowe's study (1977) attempted to find out if 40 students from two low-level tenth-grade English classes who received daily exposure to and supplementary instruction with newspapers would outperform a non-newspaper group. On a standardized diagnostic reading test and the ANPA Foundation's Newspaper Reading Test, students in the newspaper-use groups outperformed students of matched ability.

Keppler (1977) reports that 27 students in grades one through six participated in an experimental newspaper project designed to improve students' reading comprehension, vocabulary, understanding of news content, and attitudes toward reading. A standardized reading test and the ANPA test were administered. The study reports only that student improvement was demonstrated in the four areas.

Newspapers in Special Education

Six studies used newspapers in special education classes.

Stetson (1970) conducted a nine-week study of 107 secondary special education students on the effectiveness of using newspapers to teach them reading skills. The students were divided into a control group; an experimental, occasional newspaper-use group; and an experimental, teacher-directed newspaper-use group. Results on a standardized reading test used as pretest and posttest showed that the teacher-directed group had gains in scores of 6.6 months for word recognition and 5.6 for comprehension. For the experimental students who used the newspaper on their own, the average group gain scores were 3.6 months in word recognition and 1.5 in comprehension. The control group did not show any differences on the pretest and posttest.

Hirshoren, Hunt, and Davis (1974) examined the use of classified ads as reading material for educable retarded children. After taking samples from newspapers and applying a readability formula, the authors found that classified ads required a fifth- or sixth-grade readability level, and thus such ads may be too difficult for these children.

Verner, Stetson, and Thomas (1978) studied the usefulness of newspapers in helping special education junior high and senior high school students with their word recognition and reading comprehension skills. Three groups were created: Group A used the newspaper for 20 minutes each day; Group B used the newspaper as the only instructional material; and Group C did not use the newspaper. On standardized pretests and posttests, the findings showed that Group A gained 5.6 months in word recognition and comprehension; Group B gained 3.6 months and 1.5 months respectively; and Group C showed no gain in word recognition or comprehension.

Verner and Siedow (1978) evaluated the effectiveness of newspapers as the sole instructional material for improving the reading achievement of high school special education students. Group A used newspapers as a resource. Group B also received instruction in the parts and organization of a newspaper. Students were administered a standardized test, an attitude scale, and a test on knowledge of a newspaper as pretests and posttests.

Both groups made gains in reading achievement. Gains in knowledge about newspapers were noted for Group B. Students showed more positive attitudes toward politics, newspapers, and want ads after the program than before.

Curtis and Shaver (1980) examined the question of whether the exploration of contemporary problems by slow learners would affect their attitudes toward fundamental freedoms, their critical-thinking skills, self-esteem, reading comprehension, and school attendance. They used a sample of 229 students in special classes for slow learners in eight secondary schools. Using experimental and control groups for a four-to-five-month period, the program featured a wide variety of materials including newspapers, magazines, selected government reports, and books. The model for instruction was one of inquiry-problem identification, data collection and analysis, statements of position on the issues, and action plans. The authors concluded, based on their findings on several standardized tests, that appropriate and interesting social studies content for slow learners can increase interest in contemporary problems. Specifically, there were no significant differences between the two groups on attitudes toward fundamental freedoms; slight differences were found regarding self-esteem; and there was no clear support that the treatment would increase reading comprehension skills.

As reported in chapter 2, Skidell's dissertation (1986) examined the effects of using newspapers with 20 mentally retarded adults with the intent to improve their oral language ability. Both a picture-use group and a non–picture-use group made gains after instruction.

Chapter Summary

This chapter ends as it began, with a caution about making generalizations from the findings of studies using newspapers to improve the subject-matter skills of learners. Given these cautions, research tells us much, particularly when coupled with teacher/student testimony and the findings described in chapter 2.

Less caution needs to be placed on the results of studies using the ANPA Foundation's Newspaper Reading Test because of the relationship between newspaper use and testing student competency in reading newspapers, rather than in general reading skills. The 11 studies reporting experiments using this test all showed significant differences between newspaper-use groups and non–newspaper-use groups, or significant gains in scores from pretests to posttests. It may be relatively safe to say that newspaper use in education (reading classes, language arts classes, social studies classes) improves learners' competencies in reading a newspaper as measured by this test.

But what about standardized reading tests? About 85 percent of the studies that used some kind of a standardized reading test found differences in comparative mean scores between experimental and control groups, or mean gain scores from pretests to posttests, favoring those students in classes where teachers used newspapers as a major instructional resource and/or as a supplement to the textbook. More than 20 studies reported vocabulary and comprehension gains.

Even the findings of the 6 or so studies that reported no significant differences can be interpreted to mean that newspaper use was just as effective as textbook use. Newspaper use seems to help learners increase their vocabulary skills and improve their reading comprehension. A few studies report an improvement in writing skills.

Considering the results reported in chapter 2, one might want to risk a generalization that there is a good chance that newspaper use in school will improve learners' attitudes toward reading, increase their vocabulary skills, help improve reading comprehension, and may contribute to better writing skills.

In other subject-matter areas, it is apparent, as one would expect, that students who use newspapers in their classes know more about newspapers, current events, people, and places. They may be more active and interested in community events than students who do not use newspapers in class.

No general statements can be made about the influence of newspaper use in learning science and mathematics because there are too few studies in these subject-matter areas.

References

Adams, A., and Cook, S. (1977). "Seventh Graders in Raleigh Use Newspapers for a 12-Week Course." *Southern Newspaper Publishers Association Bulletin,* August 22.

ANPA Foundation. (1987). "Scores Show Newspaper Literacy Project Works." *Press To Read.* October.

Avery, L. (1973). "A Study of Integrating the Newspaper in Regular School Curricula." *Houston Chronicle.*

Avery, L. (1974). "A Survey of Integrating the Newspaper in Regular School Curricula." *Houston Chronicle.*

Berryman, C. (1972a). *Improving Newspaper Reading Skills of Minority Group Poor Readers.* Unpublished report to the ANPA Foundation.

Berryman, C. (1972b). *An Analysis of Modular Instruction of Newspaper Reading Skills to Poor Readers in Senior High School.* Unpublished report to the ANPA Foundation.

Berryman, C. (1972c). *The Influence of Sex, Race, and Prior Reading Ability on Newspaper Reading Skill Improvements in the Elementary School.* Unpublished report to the ANPA Foundation.

Bormuth, H. (1974). "Defining and Assessing Literacy." *Reading Research Quarterly* 9 (no. 1): 8–13.

The Commercial Appeal. (1980). "Achievement Soars with Newspapers." *The Teachers' Notebook.* Memphis.

Curtis, C., and Shaver, J. (1980). "Slow Learners and the Study of Contemporary Problems." *Social Education.* April: 302–309.

Diederich, P. (1971). *Test Results of Using Newspapers To Teach Reading.* Paper presented at the International Reading Association Convention, May 2, 1974.

Drake, R. (1968). *Textbook World: An Experimental Project on Secondary Education Using Newspapers as Primary Texts.* Report to the *Santa Monica Evening Outlook.* Santa Monica, CA.

Durawall, A. (1979). *The Effectiveness of the Newspaper as an Instructional Tool To Teach Seventh-Grade Mathematics Classes.* Memphis: Memphis State University. Unpublished dissertation.

East Baton Rouge Evaluation Project Board. (1978). *Report on Newspapers in Education Program.* Baton Rouge, LA: East Baton Rouge School Board.

Edfeldt, A. (1990). "Teaching Analytical Reading with Newspapers as Sole Reading Text." *Research Bulletins.* Stockholm: University of Stockholm. April: 14, 4.

Epple, R. (1975). *The Results of a Two Week Newspaper Unit on Children's Knowledge about Newspapers and Current Events.* Milwaukee: Marquette University. Unpublished master's essay.

Fox, V. (1974). *Evaluation: 1974 Summer Upward Bound Reading Program.* Boone, NC: Appalachian State University.

Gannett Rochester Newspapers (1971). *Using Newspapers in Reading Programs for Disadvantaged Students.* Rochester, NY.

Gillis, R. (1984). *The Use of Newspapers for Teaching Language Arts and Reading.* Johnson City: East Tennessee State University. Unpublished dissertation.

Hirshoren, A., Hunt, J., and Davis, C. (1974). "Classified Ads as Reading Material for the Educable Retarded." *Exceptional Child.* September: 45–47.

Hoffner, S. (1987). *Assessing the Directed Use of Newspapers in the Secondary Level Basic American Government Classroom.* Unpublished master's thesis.

Hussey, C. (1985). *Impact of Newspaper in Education in Selected Variables with Sixth Grade Students in Anchorage, Alaska.* Provo, UT: Brigham Young University. Unpublished dissertation.

Keppler, H. (1977). *Using Newspapers To Reinforce Reading Skills: Teacher Incentive Award Project, Title III.* State of Iowa Department of Public Instruction.

King, D. (1984). *The Development of a Newspaper-Based Supplemental Reading Program.* Logan: Utah State University. Unpublished dissertation.

Lewellen, J. (1976). "Mass Media and Political Participation." *Social Education*. October: 457–461.

Longley, M. (1973). *NIE Evaluations: The New York Times Mobile Reading Program*. New York: The New York Times.

Lumley, K. (1965). "Improved Reading Scores through Six Week Summer Reading." *Education Summary*. November 15, 1965.

Michalski, M. (1979). *The Effect of Newspaper Presence on Vocabulary Development*. West Long Branch, NJ: Monmouth College. Unpublished research report.

Milwaukee Journal/Sentinel. (1980). "Reading Papers Can Help Students." September 11.

NIE Information Service. (1987). "Florida Research Study Finds a Write Connection." November.

Norman, B. (1978). *Changes in Classroom Verbal Interaction as a Result of the Newspaper's Instruction Use*. Unpublished report.

Palmer, B. (1989). *NIE Information Services*. November. Also reviewed by B. Shapley, "Newspaper Use Improves Reading and Writing." *Update*. May/June 1990.

Peiler, D. (1975). *Report on the Results of an Eleven Week Newspaper Unit on Reading Achievements*. *Chicago Tribune* Educational Services.

Poindexter-Wilson, P. (1987). "The *Los Angeles Times* in Education Pilot Program: The Research Results." *NIE Information Services*. January.

Reid, M. (1972). *Evaluation of a Newspaper in My Classroom Project*. ERIC Document Reproduction Service no. ED 007 992. August.

Reynolds, P. (1975). *NIC—Why Not? Study of Newspaper Use in Seventh Grade Language Arts Class*. Unpublished report.

Riggs, V. (1972). *Title I Reading Project*. Unpublished report to the ANPA Foundation.

Ross, S. (1977). *The Effect of Using the Newspaper To Teach Reading Skills to a Select Group of Sixth-Grade Students with below Average Reading Ability*. Shippensburg, PA: Shippensburg State College. Unpublished research report.

Rowe, L. (1977). *A Study of the Effects of Using the Daily Newspaper as a Tool for Teaching Selected Basic Reading Skills to Low-Level Reading Ability High School Students*. Shippensburg, PA: Shippensburg State College. Unpublished research report.

Schofer, G. (1976). "Current Events in the Primary Grades." *Illinois School Journal*. Summer: 13–16.

Schuster, E. (1971). *Experience Report on the Chicago Tribune Reading Program*.

Seely, P. (1980). "Reading Comprehension Benefits from Use of Newspapers with Texts." *Phi Delta Kappa* 61. March: 494.

Sherman, C. S. (1980). *The Relationship between Newspaper Reading and Vocabulary Growth*. Long Beach: California State University. Master's thesis.

Skidell, M. (1986). *Using Newspapers To Effect Oral Literacy with Intellectually Impaired Adults*. Hempstead, NY: Hofstra University. Unpublished dissertation.

Smith, R. (1984). "How Consistently Do Readability Tests Measure the Difficulty of News Writing?" *Newspaper Research Journal*. Summer: 7.

Stetson, E. (1970). "The Effectiveness of Newspaper Use on Reading Achievement of Secondary Special Education Students." *Journal of Reading* 13. June: 26–28.

Update NIE. (1977). "Right To Read Succeeds in Durham." Also reported in the *Southern Newspaper Publishers Association Bulletin*. September 1978.

Update NIE. (1982). "Readership Study—Reading Levels." February.

Verner, Z., and Siedow, M. (1978). In Verner, Z. *Newsbook of Reading Comprehension Activities*. Houston: Clayton Publishing Co.

Verner, Z., Stetson, E., and Thomas, D. (1978). "Selected Methods and Materials for Teaching Secondary Reading to Special Education Students: Their Effectiveness." *English in Texas*. Winter: 31–32.

Volusia County, Florida. (1980). *Final Evaluation Report: NIE Project*. Evaluation Systems, Inc.

Wardell, P. (1973). *The Development and Evaluation of a Reading Program Designed To Improve Specific Skills in Reading a Newspaper*. Boston: Boston University. Unpublished dissertation.

West, J. (1979). *A Study of Using the Newspaper in Teaching Language Arts in Middle School*. Columbia: University of South Carolina. Unpublished master's thesis. Also reported in *Southern Newspaper Publishers Association Bulletin*. February 26, 1979.

Wilson, A. (1966). "Sixth Grade Students Gain Four Months on Control Group." *Grass Roots Editor*. October.

Woodell, P. (1982). *The Effect of the Use of the Newspaper in Teaching Critical Reading through Propaganda Techniques*. Dayton: University of Dayton. Master's project.

CHAPTER 4

Annotated Selection of Periodical Articles, 1980–1989

For years, teachers, librarians, newspaper in education managers, and others have sought information about articles published in educational periodicals on the topic of newspaper use in schools. This chapter provides a list of such references, but is limited to selected articles listed in *Educational Index* and *ERIC Clearing House* and published in the 1980s.

Each article title is followed by a short description. The listings are categorized by subject matter or other topics for easy, quick reference.

Adult Learners

Fenholt, J. (1985). "The Newspaper: Your Key to Better Living. Using the Newspaper in Adult Education Classes." ERIC Document Reproduction Service no. ED 299 546.

The author provides a series of newspaper activities to use with adult learners.

Hunter, C., and McNearney, J. (1988). "Read Today." ERIC Document Reproduction Service no. ED 298 453.

The authors include 12 lessons using newspapers with adult learners.

Kossack, S. (January 1988). "Use the News: Recording Classifieds." *Journal of Reading* 31: 372–373.

Ideas for helping adult learners to use classified ads are presented, with a series of activities.

"Literacy." (1987). ERIC Document Reproduction Service no. ED 291 873.

This special report includes a section on using the newspaper in literacy instruction.

Mattleman, M. S. (January/February 1988). "Using Newspapers for Literacy." *Media and Methods* 24: 10–11.

The author describes the benefits of using newspapers with adult learners.

Stewart, D. (June 1985). "Our Daily Newspapers—a Forgotten Medium for Adult Education?" *Australian Journal of Adult Education* 25: 15–22.

The author discusses the advantages of the print medium in adult education.

Walker, B. (April 1987). "Use the News." *Journal of Reading* 30: 652–653.

The author encourages use of newspapers to help adults improve their reading skills.

Career Education

"Spotsylvania County Intermediate Schools Resource Notebook." (1986). ERIC Document Reproduction Service no. ED 274 857.

Resource book provides lesson plans using newspaper content for career counseling.

Turner, T. N. (March/April 1982). "Newspaper—a New Resource for Career Education." *Social Studies* 73: 80–84.

The article suggests learning activities to help elementary and secondary students use the daily newspaper to explore the world of work. An annotated list of sources and materials is included.

College

Ash, B. (1986). "Nontraditional Education: Modalities and Implications for Higher Education." ERIC Document Reproduction Service no. ED 271 054.

Nontraditional approaches to education, including newspapers in the classroom, are discussed in relationship to their impact on higher education.

Beals, P. E. (March 1984). "The Newspaper in the Classroom: Its Use in Teacher Preparation Courses." *Read World* 23: 270.

The extensive use that student teachers can make of newspapers as a tool in reading and other curriculum areas is described.

Perrone, C. (1985). "Teaching Social Class Analysis: A Classroom-Based Library Exercise." ERIC Document Reproduction Service no. ED 302 455.

This document introduces college students to basic research methodology by using newspapers.

Current Events

Davey, C. (1985). "The Newspaper as a Textbook." *Geographical Education* 5: 22–26.

The author presents ideas on how newspapers can be used to develop an understanding of current affairs.

Earle, D. (1982). "Current Events Should Be Taught in Primary Classrooms." *Social Education* 46 (no. 1): 27–28.

This article suggests employing newspaper clippings when teaching current events to primary-grade students.

Economics

Hawks, G. (November 1988). "Dollars and Sense: The Newspaper as an Economic Resource." *Journal of Reading* 32: 166–168.

Newspapers can provide valuable information for an individual's three economic personalities—consumer, producer, and citizen. This article shows how and describes class activities.

Kelley, A. C. (1983). "The Newspaper Can Be an Effective Teaching Tool." *Journal of Economic Education* 14 (no. 4): 56–58.

A teacher-developed economics newspaper brings real-world problems to the college classroom.

Lee, H. C. (1985). "Your Economics Textbook. " ERIC Document Reproduction Service no. ED 260 012.

Ideas are presented on how to use newspapers and other resources to help students create their own textbooks.

Scheppler, M. (Fall 1986). "Using the Newspaper as a Supplemental Text for Teaching Basic Economic Concepts." *Georgia Social Science Journal* 17: 29–35.

The author describes how to use the newspaper to augment regular textbook instruction on economic concepts.

Skover, L., and Shapley, B. (September/October 1986). "Newspapers and Economics." *The Social Studies Teacher* 8, 11.

The authors suggest using newspapers to teach economics to secondary students.

English as a Second Language (ESL)

Acosta, J. (1989). "An Approach to Integrating Knowledge, Language Skills and Attitudes in Citizenship Materials." *TESL Talk* 19 (no. 1): 7–18.

A Canadian newspaper is used to help adult learners read English as a second language.

Baumgardner, R. J. (Winter 1987). "Utilizing Pakistani Newspaper English To Teach Grammar." *World Englishes* 6: 241–252.

The author shows how to use English-language newspapers in an English-language classroom in Pakistan.

Chimombo, M. (July 1987). "Towards Reality in the Writing Class." *ELT Journal* 41: 204–210.

ESL writing lessons that utilize newspapers are presented.

Geyde, K. (1982). "The Newspaper in ESL." *TESL Talk* 13 (no. 1): 18–30.

The article describes methods for using newspapers to teach reading, writing, listening, and culture in second language classes.

Hoekje, B. (1983). "Coping with Newspaper Syntax: Reading Strategies for L1 and L2 Learners." Paper presented at the annual meeting of the Teachers of English to Speakers of Other Languages, Toronto, March 15–20. ERIC Document Reproduction Service no. ED 252 829.

A comparative analysis of newspaper and prose syntax construction. The author suggests strategies for the reading of newspapers.

Kossack, S., and Sullivan, J. (May 1989). "Newspaper Activities for the Second Language Student." *Journal of Reading* 32: 740–742.

The authors present activities using the newspaper to teach vocabulary.

Minicz, E. W. (September 1985). "A Bag Full of Newspaper Clippings and Other Tricks of the ESL Trade." *Lifelong Learning* 9: 29–30.

Lots of ideas for ESL students using newspapers.

Patrie, J. (1988). "Comprehensible Text." *TESL Talk* 18: 135–141.

How newspapers can be used for basic and literacy levels of ESL instruction.

Reynoso, W. D. (1987). "Blacks, Hispanics, and Asians in the English Classroom: A Linguistic Approach to a Problem." ERIC Document Reproduction Service no. ED 290 166.

The author shows how newspapers help to teach English to nonnative students or those with different dialects.

Wajnryh, R. (Spring 1988). "Communicative Use of Newspaper Texts in Classroom Reading: The Read-Ask-and-Tell Approach." *Reading in a Foreign Language* 4: 107–118.

The author describes how to use newspapers in the English-language classroom.

Foreign Languages

Berwald, J. P. (1986). "Au Courant: Teaching French Vocabulary and Culture Using the Mass Media." ERIC Document Reproduction Service no. ED 276 644.

The author outlines potential uses of daily newspapers for vocabulary development and grammar review in French-language instruction.

Deutsch, R. (1984). "Advertisements: An Overlooked Resource in the Foreign Language Classroom." American Council on the Teaching of Foreign Languages. ERIC Document Reproduction Service no. ED 253 055.

Suggested classroom activities are presented in four categories: vocabulary, grammatical rules and relationships, culture, and further activities.

Smith, M. F. (1984). "Using English Language Newspapers in First-Year Foreign Language Classes." *Foreign Language Annals* 17 (no. 1): 43–46.

This article describes a flexible strategy for associating Spanish with the daily English-language newspaper interests of junior high and senior high students.

Geography

Futhey, C., and Mazey, M. E. (1982). "Classroom Strategies for Using the Newspaper." Paper presented at the annual meeting of the National Council for Geographic Education, San Diego, October. ERIC Document Reproduction Service no. ED 238 767.

Described are two approaches for using newspapers to teach local, regional, and state geography courses to college students.

"Newspapers, Football and Geography." (1985). ERIC Document Reproduction Services no. ED 300 317.

Booklet focusing on a professional football team and how to use the newspapers to learn about geography.

Woodring, P. (1984). "Geography's Place in Basic Education." *Journal of Geography* 83 (no. 4): 143–144.

The author argues that geographical knowledge is essential for daily activities such as newspaper reading.

Mathematics

Adler, J. (February 1988). "Newspaper-Based Mathematics for Adults in South Africa." *Educational Studies in Mathematics* 19: 59–78.

A case study of how newspapers were used to help teach math to adult learners.

Barson, A., and Barson, L. (March 1988). "Ideas." *Arithmetic Teacher* 35: 18–24.

Newspapers are a source of data for classroom activities.

Bellipani, L., and Casey, K. S. (1980). "Balloon Talk." *Science and Children* 17 (no. 7): 18–19.

An activity on metrics for elementary children that utilizes newspaper comic strips.

Burns, M. (1983). "Put Some Probability in Your Classroom." *Arithmetic Teacher* 30 (no. 7): 21–22.

A lesson for a sixth-grade class from an article in a Sunday newspaper is described.

Czepiel, J., and Esty, E. (November 1980). "Mathematics in the Newspaper." *Math Teacher* 73: 582–586.

The authors explain how everyday activities like newspaper reading depend in part on mathematical knowledge. Articles are classified into eight categories.

Dull, E. (1980). "Could We Split the Rent?" *Instructor* 99 (no. 7): 102–103.

Fifth graders become interested in math by learning about jobs, housing, and transportation costs based on information in the local newspaper.

Edwards, V. (May 1981). "Mixing Budget with Pleasure." *School and Community* 67: 38.

The use of local newspapers as a text, with role playing, is presented as a relevant method to teach budgeting to high school students.

Fennell, F. (October 1982). "Newspaper: A Source of Application in Mathematics." *Arithmetic Teacher* 30: 22–26.

Teachers are encouraged to apply newspaper material to produce math activities such as comparative shopping or buying and furnishing houses, in order to involve students in mathematical skills use.

Guenther, J. E., and Corbitt, M. K. (1985). "Using the Newspaper in Secondary Mathematics." ERIC Document Reproduction Service no. ED 303 334.

Ideas for using the newspaper in math instruction.

Hintz, M., and Zeigler, J. (1986). "That Figures: A Mathematics Resource Package for Intermediate Grades." (Revised). ERIC Document Reproduction Service no. ED 304 313.

A resource package for elementary-level mathematics substituting newspapers for textbooks.

May, L. J. (May 1984). "Count on Newspapers for Math Fun." *Early Years* 14: 76.

The author suggests the use of newspapers to demonstrate how math is used in real-life situations. Several math activities for various elementary and junior high grade levels are provided.

Overbeck, C. (1984). "A Survival Kit for Teaching English to Refugees." *Lifelong Learning* 8 (no. 2): 29–30.

Newspaper ads are used to teach refugees numbers and the use of money.

Rossi, T. (March 1981). "Sell 100 Shares when It Reaches $20^1/8$." *Instructor* 74: 70–71.

The author describes how he used the business section of the newspaper to teach his fifth-grade class about the stock market.

Savino, R. J. (1987). "The Stock Market and Economic Principles: A Curriculum Project." ERIC Document Reproduction Service no. ED 301 505.

How to teach macroeconomic principles through mock stock market investing. The newspaper is used as an instructional tool.

Shaw, J. (April 1984). "Let's Do It. Newspapers Add Spark to Mathematics Activities." *Arithmetic Teacher* 31 (no. 4): 8–13.

Use of the newspaper in a variety of ways to make mathematics lessons interesting and effective.

Shaw, J. (February 1985). "Ideas." *Arithmetic Teacher* 32: 31–36.

Worksheets are provided that involve using newspapers in problem-solving and information-finding activities.

Vigilante, N., and Kossack, S. (October 1988). "Newspapers Enhance Mathematics." *Journal of Reading* 32: 70–71.

Ideas for integrating newspapers into math instruction.

Music

Livingston, C. (May 1989). "All the News That's Fit for the Music Classroom." *Music Educators Journal* 75: 37–39.

Classroom activities employing newspapers and news magazines to enhance students' motivation and their awareness of current musical events.

Parents

Criscuolo, N. P. (1982). "Parents as Partners in Reading through the Newspaper." *Reading Horizon* 22 (no. 2): 120–122.

Activities based on the newspaper that parents can undertake with their children.

Criscuolo, N. P. (1984). "Parent Involvement in Reading: Surface or Meaningful?" *Childhood Education* 60 (no. 3): 181–184.

Six situations that meaningfully involve parents in school are described. One of the situations is newspaper activities.

Physical Education

Smith, G. (March/April 1980). "Newspapers in the Elementary Physical Education Curriculum." *Journal of Physical Education* 77: 91.

The author lists nine activities using newspapers in the elementary physical education curriculum as a means of working on skills such as tossing, catching, rhythmic movement, and eye-hand coordination.

Public Relations

Bishop, R. L. (Summer 1988). "What Newspapers Say about Public Relations." *Public Relations Review* 14: 50–52.

The author shows how to use newspapers to determine favorable and unfavorable public relations.

Criscuolo, N. P. (1981). "The Media and the Schools: Can Good Relations Be Established?" *Illinois Schools Journal* 61 (no. 1–4): 38–43.

Eight strategies in which educators can utilize the resources of the newspaper to improve the image of their schools.

Criscuolo, N. P. (1982). "Enhance Your Press Rapport." *Executive Educator* 4 (no. 6): 24–36.

School administrators are offered eight suggestions for increasing quality newspaper coverage.

Reading—General

Criscuolo, N. P., and Gallagher, S. A. (February 1989). "Using the Newspaper with Disruptive Students." *Journal of Reading* 32 (no. 2): 440–443.

The author describes advantages of using newspapers as reading material for disturbed adolescents. Activities are included.

Fenholt, J. S. (1988). "Ready To Read." ERIC Document Reproduction Service no. ED 302 840.

Ideas to help students learn how to use the newspaper as reading material. Workbook contains 26 lessons.

George, C. J. (November 1986). " 'Success'ful Reading Instruction." *Educational Leadership* 44: 62–63.

Reading and writing ideas using newspapers in K–2 classrooms.

Gitelman, H. F. (April 1983). "Newspaper Power." *Reading Teacher* 36: 831.

A brief article suggesting several newspaper activities to increase students' reading and writing skills.

Kautz, K. (1985). "Attitudes and Values about Reading as Conveyed by Newspaper Comic Strips." ERIC Document Reproduction Service no. ED 255 880.

Description of a study that measured how students' attitudes toward reading were influenced by comic strips.

Kossack, S. (October 1986). "Use the News: Newspapers Provide Main Gain." *Journal of Reading* 30: 74–75.

Ideas for using newspapers in remedial reading classrooms.

Kossack, S. (November 1986). "Use the News: People's Choice." *Journal of Reading* 30: 168–170.

Newspapers can be used to improve skills in nonreaders.

Kossack, S. (December 1986). "Use the News." *Journal of Reading* 30: 266–268.

Activities for teaching the skills of comparison using various parts of the newspaper.

Kossack, S. (January 1987). "Use the News: Following Directions." *Journal of Reading* 30: 360–361.

Suggestions are offered on how to use the newspaper to teach students to follow directions.

Kossack, S. (April 1989). "The Newspaper in the Content Areas: Language Arts." *Journal of Reading* 32: 646–648.

The author argues that newspapers provide a rich source of material to build listening, speaking, writing, spelling, and grammar skills.

Kossack, S., and Hoffman, E. (November 1987). "A Picture's Worth a Thousand Words: Comprehension Processing via the Comics." *Journal of Reading* 31: 174–176.

Ideas on how to use newspaper comic strips with reluctant, older, and disabled readers.

Laffey, D. G., and Laffey, J. L. (April 1986). "Vocabulary Teaching: An Investment in Literacy." *Journal of Reading* 29: 650–656.

The authors describe vocabulary lesson sequences that were used to teach sixth-, seventh-, and eighth-grade remedial readers with the help of newspapers.

Naylor, K. (March 1986). "The Newspaper in the Classroom." *Reading Teacher* 39: 749–750.

The author lists resources for teachers of basic reading and study skills, and practical learning.

"Open to Suggestion." (February 1987). *Journal of Reading* 30: 450–453.

Contributors offer suggestions for using the newspaper for vocabulary development and involving students in problem-solving activities.

Sullivan, B., and Kossack, S. (February 1988). "Use the News." *Journal of Reading* 31: 272–274.

Ways of using the newspaper to improve students' reading and writing abilities while increasing their knowledge of the world.

Taylor, W. M. (1986). "Teaching Critical Reading as a Way of Teaching Critical Thinking." ERIC Document Reproduction Service no. ED 276 432.

The author offers a series of five writing assignments that utilize political articles from newspapers and magazines.

Valeri-Gold, M. (Spring 1989). "Encouraging Reading/Writing Literacy with Young Children in the Home." *Reading Horizons* 29: 176–182.

Suggestions for using newspapers and magazines to encourage students' reading and writing skills. Ten practical suggestions for parents.

Reading—High School English

Ammann, R., and Mittelsteadt, S. (May 1987). "Turning on Turned Off Students: Using Newspapers with Senior High Remedial Readers." *Journal of Reading* 30: 708–715.

The authors describe their experiences working with remedial readers and give ideas for using newspapers with senior high students.

" 'Daily News' High School Reading Program." (1986). ERIC Document Reproduction Service no. ED 276 992.

Final evaluation report on a secondary reading program that was based on newspapers in the classroom.

Fuchs, L. (1987). "Teaching Reading in the Secondary School." ERIC Document Reproduction Service no. ED 281 165.

Ideas for how secondary reading teachers can use the newspaper in the classroom.

Hansen, C. (1982). "Start Your Own High/Middle School Newspaper." *English Journal* 71 (no. 4): 58–59.

Advice on organizing and publishing a school newspaper.

Hester, P. O. (January 1989). "The Found Poem." *Reading Teacher* 42: 342.

This article describes how free-form poetry can be created out of newspaper content.

"How To Prepare Materials for New Literates." (1986). ERIC Document Reproduction Service no. ED 276 973.

Guidebook to help educators prepare materials for people who have recently learned to read. Ideas for using community newspapers are included.

Kossack, S. (May 1986). "Realism: The Newspaper and the Older Learner." *Journal of Reading* 29: 768–769.

The author describes six advantages of using the newspaper in classes for older students.

Kritzberg, B. (March 1988). "Fire Ants, Doublespeak and the 'Vox Populi.' " *English Journal* 77: 43–44.

Students learn to respond to conflicting news media reports. Ideas on how to use television and newspapers are presented.

Linksman, J. (1983). "Teaching Mythology Creatively." *English Journal* 72 (no. 3): 46–47.

A mythology newspaper is an enjoyable way of teaching mythology.

Midgley, D. A. (Spring 1980). "A Teaching Unit on Propaganda Using Magazines, Television, and Newspapers." *The Bulletin of the CSSPAA,* 15–16.

The author presents activities and guidelines for teaching a unit on propaganda at the secondary school level.

Otten, N., and Stelmach, M. (December 1987). "Turning News into Literature." *English Journal* 76: 63–64.

The author gives ideas for classroom activities for creative reading and writing.

Rosado, M. V. (November 1982). "Reluctant Readers Respond to the Newspaper." *Journal of Reading* 26: 173.

Adolescents at a vocational high school showed increased motivation to read after the introduction of newspapers and related curriculum.

Shishin, A. (1985). "Rhetorical Patterns in Letters to the Editor." ERIC Document Reproduction Service no. ED 288 350.

The author uses letters to the editor as instructional tools in teaching rhetorical styles.

"What's a Good Way of Using the Newspaper in English Classes?" (September 1985). *English Journal* 74: 67–74.

Twenty teachers from different schools across the nation share how they used newspapers in the classroom.

Science

Guenther, J. E., and LaShier, W. (1985). "Using the Newspaper in Secondary Science." ERIC Document Reproduction Service no. ED 303 333.

The authors include ideas on using the newspaper in secondary science instruction.

Mogil, H. M. (1984). "Sharpening Your Weather Eye." *Science and Children* 21 (no. 5): 14–17.

Drawing on local newspaper weather information to create activities for the classroom.

Rayborn, S., and Tuten-Puckett, K. (November/December 1980). "Use the Newspaper To Teach Energy." *Science and Children* 18: 12–14.

Newspapers can help teach how energy can be related to our daily lives.

Robertiello, M. J. (March 1983). "Newspaper Ecology." *Science and Children* 20: 23–24.

This article emphasizes a method of using newspapers to acquaint students with the environment.

Sebastian, G. R. (1984). "Teaching Weather Concepts." Paper presented at the annual meeting of the National Council of Geographic Education. ERIC Document Reproduction Service no. ED 253 444.

Ten exercises based on the weather map in a national newspaper are used to teach intermediate-grade students about weather.

Spector, B., and Kossack, S. (March 1988). "Use the News." *Journal of Reading* 31: 566–569.

Activities use the newspaper in the science area for older, disabled students who are learning decision-making skills.

Social Studies

Callahan, T., and Felton, R. (1980). "The Newspaper in the Social Studies Classroom: An Issue Oriented Curriculum." ERIC Document Reproduction Service no. ED 221 879.

How teachers can get students involved in an issue-oriented curriculum by using the newspaper.

Chusmir, J. (February 1989). "The Origin of Newspaper in Education Week." *Journal of Reading* 32: 452–454.

The history of Newspaper in Education (NIE) Week is summarized.

Gray, L., and Burroughs, W. (January 1987). "Constitutional Issues: Separation of Powers." *Social Education* 51: 28–30.

Historical background and teaching suggestions for addressing the issue of separation of powers. The author uses a letter from a newspaper publisher as an instructional tool.

Hantula, J. (January/February 1989). "Lazy Elephants and the Constitution." *Social Studies* 80: 21–23.

An eighth-grade class produces a newspaper to help learn about U.S. history, 1787–1791.

Hefferman, B., and Casement, S. (September 1988). "The Same News Can Be Different." *Educational Leadership* 46: 63–65.

Students compare foreign and American newspapers to learn how cultural perspectives differ.

Heitzmann, W. R. (September/October 1988). "America's Political Cartoon Heritage." *Social Studies* 79: 205–211.

The author traces the history of political cartoons with the help of newspapers.

Lamb, S. (1980). "The Newspaper in the History and Social Studies Classroom." *History and Social Science Teacher* 16 (no. 1): 53–59.

Methods for using the newspaper in the secondary social studies classroom are outlined.

Lankiewicz, D. (July/August 1985). "American Press Coverage of the Execution of Louis XVI: A Lesson Strategy for Gauging Opinion." *Social Studies* 76: 184–186.

In this unit, high school students discuss newspaper articles reporting the trial and execution of the French King Louis XVI. Students look for key words and phrases that might indicate a gauging of opinion.

Mantrone, B. (September/October 1987). "Teaching Immigration through Primary Source Material." *Social Studies* 78: 235–237.

Review of a collection of source materials, including newspapers, that cover various aspects of immigration.

Morse, J. C. (September 1981). "Newspaper in the Classroom: An Important Social Studies Tool." *Curriculum Review* 20: 405–406.

The author describes the newspaper in education program and discusses the benefits of using the newspaper as an instructional tool.

Neuman, W. R., and others. (1988). "Knowledge, Opinion, and the News: The Calculus of Political Learning." ERIC Document Reproduction Service no. ED 304 389.

Research paper describes how newspapers and other sources of media affect our political and current events knowledge.

Parisi, L. (1983). "News of the Nation. A Civil War Newspaper Project." ERIC Document Reproduction Service no. ED 238 773.

Causes of the Civil War are reviewed by applying previously acquired skills and information about the newspaper.

Shoemaker, P. J., and others. (February 1989). "Involvement with the Media: Recall versus Recognition of Election." *Communication Research* 16: 78–103.

Newspapers are used to show students how people's knowledge of elections can vary.

Sorgman, M., and Sorenson, M. (1983). "Utilization of the Newspaper in a Micro-Society Classroom." *Georgia Social Science Journal* 14 (no. 1): 18–22.

Students begin to understand the forces that shape communities, the contributions of newspapers in recording community experiences, and the role students play in shaping their communities.

Susskind, J. L. (1983). "Using the Three Mile Island Accident as a Case Study To Analyze Newspaper Coverage: A Diary of Events and Suggestions for Teaching Strategies." *Social Studies Journal* 12 (no. 12): 51–60.

Methods for studying and critically examining the coverage of current news stories in several newspapers are outlined.

Tersigni, J. F. (Summer 1987). "Getting Through: The Use of Media in the Classroom." *History and Social Science Teacher* 22: 221–225.

The author argues for the use of news media as a way of teaching major ideas.

Totten, S. (Fall 1985). "Apartheid: A Unit for Secondary Students." *Social Studies Record* 22: 19–22.

A social studies unit on apartheid, based on newspapers and magazines.

Totten, S. (November/December 1985). "Human Rights: A Unit." *Social Studies* 76: 240–243.

Activities for high school students learning about human rights, including ideas using newspapers and magazines.

Tretten, R. (Winter 1980). "Interdependence—a Tool for Teaching." *Social Studies Review,* 29–33

The author outlines two units, "how things connect" and "one thing leads to another," using newspaper content to illustrate global interdependence.

Unnithan, N. B., and Scheuble, L. K. (1983). "Evaluating an Attempt at Relevance." *Teaching Sociology* 10 (no. 3): 399–405.

A study showed that students viewed news item analysis positively, reported increased media consumption as a result of it, and found it a useful technique for applying sociological concepts.

Vlahakas, R. (May/June 1988). "From TASS to Tallahassee: In Search of Today's News." *Classroom Computer Learning* 8: 82–87.

Suggestions for social studies teachers interested in doing on-line newspaper searches with their students.

Weston, D. (1988). "Teaching about Inner Asia." ERIC Document Reproduction Service no. ED 305 325.

The author uses newspapers in studying about Asia.

Wylie, G. S. (March 1988). "American Holidays: Culture and Language Learning Combined." ERIC Document Reproduction Service no. ED 295 483.

Suggestions on how to use newspapers to combine cultural exposure and language instruction.

Special Education

Firth, G. H. (Fall 1983). "Try the Newspaper." *Teaching Exceptional Children* 16: 51–52.

The newspaper is a valuable instructional tool for use with educable mentally handicapped secondary students.

LaSasso, C. (March 1983). "Using the *National Enquirer* with Unmotivated or Language-Handicapped Readers." *Journal of Reading* 26: 546–548.

Learning-handicapped teenagers are motivated to read by the *National Enquirer*'s topics, which are often relevant to teenagers' interests.

Mandlebaum, L. H. (1988). "Reading." ERIC Document Reproduction Service no. ED 304 843.

The author provides an overview of several techniques for teaching reading, including newspapers, to students with mental disabilities.

Mauer, R. A. (1984). "The 'What's for Lunch' Approach to Reading." *Academic Reading* 19 (no. 4): 457–463.

Special education students age 11–14 improve their reading skills when materials such as newspapers are used.

Monda, L. E., and others. (April 1988). "Newspapers and LD Students." *Journal of Reading* 31: 678–679.

Suggestions for using the newspaper to help learning-disabled students improve their reading, language arts, and mathematics skills.

Vail, C. O., and others. (January 1989). "Behavior Disordered Students Use the News." *Journal of Reading* 32: 364–365.

The author argues that the behaviorally disordered can benefit from using newspapers in formal instruction.

Using Newspapers—General

Aiex, N. K. (1988). "Using the Newspapers as Effective Teaching Tools." ERIC Document Reproduction Service no. ED 300 847.

Discussion of how teachers can best utilize the newspaper as a teaching tool.

Beals, P. E. (December 1983). "The Newspaper in the Classroom: A Unit Approach." *Read World* 23: 174–175.

The author presents a guide to help teachers create their own units on the newspaper.

Beals, P. E. (March 1984). "The Newspaper in the Classroom: Its Use in Teacher Preparation Courses." *Read World* 23: 270.

The extensive use that student teachers can make of newspapers as a tool in reading and other curriculum areas is described in this article.

Beals, P. E. (May 1984). "The Newspaper in the Classroom: Some Notes on Recent Research." *Read World* 23: 381–382.

New information is presented about the use of newspapers at home and in the classroom.

Becher, N. A. (1982). "Let's Make the Newspaper Connection." Paper presented at the annual meeting of the New York State Reading Association, November 2–5. ERIC Document Reproduction Service no. ED 232 137.

Guidelines, procedures, and practical activities for introducing a newspaper in education program in the schools.

Bransky, T. (January/February 1986). "Newspaper Bug Bites Kids! Flash . . . from the (Re) Associated Press." *Gifted Child Today* 9: 34–35.

The author gives suggestions for a classroom activity for gifted students using the newspaper.

Criscuolo, N. P. (May 1981). "Creative Homework with the Newspaper." *Reading Teacher* 34: 921–922.

The newspaper can be a source for many home-based assignments to take the drudgery out of homework and generate enthusiasm. Activities are presented.

De Jong, B. (1982). "The Newspaper—a Living Textbook." *Australian Journal of Reading* 5 (no. 2): 80–88.

This article describes a program that uses daily newspapers in the classroom to teach important skills.

DiGregrio, D. (1984). "Daily Newspapers Provide Real Life Teaching-Learning Materials." *Lifelong Learning* 8 (no. 1): 29–30.

A variety of activities and strategies using the newspaper as teaching material are suggested.

Edwards, P. (1985). "Hey, That's a Good Idea! Useful Hints for Busy Teachers." ERIC Document Reproduction Service no. 258 170.

The author gives ideas for newspaper uses for classroom activities. Intended for primary teachers.

Edwards, V. (May 1981). "Mixing Budget with Pleasure." *School and Community* 67: 38.

The use of local newspapers as a text, with role playing, is presented as a relevant method to teach budgeting to high school students.

Gulliksen, H. (1985). "Creating Better Classroom Tests." ERIC Document Reproduction Service no. ED 268 149.

This article includes a previously published article by Paul B. Diederich and Marvin Maskovsky, "Measuring the Effects of Newspapers in the Classroom."

Haggerty, D. (1986). "Make It Relevant: A Guide to Using 'The Morning Call' in the Classroom." ERIC Document Reproduction Service no. ED 281 199.

The author presents a wide variety of classroom activities using the newspaper.

Hatcher, B. A. (May/June 1984). "Extra, Extra! Hot off the Press: Activities for Magazines and Newspapers in Your Classroom." *Childhood Education* 60: 337–338.

Seventeen different activities to motivate students.

"Interchange." (1983). *Reading Teacher* 36 (no. 8): 828–833.

Tips are offered on using the newspaper in the classroom.

Ketzer, J. W. (1987). "Audiovisual Education in Primary Schools: A Curriculum Project in the Netherlands." ERIC Document Reproduction Service no. ED 287 766.

Ideas for how mass media, including newspapers, can affect a child's social, emotional, cognitive, sensory, motor, and creative development.

Kossack, S. (March 1987). "Use the News. NIE Week, ANPA: Resources for Reading." *Journal of Reading* 30: 552–554.

Various suggestions for the use of newspapers in classrooms of all educational levels.

Morse, J. C. (1986). "Using the Newspaper in Upper Elementary and Middle Grades." ERIC Document Reproduction Service no. ED 306 147.

The author provides a guide for elementary and middle school teachers who want to incorporate newspapers into daily classroom instruction.

Moyles, J. (June 1983). "Finding Out about Finding Out." *Child Education* 60: 26–27.

Among sources listed are the daily newspaper, which can be used to improve students' fact-finding skills.

Newton, R. (1985). "Newspaper in Education: New Readers for Newspapers." ERIC Document Reproduction Service no. ED 260 373.

Observations on the use of newspapers in education. A national movement to take newspapers into public schools is described.

Potter, J. B. (November 1983). "The Newspaper: A Terrific Teaching Tool." *Early Years* 14: 36–37.

Twenty activities are introduced to get a class started on a newspaper-reading habit.

Raimo, A. M. (March 1982). "Producing a Newspaper as a Final Exam." *Journal of Reading* 25: 595–596.

The author explains the purpose and shows how to use the creation of a newspaper as a final exam for students.

Skover, L., and Abeles, J. (February 1983). "Extra! Extra! Newspaper in Education." *Media and Methods* 19:25.

The newspaper is discussed as a natural teaching aid at all grade levels and subject areas. The NIE program is highlighted.

Sullivan, B. L. (1985). "Research on the Reading of Newspapers." ERIC Document Reproduction Service no. ED 257 045.

A review of the literature on newspaper reading includes a number of topics.

Sullivan, B., and Kossack, S. (February 1988). "Prepare Your Students To Take over the World: Celebrate NIE Week." *Journal of Reading* 31: 472–474.

The authors describe teaching-learning strategies to be used by specialists in each region of the United States as part of the celebration of NIE Week.

Vacca, J. L. (Winter 1985). "Questions To Assist in Designing Supplementary Materials." *Reading Horizons* 25: 98–102.

The author gives ideas for the design of instructional materials including using newspapers.

Vocational Education

Sullivan, B. L. (August 1983). "All the News That's Fit To Teach." *Vocational Education* 58: 36–37.

The author describes how vocational education programs can improve students' employability skills by using the daily newspaper.

Writing

Bryant, J. A. R. (December 1988). "Wacky Wire Service Records Capture Student Interest." *Journal of Reading* 32: 274–275.

Creative writing assignments motivate and capture student interest with the use of newspapers.

Chimombo, M. (July 1987). "Towards Reality in the Writing Class." *ESL Journal* 41: 204–210.

The author presents English as a second language (ESL) writing lessons that utilize newspapers.

Donelson, K., and Haley, B. (1982). "One Way to the Short Story: Newspaper Clippings as Source Material." *Exercise Exchange* 26 (no. 2): 9–14.

The newspaper can be used as a source for short story material.

Duncan, A. M. (1985). *"Liebes Tagebuch*: Abroad at Last, but Let Me Tell You *'auf Deutsch.'* " ERIC Document Reproduction Service no. ED 268 814.

German instructor uses newspapers to help with writing assignments in summer program with American students.

"Essential Skills: Writing Activities." (1985). ERIC Document Reproduction Service no. ED 294 227.

A collection of practical writing activities for classroom teachers, including ideas for using newspapers.

Evertz, S., and others. (1987). "The Write Way On." ERIC Document Reproduction Service no. ED 299 579.

A guide to basic skills that includes ideas for uses of the newspaper in class activities.

Hulce, J. (Spring 1987). "Dewriting: Breaking into Writing." *Exercise Exchange* 32: 7–9.

The author presents ideas for using newspapers to help motivate students to write.

Kearns, J. A. (1982). "Up a Writing Creek without a Paddle Oar a Book." *English Journal* 71 (no. 4): 56–57.

A number of nontextbook methods for teaching writing, including newspaper articles, are described.

Kossack, S., and others. (May 1987). "Use the News." *Journal of Reading* 30: 730–732.

This article describes newspapers as a good alternative to the traditional writing textbook and discusses how they can be used at all age levels.

Stephenson, W. (December 1987). "A Real-Life Basis for Reports in Business and Technical Writing." *Teaching English in the Two-Year College* 14: 271–272.

Ways that students can use newspapers as a source of ideas for writing assignments.

Toth, M. (1982). "We Write for a Reason." *Instructor* 91 (no. 8): 38–40.

Students are motivated to write by developing a newspaper.

Tway, E. (1985). "Writing Is Reading: 26 Ways To Connect." ERIC Document Reproduction Service no. ED 253 877.

Ideas to help elementary students integrate the skills of writing and reading with the help of newspapers.

Wahlquist, E. (March 1988). "Letters: Value to Self and Society." ERIC Document Reproduction Service no. ED 294 207.

Letters from newspapers and other sources help students learn letter-writing skills.

CHAPTER 5

Newspaper Curriculum Resources for Teachers and Librarians

Over the years, newspaper in education managers and some educational and other commercial publishers have published supplementary instructional materials to accompany classroom newspaper subscriptions. These materials were published in response to requests from elementary and secondary teachers for updated, relevant, and interesting materials for students and for guides to help teachers use newspapers to teach subject matter and other content. NIE managers and publishers sought assistance from the American Newspaper Publishers Association Foundation and brought curriculum specialists, teachers, and college professors together to develop appropriate curriculum materials.

The information about materials listed in this chapter was provided by several newspapers or found in a guide entitled *Bibliography: NIE Publications*, published by the ANPA Foundation.

These instructional resources are grouped into four separate lists: an alphabetical listing, by state, of resources available from newspapers; resources from a national newspaper; those from foundations; and material available from educational and commercial publishers. It should be noted that not all states are represented, nor are all newspapers that have a newspaper in education program. Many newspapers only offer supplementary material when classroom sets of newspapers are purchased. In most cases, a brief description is provided; in a few cases, only the title is listed because the NIE manager did not include a description.

Information about ordering these materials is also given. If no price is included, contact the newspaper or publisher directly to find out if any fees are charged.

The instructional resources written for students are motivating, interesting, relevant, and an excellent supplement to the use of the daily newspaper and the class textbook. The teachers' manuals and guides are attractively designed, useful, and filled with ideas, suggestions, and activities.

The author wishes to thank the ANPA Foundation and the NIE managers who responded to his request for supplementary instructional materials.

Newspapers State by State

Arizona

The Arizona Republic/The Phoenix Gazette
P.O. Box 1950
Phoenix, AZ 85001
602-271-8932

Arizona Business Gazette. A collection written especially for the teacher of business and economics, this binder contains 43 pages of ideas, projects, and student activities. Grades 9–12 and up. ($3.00)

Between the Lines. This 36-page, loose-leaf collection of reproducible activities can be used to teach students about the newspaper. Grades 3–8. ($2.50)

Consumer Choices and Spending. Geared for elementary and secondary students, these 40 activities help in teaching basic economic and consumer concepts.

Creating a Classroom Newspaper. This 30-page, loose-leaf guide offers complete how-to's for preparing and creating a newspaper for your class. ($2.00)

Good News Teacher's Guide. This 32-page, loose-leaf packet offers language arts, social studies, math, writing, and science activities for grades K–3, 4–8, and 9–12. ($2.50)

Language Arts. Based on the U.S. Department of Education's essential skills list, this packet contains reading, writing, and speaking lesson plans with follow-up activities and reproducible lessons. Grades K–12. ($4.00)

Math Booklets: *Count Down.* This guide contains 25 activities related to number and sequence recognition, counting and sequencing skills, place value, addition and subtraction, and math vocabulary. *It Figures.* 40 activities to teach about money management, metrics, graphing, averages, fractions, ratios, decimals, and geometry. *Secondary Mathematics.* This booklet helps students practice computation and estimation skills, study graphing and statistics, and apply mathematics to real-life problems.

The Newspaper: Your Key to Better Living. The 50-page, loose-leaf guide features activities using the newspaper to teach survival skills such as use of coupons, job hunting, finding transportation, and using the classifieds. Reproducible lessons advance reading comprehension and expand vocabulary while involving students in the community and the world around them. ($4.00)

Newspapers: Exploring the Dimensions of Thinking. This guide will help you teach your students to expand their thinking skills and apply their reasoning skills to situations around them. Lesson plans and worksheets are included. Grades 5–12. ($2.00)

Social Studies. This booklet lists more than 50 important skills and each skill is followed by a suggested newspaper activity. The booklet also offers sample 10-day lesson plans, follow-up activities, and reproducible lessons for grades K–3 and 4–8. ($4.00)

Using the Newspaper with Gifted Students. These activities for middle and high school students require in-depth study, higher-order thinking skills, self-directed learning, or open-ended responses. ($3.00)

Arkansas

Arkansas Gazette
P.O. Box 1821
Little Rock, AR 72203
800-541-9876

Cartoon Coloring Book. George Fisher's editorial symbols are used as an introduction to fact and opinion, main ideas, and satire.

Classroom Newspaper Packet. This packet is a step-by-step guide to producing a classroom newspaper.

Curriculum Guide of Activities. A guide for teachers of grades K–12 with ideas for using the newspaper in all content areas.

Gifted and Talented. A manual of higher-level thinking-skills lesson plans in all subject areas.

Global Studies. A teacher's manual illustrating the use of newspapers to teach eight themes: interdependence, culture, development, change, building democracy in Latin America, diversity, values, and conflict.

Teaching Creatively. This booklet contains suggestions for using the newspaper for creative teaching and includes student activity sheets.

Terminology Poster. A large foldout newspaper page with terms identified for easy reference.

California

The Bakersfield Californian
P.O. Box 440
1707 Eye St.
Bakersfield, CA 93302
805-395-7500

Curriculum Notebook. The notebook presents a variety of activities for teaching many subjects including math, social studies, language arts, and current events.

The Fresno Bee
1626 East St.
Fresno, CA 93786
800-877-3400, ext. 6448

The World Series of Geography. ($5.00 includes postage)

Los Angeles Times
Times Mirror Square
Los Angeles, CA 90053
213-237-4342

The Constitution in Our Times. For elementary and secondary students, these lessons are designed to provide current examples of the U.S. Constitution in action and show its relevance in daily life.

Contemporary Application in Mathematics. Lessons designed to take secondary students beyond the textbook and put math into a practical, real-life context.

Critical Thinking. Activities and lessons focus on higher-level thinking skills to help elementary and secondary students move beyond knowledge and comprehension toward synthesis and evaluation.

Discovering Your World with the Los Angeles Times. Lessons and activities across the content areas encourage language development and manipulative skills in K–3 students.

English in the Present Tense. These lessons enable secondary students to work with real-world situations as a model for contemporary English.

ESL. Lessons for topical and life-skill-oriented curricula make use of visual text to arouse elementary and secondary students' interest as they explore the English language.

Expanding Your World with the Los Angeles Times. Lessons and activities for grades 4–6 introduce students to the newspaper and reinforce the content areas.

Gateways to the World. Qualitatively different lessons designed to generate greater global awareness and higher-level thinking skills as gifted and talented elementary and secondary students study and analyze real-world events.

Ideas for Your Current Events Curriculum and News Challenge. Ideas and lessons to teach current events, plus a copy-ready quiz mailed weekly, designed to challenge and motivate secondary students to learn more about their world.

Journalism. Lessons for elementary and secondary students feature the newspaper as a model for writing news stories, features, and editorials.

Life Skills. Lessons designed to teach life skills, improve reading proficiency, and motivate the at-risk secondary student.

Making the Writing Connection. Using the California Writing Project process, these lessons and activities help elementary and secondary students improve their writing skills while connecting real-life events with literature.

Orange County Centennial Guide. This guide offers 100 elementary and secondary lessons, research and discussion topics, bulletin-board ideas, county resources, and more learning activities geared to reinforce reading, writing, social studies, and critical thinking, with contemporary Orange County applications.

Perspectives in Social Studies. Lessons designed to supplement the social science curriculum for secondary students and make instruction as current as the day's news.

Reading for Life. Essential life skills are taught while improving basic skills and critical thinking for the adult learner.

The San Diego Union
P.O. Box 191
San Diego, CA 92112-4106

Citizens on Assignment. Self-contained lesson plans and coordinated worksheets integrate reading, writing, social studies, and critical thinking. Grades 6–12. 73 pages. ($6.00)

Freedom: A Case Study. An actual U.S. Supreme Court case involving the First Amendment. Teaching strategies included. Grades 6–12. 15 pages. ($2.50)

Key to Better Living. Six units and worksheets reinforce basic reading, writing, and daily living skills. For grades 4–12 with applications for older learners, literacy, and adult education. 50 pages. ($5.00)

Mini Page Teacher's Guide. Over 100 strategies for using the Mini Page and the newspaper for reading, writing, vocabulary, and social studies with prereaders to intermediate readers, grades K–6. 123 pages. ($7.00)

The Newspaper in Secondary Language Arts. Over 200 strategies in four categories of language arts foundations, literature, writing, and speech applications. Worksheets included. For grades 7–12. 13 pages. ($6.00)

The Newspaper in Secondary Mathematics. A broad range of quantitative skills are covered in sections including numbers, working with data, probability, geometry, measurement, and real-life applications. 13 pages. ($3.00)

The Newspaper in Secondary Science. Over 150 strategies with focus on improving personal life through science, societal needs of science, science awareness, nature, and academic preparation for a scientific career. For grades 7–12. 27 pages. ($4.00)

The Newspaper in Secondary Social Studies. More than 45 strategies with worksheet included in general social studies, history, government, economics, and geography. For grades 7–12. 92 pages. ($7.00)

The Newspaper in Upper Elementary and Middle Grades. More than 10 strategies in each of five subject areas—language arts, science, math, social studies, and knowing the newspaper. Additional strategies and coordinated worksheets. For grades 4–9. 93 pages. ($7.00)

The Newspaper with Gifted Students. Critical thinking worksheets are designed around key sections of the newspaper for exploration and in-depth study of integrated curriculum. For grades 5–12. 59 pages. ($6.00)

Newspapers Make the Write Connection. Strategies for using the Kirby-Liner writing process and newspapers to develop excellent writing skills in students. Lessons follow prewriting, drafting, revision, editing, and publishing stages. Worksheets included. For grades 4–12. 72 pages. ($7.00)

NIE Introductory Guide. Students are introduced to newspapers, and the guide integrates all major subject areas. Five-day lesson plans with coordinated worksheets for elementary and secondary levels are included, plus additional strategies across the curriculum. From the International Reading Association. For grades K–12. 67 pages. ($3.00)

Telecommunications: A Time of Megachange. An exercise in futuristics details new career opportunities, possible new laws, and new sources of information with 2 pages of related activities. For grades 8–12. 8 pages. ($2.50)

Colorado

The Denver Post
1560 Broadway
Denver, CO 80202
303-820-1335

Clean Air Kids. A guide for students in grades 3–7, which helps students learn about environmental issues. Provides background information, worksheets, and vocabulary exercise.

Close Encounters of the Comic Kind. For use in grades 4–8, the guide provides ideas and activities for teaching social issues, writing, and human behavior.

Consumer Choices and Spending. Includes decision-making and practical skills to understand today's global marketplace. For grades 4–adult.

Finding the 3 R's in the Social Studies Classroom. A guide for grades 6–12 with ideas and activities in economics, geography, history, political science, sociology, anthropology, and current events.

If It's Monday It Must Be Business. A variety of lesson plans and worksheets for grades 4–12.

It's NIE K-3. Colorful and fun activities that build skills for primary students.

Math in the Real World. This guide, for grades 8–adult, uses lessons to teach and learn how to set up a budget, buy a house, balance a checkbook, and other real-life skills.

On the Sidelines. Uses the Sports section for language arts, social studies, math, and science activities. Includes supplemental activity cards. For grades 4–10.

Reading Realities. Uses the newspaper to develop reading, writing, and thinking skills. Special activities focus on skimming, scanning, and fact vs. fiction. For grades 4–adult.

The Sky's the Limit. For teachers of grades 3–6, this guide provides activity sheets and ideas to be used in all subject matter areas.

Space Travel. Activity sheets for grades 4–5 focus on language, science, social studies, math, health, and art.

Special Journalism Package. This package provides two guides to newspaper copy, including preparation for a career in journalism, job descriptions, and interviews.

Summer Workshop Yearbook. Written by Colorado teachers and presenters who attend our three-day Summer Workshop, this guide offers over 100 lesson plans that use the newspaper across the curriculum of all grade levels.

Survival Skills for the Student at Risk. For students in grades 8–12, this guide contains high-interest, low-level activities across the curriculum.

You Can Count on the Post. For teachers of grades K–6, this guide provides reproducible worksheets for teaching elementary math skills.

Florida

Daytona Beach News-Journal
901 Sixth St.
Daytona Beach, FL 32117
904-252-1511

Citizens on Assignment: A Newspaper in Education Curriculum on Citizenship. 73 pages ($5.00)

Using the Newspaper with Gifted Students. 59 pages ($4.00)

The Miami Herald
1 Herald Plaza
Miami, FL 33132
305-376-3239

Choices, Choices, Choices. This tabloid guides students through effective steps in conflict resolution and problem solving. Designed for students in grades 4–12, it enhances critical thinking while teaching self-esteem, structured ways of resolving conflict, cause and effect, and decision making. ($3.00)

Dropout Prevention. This guide contains activities geared to the at-risk student. The activities stress the development of literacy and decision-making skills, using the newspaper as a real-world and relevant text. This guide is designed for middle school teachers. ($3.00)

Ecology/The Environment. This tabloid stresses environmental danger and focuses on ways to protect the planet. ($3.00)

ESOL (English for Speakers of Other Languages). Three separate packages intended to help the classroom teacher introduce the different stages of language development within the ESOL program. Elementary, middle, and high schools are covered in separate books. ($3.00)

Florida Facts I and II. These guides cover a wide variety of topics about the state of Florida: history, economy, geography, demographics, and government. For grades 4–12. ($3.00)

Global Journalism. Designed for high school students, this tabloid presents a comparative study of international journalistic styles. It examines the many different facets of journalism from news gathering to censorship. ($3.00)

Integrated Language Arts. This program integrates the reading-writing-thinking connection with the use of real-world materials such as the newspaper. The book is arranged thematically and includes an annotated bibliography. It is oriented toward teachers of grades 4–8. ($3.00)

Integrated Language Arts: Newspaper and Theme. This booklet of activities deals with newspaper-based instruction using integrated language arts techniques. The activities emphasize a thematic approach to learning by focusing on ideas and problems rather than isolated basic skills, and integrating different levels of complexity. The newspaper provides the core idea; the teacher connects literature, writing, and spelling to challenge students' critical and creative thinking. ($3.00)

Let's Compute. This special workbook-style supplement introduces computer vocabulary and technology. It is ideal for beginning and intermediate students. Puzzles, graphics, and sample programs detail the wide use and relevancy of computers to students. ($3.00)

My Choice: The Right Choice. This substance-abuse supplement is the newspaper's all-time biggest-selling tabloid. Developed for grades 1–12, it is full of self-directed activities that involve using the newspaper. Its topics include self-awareness; peer pressure; decision making; the effects of smoking, alcoholism, and drugs; and where to turn for help. ($3.00)

A Philosophy To Live by: Dr. Martin Luther King for Kids. This Black History Week Supplement incorporates a history of the civil rights movement and the philosophy of Dr. King into a workbook focusing on conflict resolution and peace-keeping skills. ($3.00)

The World at Your Fingertips. A complete curriculum guide for teaching local, national, and world geography in elementary through high schools. Available on Macintosh disk. ($3.00)

The Tampa Tribune
Education Services Department
P.O. Box 191
Tampa, FL 33601

Classroom Va-Voom! Standards of Excellence in Writing. Each page of activities lists appropriate standards and skills as required by the Florida Department of Education. For grades 3–5.

Creating a Classroom Newspaper. Activities are based on recent research findings in reading and writing. Students who understand the structure of the text usually read with more understanding. Since newspaper structure is predictable and concise, it can become a model for student writing. For all grade levels.

Election 1990. This guide encourages the use of the newspaper as one of the best sources for teaching the process of elections and following candidates' progress throughout the election period.

Exploring the Dimensions of Thinking. For grades 4–12, this teacher's guide will help develop and expand students' thinking skills. Reproducible student worksheets cover concepts, integrating information, solving problems, making choices, and analyzing arguments.

Knowledge in Bloom. Geared to Blooms Taxonomy, this guide contains activities to stimulate higher-level, critical thinking skills. For grades 3–12.

New Beginnings in Communication Skills. This excellent text includes worksheets that can be copied for each student. It may be used with any student who is learning to read.

Newspapers & Theme: An Integrated Language Arts Approach. This booklet models a method used in research conducted with at-risk students. In the future, learning will be centered around ideas and problems rather than isolated skills. Each theme connects with real-life themes, and the activities use the whole language concept. For middle grades.

Project Success. A dropout prevention text, this guide is great for building self-esteem in at-risk students. It can be adapted for higher grade levels. For grades 3–8.

Using the Newspaper To Reinforce Communication Skills. Activities using the newspaper to teach reading, writing, and basic communication skills. For grades 8–12.

Using the Newspaper To Reinforce Mathematic Skills. Organized by state standards, suggested activities address mathematics through the use of the newspaper. With each skill, sample teaching ideas are given. For grades 3–5 or 8–11.

Using the Newspaper To Reinforce Reading and Writing Skills. These fun activities give a new look to some basic skills required by the state standards. For grades 3–6.

Georgia

The Atlanta Journal
P.O. Box 4689
Atlanta, GA 30303
404-526-5090

Citizens on Assignment. This handbook provides teachers with concrete suggestions on how to use the newspaper to teach participatory citizenship. Good for social studies or language arts, grades 7–12.

Creating a Classroom Newspaper. Written on three ability levels for elementary, middle, and upper grades, this guide provides teachers and students with lesson plans and reproducible student worksheets as they plan, write, and design their own classroom newspaper.

Improving Reading Skills. Fifty instructional modules relate to one or more of 18 reading skills such as identifying main points, locating information, judging reliability of sources of information, predicting consequences of actions, and assessing ads. For grades 5–12 in reading and social studies.

Instructional Materials for All Grades. Lesson plans, activities, and worksheets are included for working with the newspaper in math, social studies, language arts, science, and health. Material is arranged in sections for primary, elementary, and secondary classes.

It's NIE for K–3. Full of activities for developing concepts in language arts, writing, social studies, science, health, and math with a focus on the newspaper. The guide contains 60 reproducible activity sheets and 16 idea cards for enrichment. Parent/child activities are also included.

New Beginnings: Communication Skills. This adult basic-education guide contains activities and reproducible worksheets to develop and reinforce basic reading and writing skills.

New Beginnings: Mathematics. A guide that focuses on real-world math problems beginning with basic counting and progressing to percents, measurements, money problems, graphs, and tables.

Newsclips in ESL—Most Grades for Second Language Students. Methods for teaching oral language skills to students of English as a second language in an interactive, expressive way, using the content found in the daily paper.

Newspaper Primary Activities. Activities in language arts, social studies, science, math, and journalism are offered at each grade level for grades K–3. Guide contains a section on teaching a newspaper unit, which includes instructions for creating a classroom newspaper, and has reproducible worksheets.

Newspapers Make the Write Connection. Ways to teach the process of writing (prewriting, drafting, revising, editing, and publishing) across the curriculum while using various sections of the daily newspaper. Full of reproducible activity worksheets. For grades 6–12.

On the Sidelines. You can use the sports pages of the newspaper to teach language arts, social studies, math, and science in a fun, imaginative way. This guide contains lots of reproducible student activity sheets, plus supplements that may be used in individualized learning centers or for group instruction. For upper elementary and middle grades.

Primary Reading Program, Levels 1, 2, 3, 4. These manuals contain newspaper activities for developing reading skills in vocabulary, word recognition, comprehension, and study skills. Level 4 develops reading skills as pupils examine the function, content, and development of the newspaper, and contains a segment on creating a classroom newspaper. For grades K–6 (four separate books).

A Salute to the U.S. Constitution and the Bill of Rights—Levels One and Two. Two separate books are offered for grades 1–3 and 4–6. They contain model lessons using the newspaper to teach about the Constitution and introducing the Constitution through present-day experiences of elementary students. The books are designed to develop skills in critical thinking and problem solving.

The U.S. Constitution. Activities to help students use the newspaper to find real-world examples of the Constitution in action. For grades 8–12.

Using the News: A Skills Program for Georgia Studies. Correlated with skills measured on an achievement test, this guide contains activities in map skills, recognizing and stating problems, locating information, interpreting graphic aids, and evaluating information. It contains diagnostic tests, student worksheets, and extended activities.

Using the Newspaper in Adult Education Classes. Activities involve the newspaper to improve reading and life skills such as knowing the newspaper, understanding advertising, the wise use of coupons, looking for work, and much more. Activity sheets are included.

Using the Newspaper in Secondary Math and Science. This guide has activities correlated with Georgia basic skills indicators in math, as well as sections on cultivating math awareness, numbers, real-life application, working with data, probability, geometry, and measurement. The science activities are divided into four broad goals for science education: personal needs, societal issues, academic preparation, and career education in science. For grades 7–12.

Using the Newspaper in Secondary Social Studies. General social studies activities, as well as activities specifically related to history, government, economics, and geography are covered. Reproducible activity sheets are included. For grades 7–12.

Using the Newspaper in Upper Elementary and Middle Grades. Thirty activities in each of the following areas: knowing the newspaper, language arts, science, math, and social studies. Also contains reproducible student worksheets.

Using the Newspaper with Gifted Students. Activities provide experiences in content and skills that are qualitatively different from basic curriculum activities. Most activities integrate skills from a variety of subject areas, while focusing on higher-level thinking skills. For grades 7–12.

You and the Economy, a Look at Practical Economics Using the Newspaper. Activities teach understanding of economic terms and policies, big business, other economic systems, and personal economics. Supplemental charts, graphs, and tables are included. For grades 7–12.

Illinois

Chicago Sun-Times
School Services Department
401 N. Wabash, Room 245
Chicago, IL 60611
312-321-4947

The following 21 teacher guides are packed with ideas and activities to ease lesson planning in a variety of K–12 subjects.

About Journalism
Black History
Career Education
Citizens on Assignment
Consumer Education
Creating a Class Newspaper
Elections '88
Government and Politics
How To Read a Newspaper
Improving Reading Skills

Language Arts Activities
Let's Look at Comics
Mathematics and Science Activities
Newspaper Games
Primary Activities
Project FUN
Remedial Reading
Social Studies Activities
Statue of Liberty Manual
United States Constitution
Using Photographs in the Classroom

The News-Sun
100 W. Madison St.
Waukegan, IL 60085

Activity Cards. A set of activity cards with 209 individual ideas and newspaper activities for grades 4–8 and less proficient junior high students. The cards are color-coded by subject area and include sections on unit planning and lesson plan development as well as activities for science, math, language arts/reading, and social studies.

Citizens on Assignment. Twenty lessons and worksheets with suggestions on how to use the newspaper as the basis for a curriculum in language arts or most social studies courses.

Consumer Choices and Spending. Activities to help elementary and secondary students learn and apply basic economic and consumer concepts relevant to decision making and the use of money.

Creating a Classroom Newspaper. Lesson plans and worksheets cover five days of instruction for elementary through secondary levels.

Geography in the Newspaper. Objectives, overviews, and procedures for 24 activities based on current world events.

It's NIE for K–3. A curriculum guide and 76 newspaper activity worksheets.

Our Living Community. An instructional resource with activity sheets for social studies teachers. For intermediate and secondary students.

Survival Skills for the Student at Risk. Objectives, overviews, applications, and worksheets for 30 lessons or activities to heighten student interest by relating the lessons to real-life concerns.

Using the Newspaper in Secondary Social Studies. Newspaper activities and activity sheets on history, government, economics, geography, and social studies.

Using the Newspaper in Upper Elementary and Middle Grades. Newspaper activities and worksheets in the following subjects: language arts, science, math, and social studies (indicate your preference).

Using the Newspaper To Teach Secondary Language Arts. Newspaper activities and activity sheets on language arts, writing, literature, and speech.

Southern Illinoisan
710 N. Illinois
Carbondale, IL 62901
618-529-5454

Newspaper Activity Guide: Elementary and Secondary. Two ten-page booklets of activities in each of several subject areas.

Indiana

The Indianapolis Star/The Indianapolis News
307 N. Pennsylvania St.
P.O. Box 145
Indianapolis, IN 46206
317-633-9140

Display Kits. These kits provide instant bulletin-board ideas. *The Comics* displays a history of cartoons and reproductions of popular comic strips. *History's Front Page* contains reproductions of this newspaper's coverage of major events. *The Magic of Color* covers the art of presenting full color photographs. ($2.00 each)

NIE Teacher's Idea Notebook: A teacher's manual on how to begin to use newspapers in the classroom. ($10.00)

A Salute to Our Constitution and Bill of Rights. The two issues of this publication, for grades 1–3 and 4–6, each contain lessons and activities. ($6.95)

Post-Tribune
1065 Broadway
Gary, IN 46402
219-881-3000

The following instructional materials are available. (Write for cost)

Consumer Choices and Spending
Creating a Classroom Newspaper
Elementary Activity Card Set
Garfield Activity Cards for Grades K–3
How To Use the Newspaper To Prepare Middle-school Students for English
Intermediate Activity Cards
Language Arts Proficiency Testing
Newspaper: Exploring the Dimensions of Thinking

Newspaper Primary Reading Program
The Newspaper: Your Key to Better Living
On the Sidelines
Project Health
Today's Special
Using the Newspaper in Secondary Mathematics
Using the Newspaper in Secondary Science
Using the Newspaper in Secondary Social Studies
Using the Newspaper To Teach Reading Skills
Using the Newspaper To Teach Secondary Language Arts
Using the Newspaper with Gifted Students
Writing with the Newspaper

The following newspaper supplements are also offered. (Write for cost)

Back to Basics
Behind the Scenes
Census '90
Choices, Choices, Choices
Holiday Fun and Games
In Celebration of Black History, Vol. I
In Celebration of Black History, Vol. II
Newspaper Gems
The Newspaper Habit
Our Beginnings: A History of Northwest Indiana
Our World
The Stock Market Crash

Iowa

The Des Moines Register
NIE Subscription, 6th Floor
P.O. Box 957
Des Moines, IA 50304-9979
800-532-1455, ext. 8598

Along Came a Spider. This creative writing guide combines newspaper writing skills with familiar nursery rhymes. Through 60 activities, students remember to include the character, setting, action, problem, and solution in all their stories. For grades K–6.

Celebrate! Every Day Is a Holiday! This guide helps students celebrate holidays and notable occasions using the newspaper. Activities are developed from 60 famous days (5 each month), including well-known holidays and other favorites such as National Popcorn Day, Dental Health Month, April Fool's Day, Dr. Seuss's Birthday, and National Grouch Day.

Consumer Choices and Spending. The first eight lessons in this guide are designed specifically to help teach young primary- and intermediate-level consumers about money. The last four, advanced lessons may be adapted for intermediate-level instruction. Use the guide to help students learn how to apply such basic skills as reading, writing, math, and critical thinking to the real world in which they're already making spending decisions. In the course of study, students will examine the concepts of scarcity, wants, needs, resources, costs, and more. For grades 1–8.

The Des Moines Register's Teacher Manual. This collection of class-room newspaper activities is presented in a three-ring binder, and features more than 500 ideas for language arts, math, social studies, and science. For grades K–12. (With any classroom subscription order $5.00, without a subscription $10.00)

Fundamentals for Elementary Students. With this guide, teachers can help prepare students for basic skill mastery. The 60 activities focus on teaching the language arts, math, science, and social studies. Your students will learn about addition, compound words, healthy eating habits, bar graphs, fossil evidence, communication, and more. For grades K–6.

Fundamentals for Secondary Students. Teachers can use this guide to help reinforce fundamental subjects. Each of the 60 lessons focuses on skill development in language arts, math, science, or social studies. Students will learn about synonyms, writing, averages, scientific notation, astron-omy, pollution, ocean environment, government figures, history, and much more. For grades 6–12.

Geography in the Newspaper. This guide suggests geography lessons that are based on daily world events. The activities teach students to analyze coastal effects on climate, understand global interdependence, and relate geographical concepts to social problems. Lessons involve looking for examples to reinforce what is being taught, using newspaper articles to arrive at concepts in a more inductive manner, and amusing games. For grades 6–12.

Iowa Election '90. This special guide features 20 activities that focus on the 1990 Iowa gubernatorial election. Students use the newspaper to keep track of election results, learn how the governor is elected, and more.

It's NIE for K–3. Designed especially for younger elementary students, this guide contains 76 activities. Each includes a step-by-step illustrated worksheet, helping you teach newspaper knowledge, language arts, writing, social studies, science and health, math, and miscellaneous activities. Younger students learn how to identify photos; skim reading material; categorize and identify words, sounds, and numbers; and under-stand emotions.

Our Living Community. Using the activities in this comprehensive and interesting guide, you can lead your class through community problem identification, problem solving, and conflict-resolution exercises. The activities use the newspaper in connection with the student's environment in the hope of teaching young people the importance of being informed citizens in a democracy. Supplemental activities in geography, history, government, and economics give students a well-rounded view of how a community operates. For grades 7–12.

Reading Realities. Learning how to read and reading to learn are both addressed in this guide, which uses different sections of the newspaper to teach reading and writing skills. With 57 activities altogether, the lessons focus on issues surrounding general newspaper use, news stories, editorials, advertising, features, and sports. For grades 4–12.

Special Education and Cooperative Learning. Especially designed for students who are not motivated by traditional materials, this guide provides teachers with 40 activities that reinforce fundamental skills. Students use the newspaper to explore subjects as diverse as listening, eating habits, reading, personal values, and decision making. For grades K–12.

Strategies in Critical Thinking. This social studies guide develops inquiry and investigative thought among secondary students. It uses five case studies about recent news topics and includes newspaper clippings about these issues. The articles help to trigger and sustain investigative activities and a habit of inquiry among students. For grades 7–12.

Survival Skills for the Student at Risk. At-risk students are those in danger of failing to complete their education with an adequate level of skills. The guide is based on the premise that a student's interest is heightened if lessons relate to what students see as real-life concerns. This guide uses the newspaper as an instructional tool to address students' needs regarding achievement, adaptation, and attitude. Included are survival lessons for awareness and motivation, and activities in particular curriculum areas. For grades 6–12.

Using the Newspaper in Upper Elementary and Middle Grades. This comprehensive guide for elementary and middle school teachers who want to incorporate newspapers into their daily classroom instruction offers 10 lessons in each of five subject areas. Students learn about the newspaper itself, language arts, science, math, and social studies. The lessons help develop creative writing skills, understand the role of science in everyday life, learn real-life applications for math, and much more. For grades 4–8.

Kansas

The Topeka Capital-Journal
616 Jefferson St.
Topeka, KS 66607
913-295-1111, ext. 376

Comic Strips in the Classroom. This kit contains 105 activities for middle and high school students. ($8.00 includes postage)

It's NIE for K–3. Activities on such subjects as language arts, writing, science/health, math, news knowledge, and social studies. This guide contains 60 activity sheets and 16 activity cards. ($7.50 includes postage)

The Newspaper in the Curriculum. A how-to book for teachers of all grade levels. ($4.50 includes postage)

On the Sidelines. A 67-page guide containing action-packed activities creatively illustrated for elementary and secondary students and adult learners. The sports section of the newspaper can be used as a motivator to applying and practicing skills in language arts, mathematics, social studies, and science. ($7.50 includes postage)

Our Living Community. Contains 150 learning activities for middle and high school students. ($8.00 includes postage)

Using the Newspaper in Secondary Language Arts. A description of more than 202 activities related to language arts foundations, writing, literature, and speech. The 57-page book includes 30 reproducible worksheets. ($5.00 includes postage)

Using the Newspaper in Secondary Mathematics. A group of 60 activities to teach math concepts and skills with the newspaper. ($2.50 includes postage)

Using the Newspaper in Secondary Social Studies. This 92-page book contains more than 292 activity descriptions and 40 reproducible worksheets. ($6.50 includes postage)

Using the Newspaper To Individualize Instruction. How to develop activity centers from which students can work individually or in small groups on activities designed to achieve certain objectives. ($3.00 includes postage)

Using the Newspaper To Individualize Instruction in the Social Studies Classroom. Activity cards can be punched out of this work and activities performed in the classroom, using the newspaper as the primary source. ($4.25 includes postage)

Using the Newspaper with Gifted Secondary Students. A series of 60 activity sheets organized around the different sections of the newspaper. They can be used with both gifted and high-achieving students. ($5.00 includes postage)

Maine

Portland Press-Herald
390 Congress St.
Portland, ME 04104
207-780-9000

Teacher's Resource Guide. This three-ring binder guide includes activities and suggestions for using the newspaper in English, language arts, mathematics, world studies, and science. For elementary, middle, and secondary grade levels.

Maryland

Montgomery County Sentinel
P.O. Box 1272
Rockville, MD 20849
301-948-4630

Teacher's Guide. A 46-page guide for using newspapers to teach subject matter. ($4.00 excludes postage)

The Sun
P.O. Box 1377
501 N. Calvert St.
Baltimore, MD 21278-0001
301-332-6265

Body Lessons. This tabloid is designed for use in health, science, and biology classes as it examines the makeup and functions of the human body.

Consumers at Work. A work-text on functional skills for the consumer that includes articles for middle and high school students.

Newspapers and Writing. A 20-page newspaper tabloid containing writing activities that supplement language arts and English class texts.

Taking the Lead. A language arts tabloid of activities to be used in elementary and middle schools.

Michigan

Detroit Free Press
321 W. Lafayette Blvd.
Detroit, MI 48231
313-222-6411

Along Came a Spider. Packed with 60 creative ways to teach the sequence and components of narrative writing, using examples from the newspaper. For elementary grades.

Bright Ideas: Advanced Newspaper Skills. Challenges students to reach a higher level of thinking, analysis, synthesis, and evaluation in reading the newspaper and performing activities. It includes 59 pages of reproducible activity sheets. For grades 5–12.

Celebrate! Every Day's a Holiday. Five fun activities for each month that use the daily newspaper to develop reading, writing, math, or social studies skills. For elementary grades.

Celebrating the Constitution. This commemorative kit includes 45 reproducible activity sheets; two posters depicting "The Great Compromise" and "200 Years of Freedom: 1787–1987;" plus a class set of student supplements that examine the Constitution's impact on the 20th century. For grades 4–12.

Close Encounters of the Comic Kind. Students will enjoy using the comics to explore values, human behavior, and social problems and issues. Includes 73 activity sheets and 39 teaching ideas. For grades 4–12.

Current Events and Reading Comprehension Using the Newspaper. This 67-page guide incorporates current events as reported in the newspaper into interesting activities that teach students about society and social change. For grades 6–12.

Down to Business. Covers stock market transactions, the economy, and current events, while reinforcing reading and decision-making skills. For grades 5–adult.

Employability Skills: A Newspaper Approach. Helps to improve job-seeking strategies and skills, using the daily newspaper and this 116-page guide. For adult education and alternative educational programs.

Fundamentals for Elementary or Secondary Students. Two guides with 50 or more lessons in worksheet form that use the daily newspaper for a fresh approach to addressing competency in reading, writing, math, science, and social studies. A for grades K–5; B for grades 6–12.

Geography in the Newspaper. Activities focus on the news and where it is happening to give students an understanding of the basic themes of geography: location, place, relationships, movement, and regions. Includes teaching suggestions and worksheets. For grades 6–12.

Innovative Activity Cards. Using the newspaper, these 225 sequenced activity cards challenge reading, math, language arts, and social studies skills. For grades K–6 and Special Education.

Intermediate Language Arts. An interesting way to integrate newspaper exploration, while strengthening basic language skills. Includes 53 worksheets. For grades 4–adult.

It's NIE for K–3. Specially designed with children in mind, this guide offers 76 newspaper activities for language arts, writing, social studies, science and health, newspaper knowledge, and math. For grades K–3 and Special Education.

Mastering Michigan I. Students can explore Michigan from the glacier age to modern times through this 4-part program. It includes a class set of student manuals; 50 reproducible activity sheets; a Michi-game board; and a Michigan counties map. For grades 4–adult.

Mastering Michigan II: State Government and Elections. Four components combine to make learning about state government and elections informative and fun. Includes a "Bill Becomes the Law in Michigan" game; 40 reproducible activity sheets; a "Michigan Government at a Glance" poster; and a set of student manuals. For grades 4–adult.

Mastering Michigan III: Michigan and the World. Students examine Michigan's connections to the world in this 3-part program. Includes one class set of student manuals; 50 reproducible activity sheets; and a colorful poster. For grades 5–12.

Measuring Up in Mathematics. Help your students discover ways to apply mathematical formulas in real life, using examples from the newspaper. Designed according to NCTM standards. For grades K–8.

On the Sidelines. A winning combination of the sports pages and activities to reinforce math, social studies, and language arts skills. Includes 50 pages of reproducible activity sheets. For grades 4–12.

Reading Realities. A complete guide to reading and using the various sections of a newspaper. Reading, writing, and thinking skills are enhanced with 73 activities. For grades 4–adult.

Reading To Follow Directions. Choose from 60 easy-to-follow activities using the newspaper to teach alphabet sounds, words, and simple sentences. For grades K–2.

Science in the News. Junior scientists can explore earth science, health, environment, careers, technology, and general science through the newspaper and the activities in this 74-page guide. For grades 4–12.

Special Education and Cooperative Learning. Exercises using the newspaper that promote teamwork and cooperation. This 82-page guide features four competency levels. For grades K–12.

Strategies in Critical Thinking. Turn your students into private investigators using this manual and the newspaper. Includes six case studies to create competency in processing information. For secondary students.

Survival Skills for the Student at Risk. This 68-page guide is packed with newspaper activities to spark motivation and interest in students at risk of dropping out. Integrated subject areas excite students who have nonacademic interest levels and low reading levels. For grades 6–adult.

Using the Newspaper in Adult Education Classes. An interesting way to use the newspaper to teach skills necessary for everyday living, while emphasizing reading and vocabulary skills.

Using the Newspaper in Secondary Social Studies. History, government, economics, and geography lessons come alive when you use the newspaper and this 92-page guide. For grades 7–adult.

Using the Newspaper in Upper Elementary and Middle Grades. Enhances language arts, science, math, and social studies skills using the newspaper and this 94-page guide with ten lessons, worksheets, and 20 activities.

Using the Newspaper To Reinforce Math Skills. Includes activity sheets written on three levels and ways to use the newspaper to show how math concepts relate to real-life situations. Three levels for grades 3–5, 8 and 11.

Using the Newspaper To Reinforce Writing and Reading Communication Skills. Bring out the creativity in your students with this well-organized approach to studying communication skills using the newspaper. Includes 75 pages of objectives and worksheets. For grades 7–adult.

Using the Newspaper To Teach Daily Living Skills. Students learn daily living skills through reading the newspaper and completing activities. For grades 6–adult.

Using the Newspaper To Teach Secondary Language Arts. Students can use topics of interest from the newspaper and over 20 worksheets to learn language arts, writing, literature, and speech skills. Covers language arts foundations, writing, literature, and speech applications. For grades 9–adult.

You and the Government. Use this 65-page, student-oriented, self-directed workbook to supplement and bring relevance to standard American government textbooks with real-life examples from the newspaper. For grades 6–adult.

The Grand Rapids Press
155 Michigan St., NW
Grand Rapids, MI 49503

Newspapers in the Classroom. A booklet of ideas for using newspapers in several subject-matter areas plus a student-reading survey instrument and a special section on comics.

The Saginaw News
203 S. Washington Ave.
Saginaw, MI 48607
517-776-9704

Newspaper in Education Teacher Guide. A 24-page guide of activities in several subject areas.

Workbook. A newspaper tabloid on parts of a newspaper, sections of a newspaper, newspaper services, and terminology.

Minnesota

Duluth News-Tribune
Educational Services
P.O. Box 169000
Duluth, MN 55816-9000
800-456-8080

The following educational supplements are special newspaper sections 16–20 pages in length. They are designed to enrich and supplement the regular school curriculum. The minimum order accepted is 20 copies.

Blacks in American History. For use during Black History Month, this section covers the contributions and situations of Blacks from the early colonies to modern sports heroes. ($0.15 each)

The Duty of Remembering. From Philadelphia comes this sensitive look at the life and beliefs of Martin Luther King, Jr. For grades 6–12. ($0.15 each)

The Ojibwa. A second printing of an award-winning section that has been used by numerous groups to increase awareness of Ojibwa history, culture, treaty rights, and government. ($0.15 each)

Student Showcase. An annual publication of winning entries in the creative writing contest, published each May. ($0.15 each)

Winter Holidays. A popular section covering Christmas, Hanukkah, and Kwanzaa. Excellent for multicultural education. ($0.15 each)

Women in American History. A chronicle of the struggle for equal rights, highlighting outstanding women in American history. A special section on quilting is included. ($0.15 each)

The World of Architecture. Classical, medieval, colonial, and other styles of architecture are covered, with a look at buildings in the Duluth area. This supplement includes special sections on architecture in children's literature and famous architectural landmarks. ($0.15 each)

A World of Difference. Designed to help elementary students overcome prejudice and understand discrimination, this is an excellent resource for multicultural education. ($0.15 each)

The World of Stamps. Students can learn about history, science, art, and other topics through the fascinating study of stamps. This supplement is specially released for Stamp Collecting Month. ($0.15 each)

Missouri

The Kansas City Star
1729 Grand Ave.
Kansas City, MO 64108
816-234-4743

Close Encounters of the Comic Kind. Here are 73 worksheets to use as a guide to the comics and to address values and human behavior, social problems and issues, language arts, and creative writing. Grades 4–12. ($7.00)

English as a Second Language. A guide that contains activities related to structure, speaking, comprehension, writing, reading, culture, and vocabulary for grades 4–12. ($5.00)

Examining the Editorial Pages. A focus on problem-solving and critical thinking skills for grades 5–12. ($3.00)

It's NIE for K–3. More than 65 pages of activities in various subject areas.

On the Sidelines. A booklet of articles for using the sports pages in grades 5–12 to study social studies, science, math, and language arts.

Reading Realities. A 60-page notebook of ready-to-use reading activities.

Star Gazins. A tabloid filled with articles on language arts and reading for teachers and students in grades 5–12.

These Activities Are Classified. A guide to using classified advertising for general language arts, creative writing, consumer, and career education. Grades 5–12. ($5.00)

Using the Newspaper in Secondary Language Arts. A myriad of activities appropriate for grades 6–12 and adaptable for elementary language arts. ($8.00)

Using the Newspaper in Upper Elementary and Middle Grades. This ANPA Foundation publication includes activities covering language arts, science, math, and social studies. ($8.00)

Montana

The Billings Gazette
P.O. Box 36300
Billings, MT 59107-6300

NIE Idea Starters. A packet containing ideas on how to begin using newspapers in the classroom at any level. (Free)

Nebraska

Omaha World-Herald
World-Herald Square
Omaha, NE 68102
402-444-1000

Betsy Ross and the U.S. Flag. A packet including elementary and advanced stories of Betsy Ross, art and newspaper activities about the flag and Ross, instructions on how to fold and cut a perfect five-pointed star, and material on flag etiquette. Also included is a 13-star, 11-by-19-inch cloth flag. ($1.50 plus $1.00 for postage and handling)

Holiday Ideas. A packet of teaching ideas for summer, spring, fall, winter, and holidays using the newspaper. A packet of coloring sheets ready to be duplicated. Besides material for such holidays as Easter, St. Patrick's Day, Valentine's Day, President's Day, Halloween, and Columbus Day, a pattern and directions for making a pressman's hat are also enclosed. ($1.50 plus $0.90 for postage and handling)

Nebraska Anthology. A collection of articles from the *Magazine of the Midlands* about the Nebraska frontier and its pioneers, ranchers, Indians, and railroad men. ($5.00 plus $1.40 for postage and handling)

Using the Newspaper To Teach Economics. A 48-page booklet on our national economic system and its workings by Dr. James Dick, University of Nebraska, Omaha Center for Economic Education. Your local center for economic education and/or your state economic council can provide additional assistance for follow-up workshops based on this curriculum guide. Contact the Joint Council on Economic Education in New York City (212-685-5499) for the number of your local council. For grades 4–12. ($5.00 plus $0.75 for shipping and handling)

Nevada

Las Vegas Review-Journal
P.O. Box 70
1111 W. Bonanza Rd.
Las Vegas, NV 89125-0070
702-383-0211

Garfield Curriculum Card Series. Using the comic strip characters, these cards for teachers in grades K–3 provide a variety of newspaper activities. ($5.00 plus postage)

Newswoman Card Set. Using a woman cartoon character, this set of cards provides activities in the major subject areas including career education. ($5.00 plus postage)

Our Living Desert. This educational tabloid on environmental issues about the desert includes information; pictures; and activities on plants, animals, and preservation issues. ($0.10 each)

Weekly Skill Activity Sheets. Written by educators for grades K–6, the set includes activities on self-esteem, values clarification, global awareness, and many subject-matter areas. ($2.50 plus postage for each unit of 20)

New Hampshire

Union Leader
P.O. Box 780
Manchester, NH 03105
603-562-8218

Parent Activity Guide. A brochure to help parents help students learn basic skills using the newspaper. (Free to state educators and parents)

Teacher Activity Guide. A resource for using newspapers across the curriculum. (Free to state educators and parents)

Workbook for High School Newspaper Staffers and Advisors. Suggestions on writing, editing, designing, and producing a high school newspaper. (Free to state educators and parents)

New Jersey

The Record
150 River St.
Hackensack, NJ 07601-7172
201-646-4384

Creating a Classroom Newspaper. These lesson plans guide development of a class newspaper for elementary, intermediate, and secondary levels.

Exploring New Jersey. Here's a fascinating way for students to learn state history while studying contemporary issues and conditions of the Garden State. Reproducible maps and colorful stickers are included. Themes are: government and politics, geography, transportation, regional products and issues, commerce, recreational and cultural events, education, housing and real estate, sports, and community issues.

Gifted and Talented Study Unit. This 59-page publication provides activities for teaching higher-level thinking skills, including problem solving, inquiry, and creative and critical thinking.

Teacher's Manual. The elementary (K–6), intermediate (7–9), and secondary (10–12) versions each include dozens of ideas and activities for developing skills in math, language arts, science, and social studies.

Times
500 Perry St.
P.O. Box 847
Trenton, NJ 08605
609-396-3232

My Newspaper Journal. A 12-page tabloid for young readers filled with activities for reading and writing. (Free)

New Mexico

Albuquerque Journal/Tribune
7777 Jefferson, NE
P.O. Drawer J or T
Albuquerque, NM 87103
505-823-7777

Ballooning Activities with Newspapers. This fun activity-card set suggests over 90 creative ways to use newspapers with the International Balloon Fiesta (or any hot air balloon festival). Educational ideas encompass language arts, math, social studies, science, newspaper studies, and art. The set is geared for elementary and middle school students with some activities applicable at the high school level. ($5.00)

New York

New York Daily News
Circulation Department
220 E. 42nd St.
New York, NY 10017

Newsworthy: A School Curriculum Guide. Written and developed by the New York City Board of Education, *Newsworthy*'s lesson plans include aim, springboard, development, worksheets, and homework assignments.

New York Newsday
P.O. Box 4092
Grand Central Station
New York, NY 10163-4092
212-766-1204, 718-520-8062, 516-454-2181

Ads-by-Kids Contest. A study of advertising art techniques to prepare for entering the Ads-by-Kids Contest in January. Deadline for subscriptions is December 1. A workshop is required for first-time Ads-by-Kids participating teachers. For grades 5–8. ($5.00)

Blue Kit. A set of 78 teaching/learning idea cards with activities grouped by subject area in a loose-leaf notebook. For grades 5–8 and gifted elementary students. ($15.00)

Career Education and Personal Finance. A manual containing activities and materials for a 10-week study, including sample forms for job applications, résumés, and personal budgeting. For grades 7–12. ($15.00)

Cloze Testing with the Newspaper. Strategies to improve reading test scores by producing student-generated cloze paragraphs using the newspaper. For grades 2–12. ($10.00)

Improving Reading Skills through the Newspaper. A 68-page teacher's manual of reading and writing exercises for secondary students and gifted students in the upper-elementary grades. ($5.00)

Journalism Guide I. This guide for teaching journalism includes a philosophical approach, teaching strategies and activities, and two classroom posters, "Tips" and "Help," for student journalists. For grades 7–12. ($15.00)

Journalism Guide II. A guide for teaching journalism featuring a practical approach, background materials needed for each lesson, and the posters "Tips" and "Help." For grades 7–12. ($15.00)

Meeting the Challenge. A manual of activities and follow-ups, including camera-ready student worksheets. Emphasis is on the structure of the newspaper as an enhancement to learning. For intermediate and secondary special education. ($10.00)

New York City Community Studies. An innovative program designed to help teachers fulfill the New York State curriculum recommendations for fourth grade, including a teacher's handbook plus a student-activities booklet for each class member (maximum 30). For grades 4 and above. ($10.00)

The Newspaper for Second Language Learners. Some 25 teaching strategies and worksheets suggesting methods for using newspapers in ESL and bilingual classes. For beginning to advanced English proficiency. ($10.00)

NIE Language Arts/Writing Series. A set of teaching strategies and camera-ready student worksheets designed to help students develop writing skills. For grades 7–12. ($10.00)

NIE Summer Fun Program. Part 1 contains varied newspaper activities to reinforce reading, language, and math skills in grades K–6. Part 2 is a six-lesson guide for grades 7–12 with camera-ready worksheets to help students create their own newspapers. ($5.00)

Red Kit. A loose-leaf notebook featuring 52 teaching/learning idea cards with activities grouped by newspaper section and indexed by skills. ($15.00)

Science Education Series. For secondary students and gifted students in upper-elementary grades, 57 strategies plus worksheets to facilitate science teaching at the secondary level are offered. ($10.00)

Understanding the Constitution. The background of events leading up to the signing of the Constitution, plus explanations in simple terms of the three branches of government, the preamble, Bill of Rights, amendments, and more. Teaching/learning suggestions are included. For grades 4–8. ($5.00)

Whole Language Learning with the Newspaper. Ideas for using the newspaper to encourage whole language learning in the classroom. For grades K–8. ($10.00)

Press and Sun-Bulletin
P.O. Box 1270
Vestal Parkway East
Binghamton, NY 13902
607-798-1358

Activities with the Newspaper for Elementary Students. This guide contains teacher-tested ideas and activity sheets for elementary students in language arts, math, and social studies. Bulletin-board ideas are included, and all activity sheets are easily duplicated for student use. Lesson plans are set up for a week of concentrated study on the newspaper.

Citizens on Assignment. This 74-page workbook contains 20 lesson plans, hands-on experiences for students interested in becoming involved in particular issues identified in the news, and guidelines for writing about any of the 20 lessons or the community action project.

Constitutional Studies. This 20-page student tabloid, in four colors, traces the history of the Constitution, and graphically introduces the federal system, separation of powers, and the Bill of Rights. A Constitutional quiz is included; answers are in the accompanying teacher's guide.

Language Arts/Writing Series. This series contains 21 lessons designed and field-tested by teachers. Subjects covered include persuasive writing, state competency-test preparation, newspaper writing using computers, and fact versus fiction in writing. Each lesson contains accompanying response sheets to be duplicated for the students.

Science Education Series. This 57-page booklet was designed by science teachers. Part 1 contains science article activities designed to advance content goals, while part 2 contains newspaper activities such as analytical reading, graph and data table interpretation, and weather page exercises.

Using the Newspaper in Life Skills Classes. Six instructional units include reading skills such as indexing, skimming and decoding ads, and consumer education information such as comparison shopping, understanding the classified ads, and job categories.

Press-Republican
170 Margaret St.
New York, NY 12901
518-561-2300

Help for Families Using the Newspapers. (Free booklet)

The Newspaper and Content Area Activities. A 125-page curriculum guide for grades 7–12. ($15.00)

The Newspaper and Reading, Mathematics, Language Arts, and Social Studies. A 175-page curriculum guide for grades 4–6. ($20.00)

The Newspaper Content Area Activities. A 100-page curriculum guide for grades K–3. ($15.00)

Organizing a Student Press Corps. (Free booklet)

Read, Avoid Extinction Coloring Booklet. (Free booklet)

The Syracuse Herald-Journal
Clinton Square
P.O. Box 4915
Syracuse, NY 13221-4915
315-470-2129

Adult Education. A 50-page manual for using newspapers in adult-education classes.

Consumer Choices and Spending. This manual is designed to help students develop skills for becoming knowledgable consumers while applying the basic skills of reading, writing, math, and problem solving.

Creating a Classroom Newspaper. This teacher's guide provides a rationale, lesson plans, and suggestions for producing a classroom newspaper.

How To Use the Newspaper in Teaching High School and College Journalism Classes. A 14-page manual of comments and articles for use in journalism classes.

The Living Textbook. This 36-page guide offers activities for preschool and primary students and for elementary and secondary students.

Mini-Page Teaching Guide. For teachers who use the weekly mini-page, this manual provides additional activities.

Newspaper for Education: Elementary Curriculum. This manual is filled with students' activities on a variety of topics.

Newspapers in Education: Secondary Language Arts Curriculum. A 57-page manual of ideas and activities in language arts with applications for reading, writing, literature, and speech.

Newspapers in Education: Secondary Sciences and Math Curriculum. A 25-page manual of activities to help students develop skills in math, science, and health classes.

Newspapers in Education: Secondary Social Studies Curriculum. This manual contains 92 pages of activities in history, government, economics, and geography.

Newspapers in Education: Upper Elementary and Middle Grades. A 93-page manual that provides 50 lessons and worksheets in each subject area.

On the Sidelines. A manual of activities for using the sports pages to teach skills in language arts, social studies, science, and math.

Read All about It! Your Neighborhood, Your Nation, Your World. A 30-page guide to teach the five geography themes of location, place, relationships, movement, and regions.

Using Newspapers To Teach the Gifted. A 59-page manual that includes program rationale; scope and sequence suggestions; and activities for using news, editorials, advertisements, entertainment articles, and the comics.

North Carolina

The Charlotte Observer
P.O. Box 32188
Charlotte, NC 28202
704-379-6300

Newspaper in Education Teacher's Manual. A loose-leaf style notebook of 104 pages with activities for each subject area. ($6.50)

The Daily Reflector
P.O. Box 1967
Greenville, NC 27834
919-752-6166

Federal Facts Booklet and Color Wall Poster. A 14-page booklet on information about the federal government, and a 24-by-18-inch wall poster of the organization of the federal government. ($4.00 includes postage)

Lesson Plan Booklet. Of the 32 lesson plans, half are for elementary and half for secondary teachers for most subject areas. ($4.00 includes postage)

Puzzle Booklet. Educational puzzles on Black History Month, and math and history events. ($4.00 includes postage)

Students Create-a-Newspaper. Students create a classroom newspaper and learn about newspaper production. ($2.50 includes postage)

Tar Heel Trivia. This package contains 32 interesting, short articles on North Carolina. ($2.50 includes postage)

The News and Observer
P.O. Box 191
215 McDowell St.
Raleigh, NC 27602
919-829-4778

Newswriting. ($3.00 includes postage)

North Dakota

The Forum
P.O. Box 2020
Fargo, ND 58107
701-241-5437

The Centennial Story: 1889–1989. This tabloid is a useful student resource on North Dakota and its quest for statehood. (Write for cost)

Oklahoma

Oklahoman
P.O. Box 25125
Oklahoma City, OK 73125
405-231-3412

Centennial Trivia Cards. A set of trivia quiz cards for independent study on Oklahoma's centennial. (Write for cost)

Central America. A newspaper tabloid featuring history and current data on countries of this area. (Write for cost)

Drugs. A newspaper tabloid describing kinds of drugs used and abused, questions and answers about drug use, and symptoms. (Write for cost)

English Made Easy. Ideas and activities for teaching grammar and basic English are given in this newspaper tabloid. (Write for cost)

Enterprise Square, USA. A newspaper tabloid about economics and the free enterprise system. (Write for cost)

Join Oklahoma Great Race of '89. The road to statehood is featured in this tabloid, including information on trails, Indians, famous Sooners, and land development. (Write for cost)

Learning To Read. A newspaper tabloid on the rules for good spelling, spelling steps, and word games and activities. (Write for cost)

Look at Oklahoma. This hard-bound book is an album of pictures and text about the forty-sixth state. (Write for cost)

Oklahoma Heritage. A newspaper tabloid providing a synopsis of the history of the state. (Write for cost)

Oklahoma Puzzle. A 16-by-21-inch puzzle map of the state of Oklahoma with 77 die-cast counties and an early map of the state underneath the puzzle. (Write for cost)

Our Economic System. A newspaper tabloid that includes content about supply and demand, international trade, inflation, and unemployment. (Write for cost)

Problem Solving: The Faces of School Mathematics. This newspaper tabloid describes the problem-solving process including exploring the problem, devising a strategy, solving the problem, and checking errors.

Today's News—The Living Yearbook. This 425-page book is filled with ideas and activities for K–12 teachers. It covers every subject-matter area with a special chapter on cartoons and comics. (Write for cost)

Pennsylvania

Bucks County Courier Times
8400 Route 13
Levittown, PA 19057
215-949-4073

Creating a Classroom Newspaper. This 30-page guide for grades K–12 provides daily lessons that culminate in the production of a classroom newspaper. (Write for cost)

It's NIE: K–3. An action-filled guide to bridge the gap between newspapers and beginning readers. (Write for cost)

Newspapers: Exploring the Dimensions of Thinking. Lessons for teachers in grades 3–12 are designed to help students develop and expand thinking skills. (Write for cost)

Newspapers Make the Write Connection. A curriculum guide for grades 3–12 with 20 worksheets focusing on the process of writing, prewriting, drafting, rewriting, editing, and publishing. (Write for cost)

Newspapers Put the World in Your Hands. This K–6 supplement provides lessons on fundamental geography themes. (Write for cost)

On the Sidelines. A guide for teachers in grades 3–12 who wish to use sport pages to teach math, social studies, and language arts. (Write for cost)

Places in the News. A collection of 10 activity sheets to be used for teaching geography skills in grades 4–12. (Write for cost)

Read All about It! Your Neighborhood, Your Nation, Your World! This guide to lessons in reading and writing for teachers in grades 3–12 is based on five theme areas identified by the Geographic Education National Implementation Project. (Write for cost)

Rhode Island

Journal-Bulletin
75 Fountain St.
Providence, RI 02902
401-277-7230

Christmas Holiday Package. A guide to using the newspaper to teach health and nutrition. (Write for cost)

Creativity Writing Package. Ideas for using the newspaper in developing creative writing activities. (Write for cost)

End-of-the-Year Survival Package. A creative teaching guide designed to keep students motivated during the final days of school. Available every June. (Write for cost)

Exploring Rhode Island through the Newspaper. Ideas for using the newspaper to learn about the state's geography, government, culture, history, and current events. (Write for cost)

It's NIE for K–3. A creative teaching guide designed to help primary grade teachers incorporate the newspaper into the curriculum as easy as 1-2-3. (Write for cost)

On the Sidelines. A creative teaching guide designed to help teachers incorporate the newspaper sports section into the social studies, language arts, and math curricula. (Write for cost)

Science Package. A guide to teaching science with the newspaper. (Write for cost)

Special Sections and the Integrated Curriculum. This creative teaching guide provides more than 75 activities for teaching all content areas of the elementary and middle school curricula using special sections of the newspaper. (Write for cost)

Teacher Activity Booklet. Provides over 600 activities for using the newspaper in the areas of language arts, math, science, and social studies. (Write for cost)

Thanksgiving Package. A creative teaching guide to using the newspaper during the holiday season. Activities include language arts, social studies, math, and nutrition concepts. Available every November. (Write for cost)

"We the People" . . . A Guide to Using the Newspaper To Teach the Constitution and Other Law Related Topics. Over 100 creative newspaper activities designed for grades 5 and above. (Write for cost)

South Carolina

The Greenville News/Greenville Piedmont
P.O. Box 1688
Greenville, SC 29602-1688
803-298-4100

Between the Lines. A 31-page guide to the newspaper, with a variety of innovative activities for grades 4–8. ($2.00)

Creating a Classroom Newspaper. A 30-page guide designed to help a class prepare and create its own newspaper. Work is organized with a teacher's lesson plan, student worksheets on three levels of difficulty, and ideas for additional activities. Grades 3–12. ($2.00)

Elementary Activity Cards. Set I. A set of 114 cards on math, science, social studies, language arts, and newspapers. Grades 3–8. ($3.00)

Elementary Activity Cards. Set II. A collection of 105 cards in the same areas as Set I, but with different activities. Grades 3–8. ($3.00)

The Newspaper: Your Key to Better Living. A 49-page guide for adult low-level readers to develop reading and life skills. Sections on newspaper, coupons, ads, and classifieds. ($2.00)

Using the Newspaper in Secondary Mathematics. This guide contains 13 pages of activities on awareness, numbers, real-life applications, working with data, probability, and geometry and measurement. Grades 7–12. ($2.00)

Using the Newspaper in Secondary Science. A booklet of 27 pages of directed activities to help students use science to improve their lives, deal with science-related social issues, acquire academic knowledge, and learn about science careers. Grades 7–12. ($2.00)

Using the Newspaper in Secondary Social Studies. A 92-page guide in five sections: history, government, economics, geography, and various teacher worksheets. Grades 7–12. ($2.00)

Using the Newspaper To Teach Secondary Language Arts. A set of 202 activities classified as language arts foundations and writing, and speech and literature applications. The 29 activity sheets included may be reproduced. Grades 6–12. ($2.00)

The State
P.O. Box 1333
Columbia, SC 29202
800-768-2626, ext. 320

NIE Teacher's Survival Guide. This manual packet provides information and ideas on introducing the newspaper into the classroom. (Write for cost)

Tennessee

Nashville Banner
Attn: Newspaper in Education
1100 Broadway
Nashville, TN 37203

Celebration of Citizenship, We the People. A collection of articles written on the U.S. Constitution. ($6.50 includes postage)

The Constitution as a Living Document. A 70-page booklet of facts and activities. ($6.50 includes postage)

Language and Math Skill Cards. Skill cards for application, reinforcement, and maintenance of proficiency skills for elementary and middle grade students.

Pursuing the Banner. A board game.

Read, Think, Write: Beyond Basics in Communication. A collection of activity sheets to promote the thinking skills of analysis, synthesis, and evaluation. ($6.50 includes postage)

Understanding the News. A 25-page booklet of activity sheets on a variety of subjects that require reading, comprehension, and math skills. ($6.50 includes postage)

Texas

The Dallas Morning News
Communications Center
P.O. Box 655237
Dallas, TX 75265
214-977-7351, 800-431-0010

The following elementary-level guides are available from the Educational Services Department:

Basic Skills K–3

Basic Skills 4–6

Communications (Language Arts)

Mathematics

Social Studies

Teams for Grades 1, 3, 5

Your Newspaper

The following secondary-level guides are available:

Case Studies (Law), Grades 9–12

Communications (Language Arts)

Economics, Grades 9–12

Government and Politics, Grades 9–12

Life Sciences, Grades 9–12

Mathematics, Grades 7–8

The Newspaper, Grades 9–12
Read All about It (Language Arts), Grades 7–8
Social Studies, Grades 7–8
Teams, Grades 7, 9, 12

The following all-level guides and special-edition guides are also available:

Campaigns and Candidates (the Election Process)
Career Life Skills
Consumer Choices and Spending
Elections
Fun-damentals
Home Economics
It's NIE K–3
On the Sidelines

Learn To Read with The Dallas Morning News. This guide is for teachers of adult literacy. (Free to subscribers and nonsubscribers)

Houston Chronicle
801 Texas Ave.
Houston, TX 77002
713-220-7904

The following curriculum guides, geared toward elementary-level students, retell the favorite Hans Christian Andersen tales in comic book form. The format teaches and entertains. These guides are structured to use with the Sunday newspaper comics. (Write for cost)

The Emperor's New Clothes
The Nightingale
The Tin Soldier
The Ugly Duckling

Adult Basic Education Curriculum Guide. This guide provides a natural resource for adult learners. The newspaper format is repetitive in nature, yet provides real-life, high-interest material. (Write for cost)

Adult ESL Curriculum Guide. This guide, for the adult learner as well as the teacher, utilizes transitional listening and speaking activities that lead to a focus on literacy components of reading and writing. (Write for cost)

Civil Rights Handbook. Titled "The Dream Lives On: Understanding the Civil Rights Movement," this handbook for students includes information, personalities, and issues.

Economics and Essential Elements, Grades K–6, or Essential Economics, Grades 7–12. These guides meet the guidelines for teaching economics with an emphasis on the free enterprise system and its benefits. (Write for cost)

ESL and the Houston Chronicle Curriculum Guide. This guide is a current, relevant textbook for ESL students. The activities use the newspaper as a tool to reinforce listening, speaking, reading, and writing concepts and skills. For grades K–12. (Write for cost)

GED Curriculum Guide. With a frame of reference that makes learning more enjoyable and relevant, this guide approaches education from the standpoint of the daily news. Serious students may prepare for the five test sections of the general equivalency diploma (GED) examination. (Write for cost)

Geography. This unit supplements classroom geography lessons for all grade levels. (Write for cost)

Historical Front Pages—Space Travel. Blast off with space exploration from Sputnik to Discovery—and everything in between! This 20-page section chronicles the triumphs and tragedies, the successes and setbacks, of the search for the final frontier. This edition also includes educational activities, games, and ideas for teachers in science, history, and language arts at all levels. For grades K–12. (Write for cost)

Historical Front Pages—World War II: Part 1—1939–1942. Part 2—1943–1945. Your class can relive the war as the invasions, battles, bombings, and surrenders unfold in headlines and stories. These 20-page sections also educational activities, games, and ideas for educators in history and language arts at all levels. For grades K–12. (Write for cost)

Learning More through Stats and Scores: Baseball Edition. This guide features ten lesson plans that cover essential mathematical topics. For grades 9–12. (Write for cost)

Learning More through Stats and Scores: Football Edition. Teachers can supplement class lessons with this exciting guide loaded with fun and educational activities. For grades 9–12. (Write for cost)

Lesson Cycle Focus Cards. These cards contain various newspaper-related activities for different subject areas. Secondary and elementary focus cards include: math, science, social studies, language arts, newspaper fun, information to teachers, finding an ad in the *Chronicle*, and fun with comics. (Write for cost)

The Newspaper, the Constitution and You. This curriculum and teacher's guide furnishes some ideas for teaching aspects of the Constitution of the United States. For grades 9–12. (Write for cost)

Reading To Write: Using the Newspaper To Teach Writing. An effective way to teach writing is to teach it as a process of brainstorming, composing, revising, and editing. In this guide, you will find 20 lessons that cover writing complete sentences, narrative paragraphs, persuasive writing, proofreading, letter writing, and many more topics. For grades K–5. (Write for cost)

Solutions for the Future. This set of chemistry supplements helps students understand how chemistry affects their lives and provides teachers with weekly lesson plans. (Write for cost)

TASP (Texas Academic Skills Program). All college freshmen in Texas must pass the TASP test. This book presents the reading and writing portion of the test in a review format. Sample questions and answers are discussed. (Write for cost)

Teaching Texas History. This all-level resource guide contains ideas for teachers, lists of instructional aid, museum exhibits, and much more to make history come alive for students. ($7.00)

Teams. Help your students improve their test scores by applying what they have learned to everyday life. This guide allows practicing for the state-mandated objectives with newspaper content. For grades 1, 3, 5, 7, 9, 12. (Write for cost)

Texas Trivia. This collection of articles about Texas history provides a great wealth of information in an entertaining and informative manner. For grades 6–12. (Write for cost)

Using Ads To Teach. This guide provides learning activities that use newspaper advertisements; it may be used in language arts, math, science, and social studies. For grades 4–6.

Using the Newspaper in Secondary Mathematics. This guide provides teachers with a series of activities that use the newspaper as a learning resource. Included are activities for real-life applications, working with data, probability, and geometry and measurement. (Write for cost)

Using the Newspaper in Secondary Science. This guide offers a series of classroom activities that use the newspaper as a learning resource for the world of science. (Write for cost)

Using the Newspaper To Teach Secondary Language Arts. This guide contains a variety of language arts activities and worksheets that allow students to apply their language and writing skills to the newspaper. (Write for cost)

Using the Newspaper with Gifted Students. This guide encourages critical thinking, individual thought and feedback, and creativity. For grades 6–12. (Write for cost)

Using the Newspaper with Upper Elementary and Middle Grades. This guide offers ten lessons for each of four subject areas: social studies, language arts, math, and science. Each lesson describes its objective, lists materials needed, and provides detailed instructions to the teacher. (Write for cost)

A Year of Seasonal Newspaper Activities. The activities celebrate holidays and special occasions while meeting state-mandated rules for curriculum and sharpening children's newspaper skills. (Write for cost)

Your Key to Better Living: Using the Newspaper in Adult Education Classes. This guide provides teachers of adult students with a series of activities that use newspapers as a learning resource. Activities address both reading and life-skills education. (Write for cost)

Utah

Deseret News
P.O. Box 1257
30 E. 1st St. South
Salt Lake City, UT 84110
801-237-2112

Activity Card Sets:

Brighten Your Bulletin Boards. For grades K–12. ($3.50)

Comic Capers. For grades K–8. ($3.50)

Hooray for Holidays. For grades K–6. ($3.50)

Language Arts Activities. For grades 2–6. ($3.50)

Math Activities. For grades 2–8. ($3.50)

Mini Comic Capers. Language arts for grades 1–6. ($1.00)

Newspaper Games for the Classroom. For grades 4–12. ($1.00)

Newspaper Talk. For grades 3–8. ($3.50)

Our Living Community. For grades 4–8. ($2.00)

Ready, Set, Read. Basic skills for grades K–3. ($3.50)

Shopping the Classifieds. Consumer skills for grades 5–12. ($3.50)

Social Studies Activities. For grades 3–7. ($3.50)

Booklets:

Adding Life to Language Arts, Social Studies, Math, and Science. For grades 3–8. ($3.50)

Basic Journalism Workbook. For grades 7–12. ($3.50)

Citizens on Assignment. For grades 7–12. ($2.00)

Consumer Choices and Spending. For grades 1–12. ($3.50)

Creating a Classroom Newspaper. For grades 3–12. ($3.50)

Economics with the Newspaper. For grades 7–12. ($2.00)

Editing: The Do's and Don't's. For grades 5–12. ($3.50)

How To Plan and Print Your Own Newspaper. For grades 3–9. ($3.50)

Improving Reading Skills. For grades 5–12. ($3.50)

It's NIE for K–3. ($3.50)

Let's Invest. For grades 5–9. ($2.00)

The Newspaper and Secondary Social Studies. For grades 7–12. ($3.50)

Newspapers: Exploring the Dimensions of Thinking. For grades K–12. ($3.50)

On the Sidelines. Sports in language arts, social studies, math, and science for grades 5–12. ($3.50)

Science in the News. For grades 5–12. ($3.50)

Secondary Science with Newspapers. For grades 7–12. ($2.00)

Teachers Talk: Ideas from Utah Teachers for K–12. ($3.50)

Teaching Reading Skills through the Newspaper. For grades 5–12. ($3.50)

Using Newspapers To Teach Secondary Language Arts. For grades 7–12. ($3.50)

Using the Newspaper in Adult Education. For fourth grade and up. ($3.50)

Using the Newspaper in Secondary Mathematics. For grades 7–12. ($2.00)

Using the Newspaper in Upper Elementary and Middle Grades. For grades 5–12. ($3.50)

Using the Newspaper To Teach Gifted Students. For grades 5–12. ($3.50)

Workable Ideas for Career Education. For grades 7–12. ($3.50)

Writing with the Newspaper: Ideas for Teachers. For grades K–8. ($3.50)

You and the Economy. Level 1 for grades 7–12. ($3.50)

You and the Economy. Level 2 for grades 7–12. ($3.50)

Booklets for the 1991 Bill of Rights Bicentennial:

A Case Study: Freedom. For grades 7–12. ($2.00)

Free Speech and a Free Press. For grades 9–12. ($3.50)

Newspapers and Law-Related Education. For grades 5–12. ($3.50)

Understanding Advertising. For grades 5–12. ($2.00)

Understanding the Newspaper. For grades 4–12. ($3.50)

You and the Government. For grades 7–12. ($5.00)

Virginia

Richmond Times-Dispatch/The Richmond News Leader
Richmond Newspapers, Inc.
P.O. Box C-32333
Richmond, VA 23293
804-649-6901

L. D. Activity Kit. Activity cards in writing, reading, and math for learning-disabled students in grades 4–9.

Living Community. Packet of 170 activities to teach values, social studies, and citizenship. For grades 6–12 and upper-level educable mentally retarded students.

Newspaper Style as an Aid to Improved Composition. For high school English teachers, this new approach to teaching writing examines reporting style, interview style, book review style, and editorial style. For grades 9–12.

The Newspaper: Your Key to Better Living. This booklet for using the newspaper in adult-education classes provides teachers with six units of activities that address reading and life-skills education. It also contains supplementary activities.

Primary Newsfun. A teaching guide for primary teachers, with ideas for math, language arts, and social skills.

Social Studies through Current Events. A guide for high school social studies teachers on such topics as economics, history, geography, and political science.

The Special Edition or Upper Elementary Newsfun. A booklet for elementary teachers that covers activities in all subject areas for grades K–6.

Washington

The Spokesman-Review/Spokane Chronicle
P.O. Box 2160
Spokane, WA 99210-2160
509-459-5190

Special Sections. Each of the following is a 20-page tabloid that applies hands-on learning strategies to teach subjects using the newspaper.

Centennial Report (1889 edition). For grades K–adult.

Critical Thinking. For grades 2–12.

Discover Dinosaurs. For grades K–12.

Food for Thought (Nutrition). For grades K–6.

Geography. For grades 2–9.

Go Places Read. Reading skills.

The Law and Justice. For grades K–12.

Learning To Learn. For grades 3–adult.

Native Americans (Pacific NW). For grades 2–12.

Spelling Well. For grades K–8.

The Stock Market. For grades 7–12.

Summer Delights (Activities for Centennial). For grades 2–12.

A World of Difference (Self-Esteem). For grades K–6.

Writing To Learn/Learning To Write. For grades 2–12.

Teacher Survival Kit. This kit includes the following materials: activity guides, sports package, classroom newspaper guide, centennial package, activity calendar, curriculum sections, and consumer education package. ($30.00)

Washington, D.C.

The Washington Times
3600 New York Ave., NW
Washington, DC 20002
202-636-2853

Learning through the Newspapers. A 42-page booklet of activities for students in grades 4–6. (Write for cost)

Newspapers Make Learning Fun. This 62-page booklet is filled with ready-to-use activities in several curricular areas in grades K–3. (Write for cost)

Window to the World through the Newspapers. A 79-page guide for using the various sections of a newspaper ranging from advertising to the editorial pages. (Write for cost)

Wisconsin

The Milwaukee Journal/Milwaukee Sentinel
P.O. Box 661 and 371
Milwaukee, WI 53201
414-224-2653

Anatomy of a Newspaper. This unit describes the daily newspaper, its workings, and its role in society. Useful in teaching how to read a newspaper, the material is easy to understand and gives thorough explanations in a well-illustrated format. (Write for cost)

Basic and Secondary Social Studies Skills. Activities in many social studies areas, particularly history and geography, cover skills in vocabulary, graphs and maps, classification, and comprehension. Individual and group projects are included. Grades 5–12. ($1.00)

Catholic School Guidebook for Religious Education. Ideas for using the newspaper for practical application of Catholic religious teachings. Some activities relate to church doctrine; others focus on biblical themes or general religious issues. Grades 1–12. ($1.50)

Classifieds in Education Kit. This 24-card set encourages development of reading, writing, math, and critical-thinking skills, using only the classified advertising section of the newspaper. Grades 3–8; remedial 9–10. ($2.00)

Comic Universe. Ideas for using the daily comics in reading, language arts, values, critical thinking, and other areas. The well-organized and illustrated activities range from icebreakers to interest builders to introduction or reinforcement of concepts. Grades 4–10. ($3.00)

Curriculum Activity Card Kit Using Your Favorite Newspaper. This kit includes 224 7³/₄-by-4³/₄-inch cards, numbered according to ability levels, covering reading, math, social studies, language arts, and career education. For independent or class study, grades 3–8. ($8.00)

Elementary Reading Skills. A group of 180 motivating activities for developmental and remedial reading classes. Skills covered include word attack, vocabulary, comprehension, and study skills. Grades K–6. ($1.00)

Exceptional Education Rates a 10. Social-living and survival-skills activities in various academic areas to familiarize special-education students with the newspaper are presented at four different levels. Nonreader through grade 7. ($1.00)

500 Newspaper in Education Activities for Grades 1–12. Hundreds of lesson ideas for all grade levels in language arts, social studies, math, science, business education, foreign language, music, art, home economics, industrial arts, drivers' education, physical education, and recreation. ($3.00)

Holiday in the News. Activities using the newspaper to help recognize the importance of 45 secular holidays, including those noted by the Wisconsin Department of Public Instruction for inclusion in school-year study. Several curricular areas are involved. (Write for cost)

Instructional Material Using the Newspaper. This popular 1984 NIE Week booklet offers worksheets and lesson plans for language arts, social studies, reading, math, science, and health. Worksheets, teaching guides, and structured lesson plans are included. Grades 1–12. ($3.50)

Making the Right Decision—Career Education. Students are provided practice in decision making, critical-thinking skills, and goal setting through use of the local newspaper. This unit also presents job characteristics, development of job-finding skills, and positive attitudes toward self, peers, work, and society. Grades 5–12. ($2.50)

Math Skills Using Your Newspaper. Reinforcement of basic math skills through activities on topics including the metric system, graphing, ratio and percent, computation, and problem solving. Grades 3–8. ($1.00)

Newspaper Fun Trivia. What was the biggest newspaper ever printed? Where did the tabloid newspaper come from? How do you grow a newspaper tree? Learn these things and much more in this interesting booklet. Grades K–12. ($0.50)

Newspaper in Education Activities. Lesson plans using the newspaper to study U.S. foreign policy, consumer economics, art, advertising, freedom of the press, the comics, editorials, and other subjects. Grades 1–12. ($0.50)

Newspaper Workshops for Parents. How-to's and hands-on tasks are illustrated, and the booklet contains activities the parents can do at home with their K–6 children. ($3.00)

Open a New World. Newspaper-based activities in language arts, social studies, math, science, art, health, and safety for early childhood education. A special learning skills bonus section is included. Preschool–grade 2. ($3.00)

Our Living Community. This guide provides 150 learning activities based on social, political, and economic issues, allowing students to study their local communities through the newspaper. Grades 7–12. ($4.75)

Project Health. This packet contains 34 activity worksheets covering general health, mental health, fitness, nutrition, and safety. It encourages recognition of certain types of information in the newspaper and provides exercises on interpretation, critical evaluation, and creative thinking. Grades 4–8. ($3.00)

Secondary Language Arts Using the Newspaper. Detailed curriculum guide with activities in language arts foundations and writing, and literature and speech applications. Also includes more than 20 activity sheets. Grades 8–12. ($3.00)

Teaching Critical Thinking Skills. Suggestions and activities for full utilization of all levels of cognition to prepare students to apply, synthesize, theorize, and interpret curricular areas. Grades 5–12. ($1.00)

Ten Projects: Cars and Cycles and Others. Long-term activities in various skill areas. Titles include cars and cycles, women and girls in sports, patriotism, minorities, youth in the news, agriculture in the city and country, shortages, choosing a place to live, crossword puzzles, and animals in the news. Grades 1–12. ($0.50)

Ten Projects: Love and Others. Long-term activities in various skill areas. Titles include love, spring fever, being you, education, sports, fashion, careers, your local government, personality profile, and police. Grades 1–12. ($0.50)

Ten Projects: Recreation and Others. Long-term activities in various skill areas. Titles include recreation, medicine, crisis, comic strip role analysis, no news is good news, best seller books, celebrations, strange happenings, what's the story, and photo quiz. ($0.50)

Ten Projects: You the Consumer and Others. Long-term activities in various skill areas. Titles include you the consumer, heroes and heroines, human interest stories, public notices and personal messages, astrology, emergencies and disasters, words, a do-it-yourself world, vacations and travel, and television. Grades 1–12. ($0.50)

Using the Newspaper in Secondary Social Studies. A comprehensive set of options using the newspaper as a learning resource in study sections including history, government, economics, geography, and a variety of teacher worksheets. Grades 7–12. ($3.50)

National Newspaper

USA Today
Educational Services Department
1000 Wilson Blvd.
Arlington, VA 22209
703-276-5316

Basic Elementary. A guide that helps teachers introduce *USA Today* to elementary-grade students in ten lessons and in each subject matter. For K–8. ($1.00)

Earth Today: Your Place in the Environment. This guide features four instructional themes concerning 12 topics including thinning of the ozone layer, understanding weather, teaching ecosystems, forest conservation, and the dynamics of population. For grades 4–12. ($1.50 teacher's guide, $0.25 student supplement)

Economics Today. This guide helps teach eight economic themes, including you and our economic system, the global economy, our economic future, people in our economy, and creating products and services. For grades 6–adult. ($1.75)

English: Critical Thinking and Writing. A curriculum guide that offers ideas and articles for teaching writing, thinking, and problem solving. For grades 4–adult. ($1.50)

How To Read with USA Today. This guide provides objectives, classroom activities, and simple lesson plans in social studies, language arts, science, and math. For K–adult. ($1.50)

Journalism: A USA Today Perspective. This guide shows students how newspapers gather, write, and circulate news, and traces journalism's history. For grades 6–12. ($1.00 teacher's guide, $0.25 student supplement)

Scope: Science Career Opportunities. This pamphlet is designed to help students learn more about careers in science. It includes a guide and a student workbook. For grades 4–adult. ($0.50 teacher's guide, $1.00 student workbook)

Teaching Youth at Risk with USA Today. A guide for teachers seeking ways to meet the needs of at-risk students, it emphasizes seven instructional techniques for meeting these students' needs. This guide also includes lesson plans, a teaching framework, and classroom activities. ($8.00)

USA Careers. A teacher's guide complete with four lessons, worksheets, and classroom articles that provide students with information about the changing work force, the workplace, and educational options. For grades 4–12. ($1.00 teacher's guide, $0.25 student supplement)

USA Decision: Presidential Studies. This guide focuses on three themes: electing a president, changing of the guard, and the executive branch. For grades 4–adult. ($1.00 teacher's guide, $0.25 student supplement)

USA Freedom: Constitutional Studies. A guide of activities with information worksheets to demonstrate how the Constitution and the Bill of Rights are integrated into daily life. For grades 4–adult. ($1.00 teacher's guide, $0.25 student supplement)

USA Issues: Substance Abuse. Topics in this guide focus on how illegal and legal substances affect individuals and society. For grades 4–adult. ($0.25)

Foundations

American Newspaper Publishers Association Foundation
The Newspaper Center
Box 17407 Dulles Airport
Washington, DC 20041
703-648-1000

Citizens on Assignment. A 74-page workbook designed to involve secondary students in their communities. Material is easily integrated into language arts and social studies curricula. ($10.00)

Consumer Choices and Spending: A Newspaper in Education Guide. Activities at three instructional levels: primary, intermediate, and advanced. The tabloid-size, 20-page curriculum on decision making in the American economy emphasizes money and banking, scarcity, and community decisions. ($20.00)

Educators: Try NIE. This document provides a rationale for using newspapers in classrooms and summarizes recent research findings related to NIE. (Free)

Elections 1988. A curriculum to help secondary and elementary students understand presidential elections. Good as a model for newspapers developing similar units on future elections. ($20.00)

Elementary Activity Cards. Most subject areas for students in grades 4–8 are covered: language arts, social studies, science, math, and careers. Each card has self-contained activities for students to complete by using newspapers. The 108 pages can be photocopied. ($10.00)

First Amendment Poster. A full color, 20-by-25$1/2$-inch representation of our first freedom. (1–24 copies, $5.00 each; 25–99 copies, $3.00 each; 100 or more copies, $2.00 each)

First Amendment Unit. Senior high school activities on basic First Amendment cases. ($25.00)

Free Press and Fair Trial. The history of First and Sixth Amendment rights, revised to reflect Supreme Court decisions through 1986. Can be used as a primer, classroom text, or desk reference. (1–9 copies, $2.00 each; 10–49 copies, $1.50 each; 50 or more copies, $1.00 each)

FUN Supplement: Families Using Newspapers. An eight-page tabloid that provides challenges to be met by parent and elementary school student working as a team. ($15.00)

Guidelines for Newspaper Libraries. This guide describes techniques and procedures used by newspaper librarians in the United States and Canada. It covers proven methods of gathering information, systematic procedures for storing data, and benefits and costs of establishing newspaper libraries. 126 pages, loose-leaf. ($15.00, $20.00 with binder)

Internship Programs: A Manual for Journalism School Administrators. This guide includes basics for setting up internships, plus chapters on program objectives, measuring those objectives, and evaluating the newly established internships.

Journalism Career Guide for Minorities. A 56-page book designed to help minority high school and college students learn about careers in print journalism.

The Newspaper as an Effective Teaching Tool. A brief introduction to NIE, describing principle uses of the newspaper in the school curriculum. Sample activities are given. ($1.50)

Newspaper in Education: A Guide for Weekly Newspapers. A 28-page booklet that provides, for weekly and community newspapers, a brief introduction to NIE and how to budget for it. Included are sample classroom activities in language arts, social studies, mathematics, science, and health. (Free)

Newspaper—What's in It for Me? Your Complete Guide to Newspaper Careers. This four-color booklet for high school juniors and seniors and first- and second-year college students describes newspaper jobs in advertising, business, circulation, graphics, human resources, news-editorial, production, promotion, and telecommunications. (Make checks payable to Newspaper Careers Project. 2–5 copies, $2.25 each; 51–200 copies, $1.60 each; 200 or more copies, $1.10 each. Single copies to students are free.)

Newspapers and Literacy . . . "That All May Read." A 24-page booklet that describes examples of literacy programs at newspapers across North America. (1–15 copies, $2.00 each; 15 or more copies, $1.00 each.)

NIE Introductory Kit. Teachers are introduced to educational uses of newspapers at various grade levels. The kit contains a bibliography, catalog of materials, and miscellaneous photocopied articles. ($2.00)

Our Living Community. A comprehensive set of 150 learning activities for students in grades 7–12, based on social, political, and economic issues. ($25.00)

Speaking of a Free Press. Recently revised 28-page brochure spans 200 years of quotations on press freedoms. ($1.00)

Telecommunications: A Time of Megachange. An eight-page supplement to guide high school students through the many different technologies in telecommunications: telephone, cable television, satellites, and computers, plus career opportunities in these areas. ($25.00)

Using the Newspaper in Adult Education Classes. The emphasis is reading, vocabulary, and life-skills education for adults by using the newspaper, an adult-oriented medium. ($20.00)

Using the Newspaper in Secondary Mathematics. Problem solving is stressed as a fundamental skill and a key ingredient in successful mathematics education. ($15.00)

Using the Newspaper in Secondary Social Studies. Curriculum guide for grades 7–12 that helps teachers use newspapers as a learning resource in history, government, economics, geography, and other areas. ($20.00)

Using the Newspaper in Upper Elementary and Middle Grades. A comprehensive unit of activities and teacher worksheets designed to help elementary and middle grade educators use the newspaper in all school subjects. ($35.00)

Using the Newspaper To Teach about the Constitution. Real-life examples of the Constitution's day-to-day applications are taken from the newspaper. Activities are presented for elementary, middle, and secondary school levels. ($15.00)

Using the Newspaper To Teach Gifted Students. Curriculum can involve daily newspapers for middle and high school students who have been identified as gifted and talented or as high achievers. Activities involve concepts at higher levels of abstraction and emphasize higher-order thinking skills. ($20.00)

Using the Newspaper To Teach Secondary Language Arts. Activities that high school teachers can use in language arts, writing, literature, and speech classes. ($20.00)

You've Got a Lot To Offer—We've Got a Lot To Gain: Newspapers' Message to Minority Job Seekers. A 15-minute career video produced for the Task Force on Minorities in the Newspaper Business by the *Chicago Tribune*. It features minority and nonminority men and women describing jobs in sales, personnel, circulation, financial management, and the newsroom. Ideal for job fairs and school career days. ($20.00)

Florida NIE Coordinator
P.O. Drawer 2949
Ft. Walton Beach, FL 32549

Using the Newspaper To Reinforce Math Skills. For grades 3–5. A 45-page guide to explore the use of newspapers as an aid in teaching and remediating math skills, with student activity sheets. ($5.00)

Using the Newspaper To Reinforce Math Skills. For grades 8–11. A guide suggesting ways to use newspaper content to teach and learn basic math skills, with sample teaching ideas and student activity sheets. ($4.00)

Using the Newspaper To Reinforce Reading and Writing Skills. For grades 3–5. A guide to help students meet and exceed the Florida minimum performance standards for reading and writing. It's useful to others in states with minimum competency programs. ($5.00)

Georgia Press Educational Foundation
1075 Spring St., NW
Atlanta, GA 30309

The Newspaper Guide to Basic Skills Instruction. Two guides on using the newspaper to teach basic skills. Included are teaching strategies and student activity sheets. For grades 7–9 and 10–12. ($6.00 each)

North Carolina NIE Foundation
4101 Lake Boone Trail, Suite 201
Raleigh, NC 27607

Teacher's Guide. This 200-page guide is packaged in a three-ring binder and covers all subject-matter areas. ($20.00)

Educational and Commercial Publishers

Amsco School Publications
315 Hudson St.
New York, NY 10013

The Newspaper and You. Reading skills workbook that combines basic reading and writing with real-life skills through the use of newspapers. It may also be used in ESL classes. For grades 7–12. ($7.60)

Andrews and McMeel, Inc.
Mini Page Books
P.O. Box 419150
Kansas City, MO 64141

The Mini Page products, created by Betty Debnam, are valuable resources and ideal tools to help encourage use of the newspaper and the Mini Page in the classroom and at home.

The Mini Page Book of States. $4.95

Signers of the Constitution Poster. $2.50

The Mini Page Constitution Series (each set): $2.00

The Making of the Constitution Poster. $2.00

The Mini Page Language Series (six languages ordered individually): $1.00 each or all six for $5.00

The Presidents of the United States Poster. $3.00

The Mini Page Map of the USA. $3.00

The Mini Page Map of the World. $3.95

What Kids Can Do To Save the Earth Chart. $2.50

Your Newspaper Booklet. $41.50

Peter Penguin's Puzzle Parade Book. $1.25

Basset Brown's Try 'n Find Book. $1.25

Mighty Funny's Puzzle Jokes Book. $1.25

Rookie Cookie Cookbook. $7.95

The Mini Page Body Parts Book. $2.50

ABC Reading Chart. $3.50

ABC Writing Chart. $3.50

From 1 to 100 Chart. $3.50

Berkley/Small Company
P.O. Box 91460
Mobile, AL 36691

Comics as an Educational Tool. This 91-page book provides a brief history of comics and has chapters on the family, women, and children in comics; additional cartoons; drawing comics; and over 150 activities. For grades 4–12. ($5.50 plus postage)

Creating a Newspaper. A ten-lesson format with worksheets, designed to help students learn to produce their own class or school newspaper. For grades 4–8. ($5.50 plus postage)

Channing L. Bete Co., Inc.
200 Seate Rd.
South Deerfield, MA 01373-0200

About Journalism. This booklet deals with how a newspaper is organized and how news is gathered, written, edited, and printed. Useful in language arts and social studies classes. For grades 5–9. ($1.25)

Clayton International, Inc.
4384 Wheeler
Houston, TX 77004
713-741-6778

Capitalization Activities and Games. For younger or older students who need practice, these activity sheets deal with specific rules and review activities and games. All activities require students to find words in newspapers and to write words or sentences following specific rules. ($4.00)

Celebrating Holidays and Special Occasions. Teachers and parents can help children use the newspapers to celebrate each holiday with a brief history, a picture to color, a calendar, or social studies and language arts activities. ($4.00)

Collections: Vocabulary Activities. Young children and older ones who need to build basic vocabulary skills use these structured newspaper activities to make collections using direction words, contractions, nouns, adjectives, and vivid verbs. Follow-up activities include posters, dictionaries, and writing activities. ($4.00)

Elections: A Citizen's Guide. Bulletin-board captions and a booklet containing notebook, writing, and political action assignments for use during local, state, or national political campaigns. Real-life applications of textbook learning are made. For grades 6–adult. ($6.00)

Identifying ABC's. Prereaders and early readers find ABC's in newspapers, magazines, catalogs, and junk mail. This unit can be used for school or parent programs and is suitable for students of any age who have difficulty recognizing styles of type different from the textbook. ($3.00)

Math Skills Activities. Here are 50 activities for reinforcement, practice, and maintenance of basic math skills. Each page lists a specific skill, estimate of time needed, and an extension activity for able or interested students. For grades 4–8. ($8.00)

Read More about It. Newspaper activities introduce students to 11 different library resources. For grades 4–6. ($4.00)

Reading Comprehension Activities. Newspaper activities for reinforcement and maintenance of specific comprehension skills: identifying details, main ideas, sequence, cause-effect relationships; distinguishing fact, fiction, and opinion; drawing conclusions, making generalizations, and evaluating information. Suggestions for management, grading, bulletin boards, and dealing with problems of syntax, plus reviews of research supporting use of newspapers to improve achievement, attitude, and attendance. For grades 4–6; 7 and above remedial. ($18.95)

Shortages, Inflation, Currencies, Gold. These 58 newspaper activities furnish reinforcement and practice while they add meaning to social studies concepts related to free enterprise. For grade 6. ($4.00)

Dale Seymour Publications
P.O. Box 10888
Palo Alto, CA 94303

News School: Using the Newspaper To Teach Math, Science, Health. This 152-page book includes 117 reproducible activity sheets that explore the language of math, problem solving, money matters, stock market, simple statistics, energy issues, use of natural resources, and other science and health topics. For grades 6–12. ($9.75)

Newspaper Math. This text includes math problems based on feature articles, want ads, and cartoons, and emphasizes thinking and problem solving. For grades 7–8. ($9.95)

Using the Newspaper To Teach Language Arts. Reproducible activity sheets take an interdisciplinary approach for teaching word study, reading comprehension, using literary themes and topics, and nonverbal communication. For grades 5–12. ($9.75)

Using the Newspaper To Teach Math, Science, and Health. Reproducible sheets provide an interdisciplinary approach for teaching problem solving, using numbers, life science, ecology, health, fitness, and nutrition. For grades 7–12. ($9.95)

Using the Newspaper To Teach Social Studies. In reproducible sheets, an interdisciplinary approach is followed for teaching current events and issues, social choices and changes, government, career options, and geography. For grades 8–12. ($9.75)

David S. Lakes Publishers
19 Davis Dr.
Belmont, CA 94002

The Newspaper: An Alternative Textbook. A 117-page book of students' activities and ideas for using the newspaper to teach subject matter. For grades 6–12. ($6.95)

Globe Book Co., Inc.
50 W. 23rd St.
New York, NY 10010

Let's Learn about Your Newspaper. This 15-page booklet provides information and activities about newspapers from defining news to a reporter's method. For grades 3–8. ($1.50)

Newspaper Workshop: Understanding Your Newspaper. A secondary text designed to familiarize students with the newspaper while developing their reading, writing, and vocabulary skills. For grades 7–12. ($5.50 plus shipping)

Goodyear Books
1900 E. Lake Ave.
Glenview, IL 60025

Fun with the Funnies. Ideas for using comic strips to teach reading, writing, and creative expression; 50 ready-to-use reproducible activities. For grades 4–6. ($7.95)

The Writing Corner. A 178-page book filled with activities for improving writing skills. For grades 4–6. ($12.95)

J. Weston Walch, Publisher
P.O. Box 658
Portland, MA 04011

The Complete Newspaper Resource Book. This 266-page book provides more than 700 activities for helping students use newspapers in reading, writing, social studies, the arts, and consumer relations. For grades 6–12. ($20.00)

50 Political Cartoons for Teaching U.S. History. Carefully selected cartoons cover a broad spectrum of events in U.S. history, with commentary. ($25.00)

Janus Books
2501 Industrial Parkway West
Hayward, CA 94545

Using the Want Ads. This 64-page manual helps teachers teach the language arts and other survival skills using the want ads. For grades 7–12.

Knowledge Unlimited, Inc.
Newscurrents
P.O. Box 52
Madison, WI 53701-0052
800-356-2303

Three resource guides filled with creative ideas for using the newspaper to teach language arts and reading skills as well as math, science, and social studies. Each unit contains 25 pages of teacher-directed activities and 42 activity cards and independent study cards. ($29.95 each)

Using the Newspaper To Teach Language Arts/Reading Skills
Using the Newspaper To Teach Math and Science Skills
Using the Newspaper To Teach Social Studies Skills

Editorial Cartoons by Kids. A companion piece to the resource handbook, *Understanding and Creating Editorial Cartoons,* this book showcases a selection of the most original, creative, and thought-provoking entries in a national student editorial cartoon contest. In about 100 cartoons, subjects range form *perestroika* to the savings and loan crisis to the budget deficit. A fascinating, entertaining, and enlightening display of student ingenuity and knowledge. ($7.95)

NIE Activity Cards. These cards are designed to motivate students to explore all sections of the newspaper and provide activities in 11 major subject areas. For grades 4–9. ($16.00)

NIE Teacher's Guide. This 300-page guide has 16 lesson plans, a glossary of newspaper terms, and over 100 group and individual activities and projects in all subject areas. For grade 4–college. ($47.00)

Understanding and Creating Editorial Cartoons. This 129-page loose-leaf handbook is divided into several sections, each of which focuses on one aspect of editorial cartooning, such as caricature and stereotype, use of symbols, and humor and irony. An exciting and innovative way to teach higher-level thinking skills. Each section contains reproducible activity sheets and lesson plans. ($29.95)

Newspower
P.O. Box 203
Northfield, MA 01360
800-346-8330

The Bookworm News. Children in grades 2 and 3 will love to read when they can tell all about it in *The Bookworm News.* This project features a simple book report, jacket illustration, author fan letter, a student book idea, and a color-and-label library page. ($12.95 for a package of 30)

The Community Traveler. Enhance your social studies curriculum with this make-your-own newspaper. Kids write about field trips, their own neighborhoods, outdoor discoveries, and faraway friends and places. ($12.95 for a package of 30)

The Health and Safety News. Kids write about good health care ideas, foods to grow on, tips for preventing accidents, "What would you do if . . . ?" situations, and more. ($12.95 for a package of 30)

The Health and Safety Reporter. Get students thinking and writing about such topics as substance abuse, keeping fit, diet do's and don't's, accident prevention, dealing with emergencies, and more with this tabloid. ($12.95 for a package of 30)

My First Newspaper. A kindergarten and first-grade reading/writing readiness tool. Four-page, 11-by-15-inch newspapers have fill-in format, winsome cartoon characters, and large drawing spaces. Five different newspapers focus on children's interests: school, family, friends, nature, and health. ($12.95 for each package of 30; $39.95 for 20 each of all five newspapers)

The News. Two big, four-page sections with all the features of a real newspaper. Section A features a front-page story, weather box, food page, and fun page. Section B features a travel page, "Talking about Animals" page, special events page, and book review page. Package contains 15 copies of each section. For grades 2–3. ($12.95)

The News Kid-Pack. One each of the five newspapers for grades 2 and 3. ($3.95)

The News Variety Pack. This contains 20 each of the five newspapers for grades 2 and 3. ($39.95)

Newspower. Each book in this series helps students master essential reading and study skills. Directed exercises send students to their favorite newspapers to practice skills learned in the workbooks. Each book is 32 pages. For grades 5–8. ($3.95 each or $39.50 for all ten)

Building Word Power: Vocabulary Development

Getting the Facts Straight: Organizing Information

How To Read and Follow Instructions

How To Read Faster and Remember More

Making Decisions: Judgments and Conclusions

Reading and Thinking: Critical Reading

Reading between the Lines: Making Inferences

Reading, Studying and Learning: Reading-Study Skills

Seeing the Big Picture: From Preview to Main Idea

Understanding New Words: Vocabulary and Context

The Reporter. Two big four-page newspapers for grades 4–8. Two sections feature a news story and weather report; columns for school, town, and world news; and interview, fun, editorial, leisure, sports, and classifieds pages. Package contains 15 copies of both sections. ($12.95)

The Reporter Book Review. Kids write about what they're reading at home or in school. Features include a book review, a jacket illustration, places to list or write about favorite books, a book ad to create, and much more. ($12.95 for a package of 30)

The Reporter Kid-Pack. One each of the five newspapers for grades 4–8. ($3.95)

The Reporter Variety Pack. This contains 20 each of the five newspapers for grades 4–8. ($39.95)

The Travel Reporter. Reinforce social studies and geography lessons with this tabloid. Kids write about foreign countries, hometown views and news, adventures, plus a special correspondent letter-writing feature. ($12.95 for a package of 30)

NIE Information Service
P.O. Drawer 160
Pittsford, PA 14534
716-248-5385

Subscribers to the information service receive the following information each month:

Art Pages. Sparkling, original, reproduction-quality art for use in activities, displays, and newsletters.

Articles. Stories by NIE coordinators and education professionals about their programs, philosophies, and what they have found to be successful.

Learning through the News. Camera-ready student worksheets accompanied by step-by-step procedures and description of the activity for teachers.

Periodic Surveys. With results of NIE effectiveness, development of NIE programs, funding, seminars, and more.

Reprints of Materials. Items developed for NIE programs, workshop techniques, and school projects. (Write for cost)

READ, Inc.
P.O. Box 994
Columbia, MD 21044

Motivational Activities for Reluctant Readers. This manual provides teachers with motivational ideas and activities focusing on listening, reading, and writing skills. For grades 6–adult. ($4.00)

Scholastic Inc.
P.O. Box 7501
2931 E. McCarty
Jefferson City, MO 65102

Political Cartoons. This guide presents a scope-and-response chart of skills and subskills used when interpreting political cartoons, duplicating masters and activities, and lesson plans. For grades 4–9. ($22.95)

Teacher Created Materials
5445 Oceanus Dr.
Suite 106
Huntington Beach, CA 92649
714-891-7895

Newspaper Reporters. Student reporters learn to research facts, plan interviews, take notes, write leads, and plan layouts, using this 48-page reproducible booklet. ($5.95)

The School Times. This booklet provides 15 ready-to-use newspaper forms in which students write their own stories. ($5.95)

CHAPTER 6

Newspaper Strategies for Teachers and Librarians

> "Mankind will write their book day by day, hour by hour, page by page
> . . . the only book possible from day to day is the newspaper."
> La Martine, French statesman

The purpose of this chapter is to describe to you, the teacher or the librarian, ways to use the daily newspaper as you go about teaching subject matter to students. The ideas are designed to encourage you to use newspapers as a supplement to the textbook and as an essential part of your daily curriculum and library activities.

This chapter is not all-inclusive. Its purpose is to get you started, to motivate you to use the resources described in other chapters, to encourage you to use your own creative ideas to enhance students' learning, to help your students get into the habit of daily newspaper reading, and to develop their critical-thinking skills as you teach and they learn subject-matter content. The strategies in this chapter need to be modified by you to match the needs, interests, and abilities of students in your classes or libraries. Once you have tried a few of the strategies you may want to obtain the resources described in other chapters to enrich the curriculum in your classrooms and libraries.

Sample Strategies for Teaching Mathematics

The daily newspaper affords students the opportunity to apply their math skills to real-life problems. The newspaper contains material that helps you teach the structure of numbers, sets, and relations and functions of numbers; the use of mathematics language and symbols; and so on. With the daily newspaper, students can understand relationships between the abstractedness of numbers and math processes, and the concrete application of these to daily living.

General

¶ Have each student cut out numbers from the advertisements in the newspaper. When each student has about 25 cutouts, have him/her place them in envelopes marked as follows: fractions, odd numbers, even numbers, money numbers. Then have the students make up math problems for their classmates to solve.

¶ Use the won-and-lost records of the local high school team or professional team to find percentages.

¶ Have each student find and cut out headlines that use numbers or mathematical words and symbols, and make a poster of these.

¶ Using the obituary column, students can determine the average number of deaths per day for a week and the average age of death.

¶ Have the class use the list of professional teams in a sport and compute distances the teams have to travel to play one another.

¶ Have each student prepare a mathematics problem using some part of the newspaper. Each problem is placed on a sheet of paper with the newspaper clipping attached. Each student solves his or her own problem. Then all problems are placed in a box. Each student draws a problem from the box, solves it, and checks the answer with the student who wrote the problem.

Money

¶ Assign each student to clip out of the newspaper pictures of several products and the cost of each. Have them make up problems in addition, subtraction, division, and multiplication using the clippings.

¶ Collect automobile ads for one or two days. Have each student select a particular make and year of car and compare how dealers price the car. What is the average cost? Highest price? Lowest price?

¶ Tell students to pretend that they must buy enough food for a family of three for one day. The total amount of money they can spend for this is $24.72. Using newspaper ads, have them determine what products they would purchase. How much did they spend? Did they have any money left? How much?

¶ Have students clip from the newspapers five ads for houses that give the price of each house. Ask them to determine the average cost of the five houses.

¶ The daily newspaper provides many advertisements about borrowing money, loan rates, and credit card enticements. You can discuss with the class the pros and cons of borrowing to pay for merchandise. The class can investigate the advantages and disadvantages of borrowing money from a loan company or a bank, charging items on a credit card, or saving one's money and only buying something when one has the cash to pay for it.

Graphs

¶ There are four major kinds of graphs: circle graph, line graph, pictograph, and the bar graph (vertical and horizontal). Some activities involving graphs follow:

1. Have students cut out a variety of graphs used in their local newspaper.
2. Discuss why graphs are used. The students should understand that graphs are used to depict facts quickly and easily for the reader.
3. Discuss characteristics of bar graphs they have found in the newspaper:

   Bars can be horizontal or vertical.

   They are usually labeled by date or time or amount.

4. Discuss characteristics of line graphs found in the newspaper:

   Heavy line connects horizontal and vertical quantities.

   Points usually indicate amount, date, or time period.

5. Discuss characteristics of pictographs they have found in the newspaper:

   Use of symbols—stick figures, cars, other symbols.

   The symbol is usually placed to the right of name, dates, or time periods.

6. Discuss characteristics of circle graphs they have found in the newspaper:

   The circle represents the whole amount.

   Each wedge represents percentage of entire amount.

7. Make a bar graph showing the number of students in class who ride a bus to school.
8. Make a bar graph of the following information. Jim recorded the time it took him to read the newspaper each day. His data looked like this:

   Monday—10 minutes

   Tuesday—20 minutes

   Wednesday—15 minutes

   Thursday—30 minutes

   Friday—1 hour

   Saturday—5 minutes

   Sunday—75 minutes

   What would be appropriate units to use on the number line?

   Make a bar graph of Jim's data.

   How many hours did Jim take to read the newspapers this week?

9. After the students have practiced reading and making graphs, have them try to interpret graphs that appear in the newspaper.
10. Select several articles having information that students can apply to graphs. Have students make graphs of the contents of these articles.
11. Graphs also appear in many of the textbooks students use. Select a few graphs from their social studies, science, or math books to determine students' ability to interpret these graphs. Compare them to the graphs that appear in newspapers.

Geometry

Another area in which the newspaper can be used in mathematics is geometry.

¶ Have students use their daily newspaper to find examples of geometric shapes such as a circle, square, triangle, semicircle, and rectangle.

¶ Tell each student to select pictures from the daily newspaper that illustrate geometric shapes, perspective, and/or shading.

¶ Have students find a newspaper ad or picture that illustrates:

A rectangle that is not a square.

A parallelogram that is neither a square nor a rectangle.

A parallelogram with all sides equal.

A parallelogram that has no equal sides (impossible).

A square that is not a rectangle (impossible).

¶ Let the students collect several house floor plans from the real estate section of the newspaper. After discussing the purpose of the plans and the various symbols, have the students develop plans of their own houses or apartments.

Vocabulary

¶ Vocabulary lists can be developed by students and used in the weekly spelling lessons. The following list is a sample of the many math words used in daily newspapers.

account	bonds
annual	budget
asset	collateral
average	credit
billion	discount

finance	payments
fraction	percent
income	rates
interest	savings
liability	security
million	stock market
money	treasury

¶ Have students cut out several words that relate to math. Paste the cutouts in a word-bank book. Hold a spelling contest using the words in the list and other words selected by the class from their word bank.

Measurement

¶ The newspaper can be used to help students develop concepts of measurement.

1. Students can study measures of length (inch, foot, yard) by selecting ads that deal with carpeting or floor tile. They can determine the price to install carpet or tile in the classroom or a room at home.
2. Measures of quantity (dozen) and weight (ounce, pound, ton) can be illustrated by content in the daily newspaper. For example, the students can use grocery ads to examine differences between "family size" and "economy size." Students can also figure the cost per ounce or pound of different products.

Sample Strategies for Teaching Social Studies

The daily newspaper plays a vital role in the new social studies curriculum. It provides a "living textbook" from which teachers can help students learn the concepts and generalizations underlying the social studies program. The content of the daily newspaper allows students to develop their thinking skills and problem-solving abilities. The case study method of teaching lends itself well to the numerous human interest stories and news articles appearing in the newspaper.

This section provides you with a sample unit for teaching about your state and then suggests activities for teaching other social studies content.

Social Studies: A Unit on the State

The daily newspaper is an excellent resource for specific units in the social studies curriculum. In the primary grades, for example, units utilizing newspaper content can be developed for such topics as home and school, city and neighborhood, community services, transportation, and safety. In the upper grades, units can be developed on countries such as Japan, China, Brazil, and Canada. A unit on your state can be interesting and informative for youngsters when newspaper content is used. It is the task of the teacher and the librarian to begin a collection of newspaper articles and pictures about the state the students are about to study.

The following unit will serve as an example of how newspaper content can help youngsters find meaningful material for a study of their state.

Title: <u>(State's Name)</u> Today

OBJECTIVES

¶ After this unit, students should know and understand the cultural, economic, political, and historical aspects of the state of _____ .
¶ After this unit, students should appreciate _____ , its heritage, current problems, and leadership.
¶ After this unit, students should have improved their reading, writing, and thinking skills.

INITIATING ACTIVITIES

¶ Have the entire class prepare the classroom for this unit of study on your state.
¶ Assign students to one of the six cooperative learning groups:

Cultural/social life

Economics—agriculture

Economics—industry

Political—local

Political—state

Historical life

¶ Have each group follow a plan to enhance problem-solving skills, such as:

1. What do we want to find out about the cultural/social life of the state?
2. How will we locate, gather, organize, review, and evaluate information about this state?

3. In what ways can we summarize our material and present it to the class or others who may be interested in our findings?

DEVELOPMENTAL ACTIVITIES

¶ Assign selected students to prepare a large (4-by-4-foot) paper outline map of the state. Have them identify and label the capital and other major cities. Make thin, 1-inch slots on the map, and clip to them newspaper articles that highlight state affairs each week.

¶ Have each student use daily newspapers to collect news articles about the state, collect pictures of state officials, and facts about living in the state.

¶ Make a chart on state affairs to teach the students how to read charts and graphs. Use the same procedure for map reading.

¶ Invite a reporter of state news to class to explain to the students how he or she gets the news.

¶ Have students select a controversial issue on the state level, use the newspaper to collect data, and plan a debate.

¶ Have students report on human interest stories and fads that are peculiar to the state.

¶ Assign students to keep a record of economic terms that relate to the state's economy.

¶ Have the cooperative learning groups prepare booklets for other grade levels on some of the following topics: Indian/early pioneer life; what the state produces for others; do you know your state government?; places to visit in the state; famous people.

¶ Have students collect articles that indicate problems of conservation, environment, or employment.

¶ Assign each student a chapter from a textbook on the state and use daily newspapers to update the content in the textbook.

CULMINATING ACTIVITIES

¶ Have each of the cooperative learning groups present their information to the class.

¶ Have the class prepare a newspaper of their own about the state.

¶ Ask the librarian to create a file in which the information can be stored and used by other classes.

Geography

¶ Have students use datelines in newspaper articles as a means of finding out the city and country to which the article refers. Locate these on a map.

¶ Assign each student to select a dignitary who is touring the world. On an outline map of the world have the students trace the trip, using newspaper articles as the source of information.

¶ Let students select professional baseball, basketball, or football teams. Provide each student with an outline map of the United States. Have them locate the home cities of all the teams in the league. Numerous activities can result from this suggestion. Students can explore: What rivers and mountains will one team cross when they go to play another team? What teams are in the West? East? North? South? What are the distances between team locations? How should the divisions be rearranged, especially in baseball, if the criteria were location and limited travel?

¶ The daily newspaper provides many words that are part of the vocabulary of geography. For example, the students can search for articles that use such words as bay, delta, earthquakes, equator, gulf, latitude, longitude, monsoons, peninsula, and plains.

¶ Using a weather map, the students can learn how subject matter is interrelated, particularly with regard to geography, science, mathematics, and language arts.

1. Map reading.
2. Use of symbols and definition of special weather words.
3. Cities, states, countries.
4. Fronts (warm, cold, stationary).
5. Pressure areas (high, low).
6. Prediction of tomorrow's weather based on the information provided on today's weather map.
7. Are the cities with the most precipitation in low pressure areas? What is a low pressure area? What does "pressure" refer to? How does low pressure differ from high pressure? The teacher can also discuss the meaning of fronts, air masses, clouds, and isobars.

¶ Have a group of students collect daily weather maps in order to report to the class each morning a prediction of the weather. They can also explain to the class the causes and effects of high and low pressure systems, barometric pressure, temperature changes, and the vocabulary used by meteorologists.

1. Use of numbers.

   Find the city with the greatest variance between the high and low temperatures.

   Find the coldest city listed on the chart. Where is it located? Warmest city? Where is it located?

2. Decimals.

The decimal numbers used on the weather chart are expressions of what measure?

What city had the most precipitation? The least?

3. Describing or predicting the weather in their own words.

Economics

¶ Clip articles and pictures from the newspaper that tell about services the government provides the community.

¶ Assign a group of students to find articles that show how taxes pay for the services the community receives.

¶ Assign students to find out the differences between individual income tax, corporate taxes, and the kinds of taxes used to raise money to pay for services. Use newspaper articles to illustrate these.

¶ The daily newspaper provides numerous opportunities for students to develop their economic vocabulary. Here are some terms students should try to find and define based on newspaper articles.

bonds	production
federal income tax	profits
income	retail prices
insurance	stock
investments	stockholders
labor unions	strike
net profit	wages
prices	

¶ Discuss the use of advertising as a means of promoting business and of paying for the daily newspaper.

¶ Have students collect articles and pictures showing the economic problems of underdeveloped areas of the world.

¶ Study the stock market pages with the class for a discussion of these details:

1. Discuss the purpose of listing stocks in the newspaper.
2. Ask the students where the name of the company is located on the page. Why is it abbreviated?
3. Point out that the column titled "Div." means dividend, that is, the amount paid to shareholders.

Students may be familiar with the word "dividend" from their math lessons as the number to be divided by another number.

Ask what they think the word "dividend" means on the stock lists.

4. Ask the class what they think the column "Sales (Hds.)" means. Explain that this column shows the number of shares traded for the day. Since this column is expressed in hundredths (Hds.), shareholders traded that number times 100 or _____ hundred shares.
5. Ask the students to tell what they think the two columns called "High" and "Low" mean. Explain that the high column gives the highest price paid for a share and the low column lists the lowest price paid for the stock.
6. Explain that the column labeled "Last" is the closing price for the stock.
7. The final column, "New Chg.," represents the change per share compared to the closing price on the previous day. A notation of "-1/8," for example, would mean that a stock closed at about 13 cents (one-eighth of a dollar) less than the previous day.

¶ Have students select one company from the stock market listings in their newspaper and provide the following information to the rest of the class:

1. What is the name of the company?
2. How much does it cost to buy one share of the company's stock?
3. What was the closing price of the stock?
4. Was the closing price "up" or "down"? What is the actual figure?
5. How many shares were sold during the day?

¶ Give each student $9,000 in imaginary or play money. Have two students serve as brokers and sell stock. Each student in class is to buy shares in three companies on the New York or American stock exchanges from the brokers.

1. Have each student find the sale price of the stock he or she wants to buy.
2. Each student is to chart the progress of the stock for one month.
3. They may buy or sell whenever they wish.
4. Each student must keep a list of his or her transactions, profits, losses, etc. This is to be checked by the teacher and brokers each week.
5. At the end of one month, have students determine whether they made a profit or suffered losses. Have them analyze reasons for this.

History and Political Science

¶ Have students prepare a classroom newspaper of one or two pages on some historic event. For example, on the topic "Columbus Discovers America," a cooperative learning group can prepare the front page, while another group prepares articles and interviews for the second page. Each youngster can pretend he or she is an editor or reporter at the time of the discovery. Have another cooperative learning group prepare a front page of the same event from the Native Americans' (Indians') point of view.

¶ Many times youngsters fail to recognize the importance of the individual in a democracy. Some individuals serve as excellent examples of the power or influence that one person can exert on the government, on industry, or on other people. Have students collect stories of the achievements of national figures or of persons in the local community.

¶ Assign students to read the newspaper regularly to obtain information about their city and state governments. Have them prepare an organizational chart of the government, based on what they are reading in the newspapers. Also, have students keep current a bulletin board of local issues, concerns, or problems.

¶ Prepare a bulletin-board display on the question, "Is there history in the daily newspaper?" Tell students to read several newspapers for one week. From these, have the students clip out all the pictures and articles dealing specifically with things of the past. Each time they find pertinent information they should summarize it in writing and then tack it to the bulletin board.

¶ Assign each student a holiday that commemorates our historical heritage. Have each student write for a copy of the newspaper published on that day of commemoration. For example, a group of students may request the July 4, 1960, 1970, 1980, and 1990 editions of the same or different newspapers to compare articles about the historical event. From this the student can prepare a scrapbook of articles and pictures of the material each newspaper provides.

¶ Have the students write a newspaper article or editorial on the need for rules at home and school. Some students can prepare lists of rules. Others can interview the principal, parents, teachers, and other students for material for the article.

¶ Direct students to clip out articles from newspapers that illustrate different forms of government such as democracy, monarchy, or dictatorship. Have a group of students study the articles under each category and prepare a report on related issues, problems, and concerns.

¶ Using an outline map of the world, have the class identify major countries and indicate the kind of government each has. Students also can identify the leaders of these countries by finding pictures in the newspapers.

¶ Tell students to collect newspaper articles that illustrate the different forms of local government within their state. For example, some communities have a mayor and council; others have a manager or a board of trustees.

¶ Since the U.S. Constitution is the law of the land, have students find newspaper articles that are related to what is written in the Constitution. You may also assign certain amendments of the Constitution to groups of students and have them find articles related to that amendment.

¶ Ask the students to find and read articles that illustrate that individualism and equality of opportunity are basic to our democratic way of living.

¶ Assign students to find articles and pictures that illustrate people working together to meet the needs of other people.

¶ Have each student select a particular branch or agency of the federal government and prepare a scrapbook on its organization, purposes, personnel, and activities. Use the daily newspaper for articles and pictures of these agencies.

¶ Have students collect pictures from newspapers that depict how people work together. A bulletin-board display can be prepared showing the various services the community provides its citizens such as schools, hospitals, protection, safety, and security.

¶ Articles and letters to the editor that illustrate conflicting opinions in a community can be collected. These conflicts could be discussed in class. Students can collect information that presents both sides of an issue. Debates or panel discussions can be developed on the material in the daily newspaper.

¶ Newspaper articles can be the basis for studying specific social, economic, or cultural problems in the community.

¶ Students can study the various social, ethnic, and economic differences within their own state by using newspapers published throughout the state.

Sample Strategies for Teaching Science, Health, and Safety

Science is such a rapidly changing subject that many textbooks are obsolete before they are printed. The newspaper, however, is one medium that consistently reports up-to-date scientific information. Using daily newspapers in science class supplements, very effectively, the content in the textbook.

Science

A recent informal survey of several newspapers indicated that science content is plentiful. The author found pictures and articles on rock collections, weather, space travel, the body, vitamins, conservation, the planets, health, pollution, earthquakes, oceanography, science personalities, and so on.

¶ Have the class plan a school display for a modern "Who's Who in Science."

¶ Each student should select a science topic in which he or she is especially interested and prepare a scrapbook or science newsletter on this topic.

¶ Another group of students can design quiz games based on scientific information found in the newspaper. Each week the quiz games can be used for evaluating students' science reading.

¶ Have students prepare biographies on people in the science field.

¶ The class can start a science library by cataloging science articles and pictures. This is an excellent way of introducing students to the science specialities such as astronomy, biology, chemistry, zoology, and the Dewey decimal system.

¶ Encourage each student to make a science vocabulary notebook. This list can be used for individual spelling quizzes, vocabulary tests, or dictionary exercises.

¶ A science concept can be "discovered" by students in class and then illustrated by newspaper articles and pictures. For example, you could choose "For every action there is an equal and opposite reaction." Students can bring in examples of this concept published in their daily newspaper.

¶ Class discussion and individual reports can be presented on some of the following topics frequently written about in newspapers: air and water pollution, body transplants, space flights, archaeological discoveries, health topics, weather phenomena, drugs, or tobacco and smoking.

¶ A group of students may enjoy preparing a radio script on some recent scientific discovery. Invite a scriptwriter from a local radio station to help them. Maybe the class could present their script on a local radio station.

¶ Have students collect newspaper articles, pictures, and advertisements illustrating how machines help humans do work. This collection can include such items as power tools, construction machinery, transportation farm equipment, home appliances, convenience machinery, i.e., electric toothbrushes or shavers, and, of course, the microcomputer.

¶ Let the class prepare a mural on space flight from countdown to touchdown, based on articles and pictures from the daily newspaper.

¶ Have students collect information concerning specific topics in the field of communication such as telegraph, telephone, radio, television, printed material, computer, videos, and recording devices.

¶ The subject of housing can be introduced and supplemented by newspaper articles and pictures to provide material for studying the following content:

1. Where people live: climate, geographical location
2. Parts of houses affected by climate: foundation, framework, floors, roof, fixtures
3. Heating or cooling the house: air conditioning, humidifier, hot air heat, hot water heater, steam heat, radiant and solar heat
4. Protecting the house: fire, water, security, hazards

¶ Invite the science editor from the local newspaper to talk to the class about his or her job. Prepare a list of questions for the editor, such as: How did you become interested in writing about science? How does your preparation as a science editor differ from that of your colleagues? Did you take many science courses in high school or college? How does one become a science editor?

¶ Students will find it enjoyable and informative to collect science articles on such legends as the Loch Ness monster in Scotland, life on other planets, moon exploration, and the invisible world of microbes.

¶ Have students clip and save science columns such as "Ask Andy." Have them study the relationship of the material in their science textbook to the questions answered in the column.

¶ Select several students for the special events section of the bulletin board. This section would inform the class of special events about science on television, in newspapers or magazines, or in the local community. For example, a special program on oceanography may be presented on television. These students would have the responsibility of informing the teacher and classmates about the program before it is shown.

¶ Have students find articles about science fiction. Analyze the articles using the following questions as a guide: Can science fiction be true? Where do the writers get their ideas? How much science is there in science fiction? Is there any science fiction on the comic page?

¶ Tell students to collect science articles for a week and put them in a box in the classroom. At the end of the week have students decide in what area of science each article belongs: physics, astronomy, biology, chemistry, meteorology, archaeology, zoology, etc.

Health

¶ Assign a group of students to put a health news section on the bulletin board. The committee should select articles that will help the class with their personal health habits.

¶ Have students read advice columns on health or behavior and discuss why people write to the editors seeking help. Ask the students if they feel that the people who write to the writers of advice columns usually follow the advice given.

¶ Use newspapers to develop a unit on man and his diseases with a list of vocabulary words from the newspapers: AIDS, antibiotic, cancer, epidemic, immunization, influenza, insulin, measles, microbe, penicillin, plague, pollution, transplants, vaccine, virus.

¶ Use the daily newspaper to develop a unit on food around the world. Select recipes that are common in other countries. Parents of students could prepare some of these for sampling by the class.

¶ Have students find articles that discuss the pros and cons of dieting and the many diet plans advertised.

¶ Assign students to find articles that describe the functions of the U.S. Food and Drug Administration.

¶ Have students find articles on food supplies, population growth, and countries where people are experiencing hunger and starvation.

¶ Direct students to find articles discussing the importance of water to the human body.

¶ Have students collect articles about vitamins, dieting, food fads, and balanced diet.

¶ Students can learn about themselves and their relationships with others by discussing articles that deal with prejudice, relationships between individuals and groups, gangs, and relations between countries.

¶ Have students discuss the meaning of competition. Find articles that illustrate people in competition or show what it means to be a good winner or loser. Discuss these topics with the class.

¶ Discuss with the class the concept that groups are people who work together because of common goals or aims. Have students illustrate this concept by clipping articles that show people in groups working for a common goal.

¶ Have students select articles that deal with the family and discuss the content.

¶ Have students select articles that illustrate the need for rules, regulations, and laws.

¶ Let students prepare a bulletin-board display of newspaper articles and pictures of good grooming habits and proper manners.

¶ Several articles and pictures can be collected and discussed that relate to the important organs and systems of the human body.

¶ Students can prepare a display of articles and pictures that illustrate outdoor play and muscle-building activities.

¶ Clip and discuss syndicated columns that focus on health problems.

¶ Most schools must teach a unit on alcohol, drugs, and tobacco. Use the daily newspaper to collect articles on each of these subjects.

Safety

¶ Have each student make a booklet titled "Safety First" using articles and pictures from newspapers.

¶ Make posters depicting safety rules about things a child should not touch, smell, or drink.

¶ Have the class prepare a safety booklet for younger children based on newspaper articles and pictures.

¶ Students can prepare posters or comic strips on what to do during such disasters as floods, hurricanes, tornadoes, and earthquakes.

¶ Have students analyze stories about traffic accidents to determine how they might have been avoided.

¶ Have students find instances where people have risked their lives to save others.

Sample Strategies for Teaching Language Arts

The daily newspaper is a natural instructional resource for teaching the language arts. Such objectives as increasing vocabulary, developing reading skills, and improving writing ability can be better attained when teachers and librarians utilize the daily newspaper, as was suggested in the research described in chapter 3.

¶ Since most primary-grade students use the daily newspaper for pleasure reading, its pictures, comic strips, and cartoons can be a means for developing the skill of using picture clues to understand content.

¶ Newspaper headlines can be used to provide activities for developing word recognition skills. For example, students can cut out and paste in a folder all words, in various headlines, that they recognize. They can be encouraged to learn new words by cutting out words that begin with the letters of their first names.

¶ Prepare a game called Down with Vowels. Select a couple of headlines, cut them out, and covers the vowels with correction fluid. Make an overhead or handout of these headlines and ask students to tell what vowels are missing, read the headlines, and tell what the headline means. Example: B_sh S_ys: N_ N_w T_x_s.

¶ Students can prepare their own weekly newspaper based on their experiences and these can be used as experience charts in reading.

¶ Students can make their own sentence strips from words cut from the headlines.

¶ There are several exercises that you can create for using newspaper content to develop structural clues or visual scrutiny.

1. Have each student find words on the sports page that are compound words (sportsmen, fishermen, basketball, football, baseball).
2. Have each student use the front page to find words that utilize a prefix or suffix.
3. Using an article of particular interest to the class, the teacher can have the students identify:

Plural words

Words that look alike (game-same, where-were, was-saw)

Words ending in -er or -ing

Words that begin with a vowel, a consonant, or a consonant blend

¶ Human interest stories can be effectively utilized for developing interpretive skills. For example, you can discuss with students the motives of the characters, their attitudes, the problem, and ways to solve the problem.

¶ Newspaper articles can be used to help students:

1. Distinguish between fact and opinion
2. Find proof of a statement in some other source—a textbook or an authority
3. Determine the setting of the article—where and when
4. Judge the merit or value of the article
5. Find the main idea of the article
6. Distinguish the important facts
7. Make a summary of the article

¶ Have students collect pictures that show how people react to an incident or event. Examples would include surprise, fear, happiness, sadness, or other emotions.

¶ Dramatization of a comic strip or cartoon can be effective in developing skills of interpretation.

¶ Each day have students select an article of interest; then underline each new word, find its meaning, and use it in other writings.

¶ Have each student read a particular newspaper article. Then ask a series of questions to evaluate reading comprehension.

¶ Have the class label four envelopes for nouns, adjectives, verbs, and adverbs. Then help them develop sentence-building skills by completing this activity:

1. Have each student cut words from newspaper headlines and place them in the appropriate envelopes.
2. Have each student select words from the envelopes marked "nouns" and "verbs," and make sentences with them.
3. Each student can then select adjectives and use these with the nouns. Do the same using verbs and adverbs.
4. Have students make numerous sentences using this procedure.
5. By varying this activity students can learn many aspects of sentence building. For example, by placing the adjective after the verb, the student can learn about linking verbs and adjective transformation.

¶ Have students clip words from several headlines until they have collected about 50 different words. Then complete the following:

1. Tell them to place the words in two major columns—those beginning with a vowel, the other column for consonants. Have the students record these words in a notebook.
2. Have students record all the rhyming words.
3. Make them arrange the list in alphabetical order.
4. Have the students record all words with silent letters.

¶ Have students find at least five words in the newspaper that are used with at least two different meanings.

¶ Have students search for foreign words and phrases in the newspaper and find their meanings.

¶ Assign students to read a news article and outline the important facts by answering the questions: who, what, where, when, why, and how.

¶ Have students read a news article, then write a one-sentence summary of each paragraph or find a sentence that summarizes the entire paragraph.

¶ Have students keep a log of words from newspaper headlines that are synonyms and antonyms.

¶ Have students write about an incident in their lives as a newspaper article. Use the reporter's five W's—who, what, when, where, and why.

¶ Remove headlines from articles. Have students read the article and then write the headline. Compare their headlines to the original.

¶ Have students write headlines and lead sentences for an article about an incident at school or at home.

¶ Assign students to read several letters to the editor. Ask them to write one-sentence summaries of the issue, concern, or problem being addressed.

¶ Select a picture from the newspaper and remove the caption. Let students write their own captions.

¶ Have several student groups prepare their own comic strips. Test the comics for interest and appeal by giving them to other students and watching their reaction.

¶ Have each student select and study advertisements that interest them. After their analysis, have them write their own advertisement on a product they select.

¶ Tell each student to watch all or part of a sporting event on television. Then have them write an article on the event as a sports reporter would.

¶ Assign each student the task of writing a classified ad for something he or she would like to buy or sell.

¶ Students will enjoy rewriting comic strips in prose form. Have them write an opening paragraph, use quotation marks, and conclude the story.

¶ Assign each student the task of finding at least three different types of sentences (imperative, declarative, and interrogative) in a story on the front page of the paper.

¶ Have students clip from the newspaper two different uses of quotation marks.

¶ Students can cut out three newspaper headlines and rewrite them into complete sentences.

¶ Have students cut out five or six headlines. Using words such as while, as, before, because, so, for, or that, have students put these headlines together to make simple or compound sentences.

The Daily Newspaper and Independent Study

In the middle and high school grades, teachers and librarians may wish to create independent study opportunities for individuals or cooperative learning groups. Independent study for individuals or small groups is a process by which students learn content and develop research and learning skills with limited assistance from teachers and librarians.

One might ask, "Why provide students with independent study opportunities?" The answer is that self-direction is one of the major objectives in education; that is, we want to help students to learn how to learn. Most people learn best when they discover things on their own.

To date, too much emphasis has been placed on the teacher as a transmitter of information. The teacher's or librarian's role should be to create situations and provide materials that encourage students to research, study, create, and report.

Newspapers lend themselves well to independent study because the content, along with supplemental materials such as magazines, pamphlets, and videocassettes, helps students bring reality, relevance, and purpose to their work. For example, teachers, students, and librarians could create independent study packets on a variety of issues, including: economic issues (global economy, multinational corporations, debt crisis, overpopulation), political issues (immigration, foreign policy, national self-interest, international relationships), ecological issues (acid rain, pollution, land use, endangered species), technological issues (military power, transportation, weaponry, developed vs. underdeveloped countries), and quality-of-life issues (equality, justice, security, the freedoms, housing, food). Teachers, librarians, and students can also design independent study units about local and state problems.

Here is a suggested format for an independent study unit, followed by an example.

Learning Strategies

This strategy is designed to encourage students to learn about a specific body of content, a problem, or an issue, using daily newspapers and supplementary materials.

Exercises and activities—some designed by the teacher or librarian, others by the students—should be interesting to do and should focus, whenever possible, on the processes of learning: questioning, reading, collecting evidence, classifying data, discovering principles, making hypotheses, summarizing, and reporting and evaluating results.

Reporting Strategies

The teacher or librarian determines the methods the students will use in reporting what they are learning. For example, will there be discussion groups, informal reporting sessions, oral reports to the class, or written reports to the teacher?

A student's or group's specialized knowledge should be shared with other students in some way. The old cliché, "If you want to know something well, teach it," is valid here. Each student or group who completes an independent study unit should teach the class if time permits. Some teachers and librarians hold a once-a-week independent study seminar session where students come together to share what they have learned. Students may suggest other ways of reporting or sharing this knowledge.

Materials

Daily newspapers are the basic resource material to be used in this study. Supplemental materials such as magazines, textbooks, encyclopedias, pamphlets, booklets, commercial television, and cassette tapes may also be used.

Time

Depending upon the amount of work a student or group has to do in and out of school, it is suggested that each independent study unit encompass a two- to three-week period.

Assessment

Teachers or librarians should keep an independent study folder or have some other system that enables the students to store their materials and allows the educator to check student progress at any time. Then, teachers or librarians should also assess, in some way, the extent to which students cooperated with one another and their attention to time management and the processes of learning.

Example: Impeachment

The following example of an independent study unit may be a helpful model for creative work for students in your classes or libraries.

Topic

A historical perspective on the investigations and procedures for impeachment of presidents and vice-presidents.

Materials

Daily newspaper articles (in folder)

Magazine articles (in folder)

Textbooks and reference books (on shelf)

Library resources

LEARNING STRATEGIES

The student or group may select five or more of the following strategies. However, they must do numbers 7 and 11.

1. Read the newspaper articles in the folder. (10 points)

   What is the basic problem?
   What are some of the issues?
   What procedures are being followed to solve these problems?
   What do you think will happen? Why?

2. Prepare a news story on each of the following vice-presidents and the issue or scandal he was involved in. (20 points)

   Aaron Burr
   Schuyler Colfax
   Daniel Tompkins
   John C. Calhoun
   Spiro Agnew

3. Write an article (newspaper feature story) that develops the similarities and differences among the Crédit Mobilier scandal of the 1870s, the Teapot Dome scandal of the 1920s, and the Watergate issue of the 1970s. (20 points)
4. Prepare a video- or audiocassette tape that will be informative and instructive to other students on the topic of vice-presidents and scandals related to that office. (30 points)
5. Prepare a 30-minute lesson on impeachment that you or your group would be willing to present to the class. See the teacher about methods of presentation. (50 points)
6. Write a feature article on vice-presidents throughout U.S. history focusing on their contributions, problems, scandals, and their relationships with the presidents they served. (50 points)
7. Outline the procedures that must be followed to impeach a president, vice-president, or member of Congress. After the outline is complete, identify presidents, vice-presidents, and congressmen who have been impeached or were considered for impeachment. Give the reasons for the procedures against them. (20 points)
8. Write a feature article on the purposes and functions of grand juries. Outline the similarities and differences between grand juries and congressional investigating committees. (25 points)
9. What do the following words mean? (10 points)

   allegation
   impeachment
   indictment

precedent

prejudicial

10. Keep a record, based on newspaper articles, of the work, travels, and public statements of the current vice-president. Write a summary of how this person seems to be treated by the press. Identify the specific work the vice-president is doing for the president. (15 points)

11. In your opinion, and as a result of the reading you have done, which of the following three statements would you support? Tell why! (25 points)

A vice-president cannot be indicted for any crime until he is first impeached.

There is no constitutional requirement that impeachment must precede indictment.

Impeachment is a prerequisite to indictment for a president or vice-president.

GRADING PLAN

1. Total possible points: 275.
2. The student may select any five or more activities.
3. Based upon the quality of the work, a student may receive

Points	Letter grade
200+	A
150–199	B
100–149	C
Less than 100	D

The Daily Newspaper and Activity Cards

There are nine reasons to create activity cards involving newspapers for students to use in your classrooms or libraries.

1. Activity cards encourage your students to engage in independent learning.
2. They provide interest and variety in the learning tasks.
3. They engage the student in reading and writing activities.
4. They ask the student to do something constructive while you are working with small groups or individual students.

5. They are easy to construct both for you and the students.
6. They are more creative than ditto sheets.
7. They help promote cooperative learning and small-group work.
8. They help reinforce the skills and content you are teaching.
9. They enable you and your students to utilize real-world instructional materials.

Activity cards are simple, quick, and easy to make. They can be made out of cardboard, manila folders, or any other available materials that are useful to students. Of course, lamination extends the use of activity cards. Students should be encouraged to make activity cards based on content they are studying in class or on things that are of interest to them.

One teacher has a box of 30 activity cards on reading comprehension, half of which were created by the students. Another teacher created cards about math words and symbols. Another has weekly activity cards on local and community problems. Here is a description of two activity cards—one created by a teacher, the other by a student.

The teacher's intention was to create a series of activity cards on reading comprehension. On the front of a manila folder, she placed a picture of a tennis game with the words "love" and "deuce" on the cover. Inside the folder, the teacher pasted a Sunday newspaper cartoon, in color, of Bil Keane's "Family Circus." The frames showed a father trying to explain to his son how one keeps score in tennis.

On the back of the folder, the teacher asked a series of comprehension questions, with the number of points students receive for answering each question correctly. There is also an optional bonus assignment that requires the student to rewrite the cartoon in story form.

A sixth-grade student designed an activity card using a single piece of cardboard. The student cut out a newspaper filler (a two-sentence article) about a woman who found $4,150. The student pasted the filler on the card along with an ad about toys and their cost. She then asked, "If you were to purchase all of the toys in this ad and pay the sales tax, how much of the $4,150 would you have left?" A bonus question asks the user of the card to compute how many subscriptions to the local newspaper could be purchased with this amount of money.

Newspaper content, its color, its format, and its variety provide some very special materials for making activity cards. The nine reasons for using activity cards will be apparent when you try this idea in your classroom or library.

Be a Reporter

Teachers and librarians should encourage the students to be "reporters." The purpose of this strategy is to help a student collect data on a topic, synthesize and evaluate it, then write about the topic.

A variety of current topics in the news should be of interest to young reporters in your classes and libraries. For example, students may wish to be investigative reporters researching such topics as abortion, censorship, child abuse, use of steroids, endangered species, pollution, gun control, or the homeless.

Each student reporter uses a notebook, box, or pocket folder to store the data. For example, if a pocket folder is used, the student would design a cover representing his or her topic. In the left pocket of the folder, the student collects data from newspapers, magazines, and reference books about the topic. In the right pocket, the student prepares a preliminary list of questions about the topic. Additional questions are added as the student studies the data.

Each piece of data (newspaper articles, editorials, etc.) is coded by number or letter, and in the right pocket the student writes a summary of the data with the code numbers. The student reporter uses the summary to try to answer the questions posed or goes back to the original data should additional information be necessary.

Either the teacher or the librarian can show the students how feature stories are written in daily newspapers and magazines. Using one or two newspaper models, the reporter uses the questions posed earlier, writes a synthesis of the topic, evaluates his or her summary, and then writes a feature story on the topic.

The teacher or librarian provides a space for collection of these newspaper feature stories to be read by other students in class or to be shared with students in other classes.

A Sample Unit on Newspapers

The major purpose of this five-day unit on the daily newspaper is to help students understand and appreciate the newspaper as a source of information, entertainment, and service. After this unit, students will have learned newspaper terminology, how a newspaper obtains the news, how a newspaper is printed each day, and how best to read a newspaper.

First Day: Newspaper Terms

OBJECTIVE

After this lesson students will understand newspaper terminology.

FOR THE TEACHER OR LIBRARIAN

The newspaper business uses specific terms. Students should become familiar with these terms, but there is no need to have them memorize each term. Many of the resources listed in this book provide a comprehensive list of terms. A selected list is presented in this unit. In this lesson we will focus on ten terms and define them as you implement the lesson.

LEARNING NEWSPAPER TERMINOLOGY

¶ Give each student a newspaper.

¶ Tell the class that you are going to read a list of ten newspaper terms and you would like them to mark an example of each on the front page of their newspapers when they think they have the correct answers.

¶ Say, "Circle a 'headline.' " All students will probably be able to do this correctly. You could also point out that there are generally two kinds of headlines in the newspaper: a 1-2-3 label headline which you will find on the front page almost every day, and a "banner" headline which is used for special events and stretches across the top of the front page.

¶ Second, have the students find the "index." You might ask them the purpose of a newspaper index and ask them to tell you what a similar item is called in their textbooks (table of contents).

¶ Third, have them try to find a "dateline." This is the place or location from which a story comes—Washington, D.C., Moscow, Berlin, Tokyo. Why do newspapers call it the dateline when there is no date? In the early days, stories would appear in the newspaper days after the event happened. Then, one would find the date and place listed, i.e., July 4, 1846, Washington, D.C. Today, with instant communication, the newspaper usually prints news that has happened within the last 24 hours. Therefore, a date is not required but the location is.

¶ Fourth, ask the students to circle a "byline." This is the name of the person who wrote the article or column. Ask, "What word is used to name the person who wrote a book?"

¶ Fifth, ask students to circle a "credit line." In many cases, lines such as Associated Press wire services or New York Times News Service follow the byline or appear alone. Thus, the reader knows that the story or picture was taken from a news-service agency.

¶ Tell students to circle the sixth newspaper term, "jumpline." This term tells the reader to turn to a certain page to continue reading the story.

¶ The seventh term is "cut." A "cut" is a picture.

¶ Eighth, say to the students, "If a 'cut' is a picture, what is a 'cutline'?" It is the wording under the picture. Ask what another name might be. The answer is "caption."

¶ Ninth, ask the students to find the "flag" or "nameplate." That's the name of the newspaper.

¶ The last of the ten terms is "kicker." A "kicker" is sometimes used over a picture or major headline. It is a smaller headline designed to attract the reader to the picture or headline or to explain either one in some way. Your students may not find "kickers" in the edition of the newspaper they are using.

NEWSPAPER TERMS DEFINED

AP—Abbreviation for Associated Press.

Assignment—A story that a reporter has been detailed to cover.

Banner—A headline in large letters running across the entire width of the front page.

Beat—Reporter's regular routine for covering news sources.

Byline—Signature of a writer appearing at the beginning of a story.

Caps—Abbreviation for capital letters.

Compose—To set type.

Copy—All material for publication, whether written stories or pictures.

Copy Desk—Desk at which copy editors sit, sometimes horseshoe-shaped (see Copy Editors).

Copy Editors—A newspaper worker who corrects or edits copy written by a reporter. He or she may also write a headline for the article.

Copyright—An author's exclusive right of property in his work for a certain period of time. This means an article cannot be reprinted unless credit is given to the original author.

Cover—To get all the facts for a news report and write it up.

Cutlines—The words describing a picture.

Dateline—The line at the beginning of a story giving the place and date of the event reported.

Deadline—Time at which all copy for an edition must be in.

Dummy—A diagram or layout of a newspaper page, showing the placement and size of stories, headlines, pictures, and advertisements.

Feature—A story in which the interest lies in some factor other than the news value.

Fourth Estate—Traditional phrase for the press, originating in the eighteenth century. During a speech in Parliament, British statesman Edmund Burke pointed to reporters' gallery saying, "There are three estates in Parliament, but yonder sits a fourth estate, more important than all of them." He was referring to the three classes of people recognized under British law—the clergy, the nobles, and the commons. Thus newspapers became the fourth estate.

Kill—To strike out copy not to be printed.

Lead—The first few sentences or the first paragraph of a news story, containing a summary of who, what, when, where, why, and how.

Libel—Publication of material unjustly injurious to someone's reputation.

Library—File of stories, biographies, pictures, and other material available for reference in the newspaper plant. (Sometimes called "morgue.")

Makeup—The arrangement of stories, headlines, and pictures into columns in preparation for printing.

Masthead—The matter printed in every issue of a newspaper or journal, stating the title, ownership, management, subscription information, and advertising rates.

Plagiarism—Literary theft; passing off as one's own the words or ideas of another.

Proofreader—One who reads proof and marks errors.

Style Book—The printed book of rules on typographical style to be followed by the newspaper's reporters, editors, and printers.

Subhead—Headings used in the body of a story to break the monotony of a solid column of type.

UPI—Abbreviation for United Press International.

CREATING A FRONT PAGE

Have students make their own front pages by following this procedure:

¶ Group students in teams of three. One student is the reporter, the other the editor, the third the printer.

¶ Give each group a piece of newsprint larger than 8½-by-11 inches.

¶ Have enough editions of newspapers so that each group has about three to scan.

¶ Then give each group a focus for their front page. For example, one group is a disaster newspaper, that is, the students will compose a front page of disaster news. Another is a food-news newspaper, another a weather newspaper. You can also focus on sport news, economic news, transportation news, or science/technology news.

¶ On the newsprint, the group is to design the newspaper's nameplate based on the topic you assigned.

¶ Then, the reporter goes through the stack of newspapers and cuts out articles and pictures for the front page of the group's newspaper, all of which must focus on the topic.

¶ After the reporter has collected a variety of articles and pictures, the material is given to the editor, who decides what should be used on the front page. The editor and printer decide the layout.

¶ Then the editor gives the material to the printer, who will glue the material on the newsprint under the nameplate in a neat, attractive, appealing way.

¶ After the work has been completed, have each group share their work, telling the topic and whether they had difficulty finding material for the front page. Ask them how much news they used, how much they did not. You might want to discuss the fact that editors are "gatekeepers" who select the news they think will be of most value and interest to their readers. All the news that's fit to print cannot be printed.

¶ Display the students' front pages around the class or library for others to view.

Second Day: Getting the News

OBJECTIVE

After this lesson students will understand how newspapers get the news.

FOR THE TEACHER OR LIBRARIAN

The news that newspapers obtain is of four kinds: local, state, national, and international or world news.

Newspapers get their news from various sources:

¶ The city editor and staff cover all local news events in the community.

¶ Reporters are assigned specific tasks on a particular beat, such as city hall, the courthouse, or the police station.

¶ Readers and other people connected with local industry, commerce, and government many times "tip" newspaper reporters about a news story.

¶ Most newspapers use the wire services to obtain the news of the day. The Associated Press (AP) wire service is available to newspapers who join the organization and thus get the benefit of the news coverage of other newspapers. The United Press International (UPI), a private organization, sells its services to newspapers. The wire services also transmit pictures electronically.

ANALYZING THE NEWS

¶ Have students mark the front page of a copy of the daily newspaper as follows: "L" for local news articles or pictures; "S" for state news; "N" for national news; "W" for world news. Have them count the number of news items in each category. Which category has the most news on the front page? Does the paper have a special section for local news?

¶ Invite a reporter to tell the class how he or she gets assignments and other tasks.

¶ Invite a member of the city editor's staff or the city editor to talk to the class about his or her tasks.

¶ Have the students find out if there is a wire service in their community. Invite one of the wire service reporters to talk to the class about his or her tasks.

INDIVIDUAL ACTIVITIES

The following activities are designed to serve as individual classroom study problems or as homework assignments.

¶ Outline the main points made by the speakers who talked to the class. What are your impressions about what the speakers said?

¶ Find out how news is transmitted from the wire services. Sketch a picture showing what you have found.

¶ Pretend you are a reporter. Prepare a short news article on some event in your home or school. When writing the news article use the guide that reporters use, the five W's: who, what, when, where, why.

¶ What is meant by a reporter's beat? How does this differ from a policeman's beat?

¶ Can you tell if your daily newspaper subscribes to a wire service? How?

Third Day: Newspaper Content

OBJECTIVE

After this lesson students will know what the daily newspaper contains.

FOR THE TEACHER OR LIBRARIAN

The daily newspaper is made up of content that provides current information, entertainment features, interpretations, opinions, arguments, and special features.

As one studies the newspaper, one finds that factual information can be found anywhere within the newspaper. Interpretation usually appears in news columns, editorial pages, columns, and special features. Opinions can be found in the editorial pages, letters to the editor, the writings of critics, and signed columns. Most newspapers never express opinions when reporting the news. Argument and special pleadings are usually found in the editorials.

The four basic functions of a newspaper are to inform, to interpret the news, to provide a service to readers, and to entertain.

IDENTIFYING CONTENT

¶ Give each team of three students a newspaper and red and blue pencils or markers. Have one or more teams mark every item that they consider a service in red. The other teams mark entertainment items in blue.

  1. How many service items did each team find?
  2. How many entertainment items did each team find?

¶ Have each team take all stories or items not marked as service or entertainment and place them in one of the following categories:

  1. Current information
  2. Interpretation
  3. Opinion
  4. Argument or special pleading

¶ Have each team categorize the service items as

  1. Recipes, hobbies
  2. Child care
  3. Health or home problems
  4. Etiquette
  5. Fashion news
  6. Theater, radio, television
  7. Sports

¶ Have each team categorize the entertainment items as

  1. Comics
  2. Cartoons
  3. Personality sketches
  4. Sports
  5. Films
  6. Television
  7. Radio
  8. Other

INDIVIDUAL ACTIVITIES

¶ List your favorite entertainment features in the daily newspaper. Why are these your favorites?
¶ Cut out three examples of each of the four basic functions of the daily newspaper.
¶ Record the main topics of letters to the editor for three days. What topics are most of the letters written about?
¶ Prepare a scrapbook of newspaper articles and pictures on a subject you enjoy. For example, you could prepare a small scrapbook on recipes, your favorite football team, your favorite comic book, or cartoons.

Fourth and Fifth Days: Reading the Newspaper

OBJECTIVES

After this lesson students will know various ways of reading the daily newspaper. They also will appreciate the daily newspaper as a source of information and entertainment.

FOR THE TEACHER OR LIBRARIAN

The purpose of this section is to illustrate the "how" of newspaper reading. It is important to appreciate the fact that editors are trying to meet the needs of all types of readers who vary in ability, age, income, occupation, interest, education, and so on.

First, newspapers present accurate, objective information. Second, they provide commentary to help readers evaluate the news. Third, newspapers include a variety of material to meet the interest of many readers. Fourth, newspapers take an active part in supporting worthwhile community projects. Fifth, the most important obligation of the newspaper industry is to guard the freedom of the press. The importance of this responsibility was highlighted when Thomas Jefferson said, "Were it left for me to determine whether we should have government without newspapers or newspapers without government, I should not hesitate a moment to prefer the latter. But I should mean that every man should receive those papers and be capable of reading them."

Each of the following three principles provides guidelines for appropriate newspaper reading. Each principle will be followed by several classroom and individual activities that will help make newspaper reading more meaningful to students.

PRINCIPLE ONE

Students should learn about the following techniques of newspaper reading—using the index, skimming, and critical reading.

¶ Give each student a newspaper. Tell them to find the index. Ask how this index helps us in our newspaper reading.
¶ Ask the students if they know what the word "skimming" means. Explain that skimming is a method by which one is able to use his or her eyes and brain to read rapidly and pick up the most important impressions. Most skimmers are guided by the headlines, leads, subheads, and other visual clues.
¶ Explain that when reading an article in the newspaper students should be aware of the content they are reading. This is called critical reading. Explain that when one reads critically, his or her reading rate may slow

down because the reader is thinking about what is being read. For example, as you read a news story, a feature story, or a columnist's comments, you determine how "right" or "wrong" the information is, your opinion of it, how it relates to the other things you know, what facts are presented, what new words you must learn the meaning of, whether the statements are facts or opinions, and so on.

Critical reading helps you to define a problem, gather the facts, come up with some ideas of your own, evaluate these ideas and the ideas you have read, and then summarize and conclude on the basis of the information you have gathered.

READING ACTIVITIES

¶ Have students read the headlines and subheads on the front page. Have them fold the paper so that the front page cannot be seen. Ask them what the front page contained. Select students to list their answers on the blackboard. Compare the actual page with their answers.

¶ In order to get the main idea of a news story, have students read the headlines, subheads, and the first paragraph. Discuss the story. Now have them read the entire article to find out what additional information is provided. Ask if they got the main idea by skimming.

¶ Have each student select a feature story or a column. Have each student measure the column and draw two lines with a crayon, breaking the column into thirds. Tell them to read the article but to make an effort to keep their eyes within the area between the two vertical lines. Ask, "Can you tell me what the article is about and some of its specific information?" Have them practice this technique.

¶ Have half the students read an article. Record their time. Have the other half skim the article as suggested above. Record their time.

1. Which group read the article more quickly?
2. Which group has the greatest comprehension of what they read?

¶ You can have the class conduct this experiment on their own. As the teacher, all you have to do is prepare the posttest to measure comprehension. Students can serve as recorders and timers.

¶ Have each student select a story from the newspaper. Tell the students to read the articles carefully using the following questions as a guide.

1. What is the main idea or problem?
2. What facts support the idea?
3. What opinions are expressed?

4. Are reliable sources quoted?
5. What is my opinion of what is presented?
6. What conclusions does the article make?
7. Do I agree with these conclusions? Why?

PRINCIPLE TWO

Students should decide for themselves why they should read the newspaper daily.

¶ Discuss with the class the statement by Thomas Jefferson.
¶ Discuss with the class this quotation: "Reading is to the mind what exercise is to the body." (Joseph Addison)
¶ Discuss the answers to the following questions with the class.

1. What does the newspaper provide us that other sources such as books, magazines, radio, and television do not?
2. What makes the newspaper different?
3. Why do we need the information the newspaper provides?
4. What do you consider our best source of information—newspapers, radio, or television? Why?
5. What do you consider to be our most reliable source of information—newspapers, radio, or television? Why?

THINKING ACTIVITIES

¶ Students often say they do not have time to read the daily newspaper. Have them keep a log of their activities for three days. On the fourth day help them analyze their logs. What times would be available for newspaper reading?
¶ Have each student pretend to represent a person in a specific occupation. For example, one student can pretend to be a minister, another an ambassador, another a plumber, housewife, mechanic, etc. Have each student read one newspaper from the point of view of a person in the selected occupation. Ask the student to list or cut out articles that may be of special interest to this person.
¶ Have each student select an issue, either local or national. Have them study the newspaper to find material that gives both sides of the issue. Then the student can select a point of view and justify the selection.
¶ Ask students in what ways newspaper reading helps them in their daily living.
¶ Let the class prepare a skit or play on what life would be like without newspapers.

¶ Have the class prepare a debate on the value of newspapers in a democratic society.

¶ Tell students to list the kinds of information the newspaper provides.

¶ Have each student outline the entertainment features of a newspaper.

¶ Each student should prepare a scrapbook on any subject about the newspaper that is of interest to him or her. For example, some students can make scrapbooks on foreign newspapers printed in English. Others can choose topics such as how trees become paper, how a newspaper is published, or occupations in the newspaper business.

¶ Have the class discuss how a newspaper is similar to a textbook and how they differ. Why is it called a "living textbook"? The class will also benefit from a discussion on the similarities and differences between newspapers and magazines.

¶ Have each student state an opinion about some idea, issue, or problem to the class. You can begin by asking each student, "How do you feel about . . . ?" Record the opinions. Anyone who disagrees with the opinion is next to speak. Within the next week, students who stated opinions must try to support them with information from newspapers.

¶ Ask students to interview their parents and get their opinions of the newspaper in their daily lives. Discuss appropriate questions for the interview.

¶ Have a committee of students prepare a test on the newspaper—how to read it, its major parts, how it is published. Try the test on other classes in the school.

¶ The daily newspaper provides information about another entertainment medium—television. Several activities can be based on this service of the daily newspaper.

1. How does the daily newspaper help with our daily television watching?
2. What information does the newspaper publish about television programs?
3. Does the newspaper tell whether the program is good or bad? How do you decide whether to watch a program?
4. How does the newspaper get the material it publishes about television programs?
5. Does the newspaper provide a review of the programs you watch?
6. Write a review of a television program for your class newspaper.
7. Have the class write their own TV guide each week for a month. Have each student suggest programs that the entire class should watch.
8. Use the daily newspaper to study the published programming format of each station in your area. How are they similar? Different?

9. Use the daily newspaper to illustrate the variety of programs on commercial stations, independent stations, and educational stations.
10. Have each student select a country and prepare a newspaper story on what they think might be a typical night of television in that country.
11. Some students may be interested in finding out how television stations get their call letters and numbers.
12. Several students may wish to find out how television works. How does the picture get from the station to their homes?

PRINCIPLE THREE

Students should appreciate newspaper reading as a source of knowledge and entertainment.

¶ Discuss with the class why the newspaper is a source of knowledge and entertainment.
¶ Discuss how reading for information is different from reading for entertainment.

Target Day: Newspapers' Names and Addresses

Chapter 7 provides a list of addresses of major newspapers in the United States and in other countries that publish English-language newspapers and that have newspaper-in-education programs. With this information, you can apply any of three strategies described below. Remember that there are many variations on these strategies and you should draw from them to spark your own creative ideas for using newspapers from around the country and the world.

As you know, newspapers reflect to some extent the communities they serve. Students can broaden their knowledge and perspectives on world and local events by reading newspapers published in other cities and countries. Chapter 1 briefly referred to students' lack of knowledge of current events, geography, and international affairs. Target Day is one of many teaching strategies that may help improve students' knowledge of local, national, and world events. So here's how you get started on Target Day.

The intent is to focus on some significant event such as a presidential election, a space project, Independence Day, the Super Bowl, or the World Series. After completion of the Target Day activities, students should have demonstrated a variety of reading and thinking skills, improved their research and study skills, and enhanced their knowledge of the event. Once the event has been selected, the following steps should be completed.

¶ Have each student write to a newspaper in the United States or another country and request a copy of that newspaper's issue for the day after the event.

¶ Each student should include $0.50 in the letter and request that the newspaper be sent to their home address.

¶ Each student should address the letter to the Educational Services Department of the newspaper.

¶ The letters should be mailed at least two weeks before the event. The activities that follow should begin at least two weeks after the event or when all or most students have received their newspapers. Some students should use a copy of the local newspaper.

LESSON 1: FRONT PAGE COMPARISONS

Activity 1

Comparisons should be made as follows: students who have morning newspapers and students who have afternoon newspapers; students with newspapers from other countries and students with local or state newspapers.

Both groups should compare their front pages and discuss similarities and differences using the questions below as a guide.

¶ What is the content of the major news story?

¶ Did the newspaper use a banner headline?

¶ How many pictures were used?

¶ Was a picture relating to the major event placed a little above the fold?

¶ How many event stories are on the front page? National stories? State stories? Local stories?

¶ How many stories and pictures deal with the event?

¶ How many column inches were given to the event?

¶ How many wire service stories were printed?

¶ Is any front page unusual or different from the others? How?

Activity 2

Using some or all of the questions listed in activity 1, compare and contrast the editorial content of the morning newspapers with that of those published in the afternoon, and do the same with newspapers published in the United States and those published in other countries.

LESSON 2: PICTURES AND POLITICAL CARTOONS

Activity 1

Have each group compare the editorial cartoons in their newspapers using the following questions as a guide.

¶ How many editorial or political cartoons were published in your newspaper?

¶ Of these cartoons, how many were about the Target Day event?

¶ Did some newspapers have more than one political cartoon?

¶ On what pages did these political cartoons appear in each newspaper?

¶ Make a list on the board of the cartoonists from each newspaper. Are some of the cartoonists printed in more than one newspaper?

¶ How many students have newspapers in which the subject of the cartoon is also the subject of an editorial? Of a front-page news story?

Activity 2

Have each group compare the pictures in their newspapers using the following questions. Exclude the sports section.

¶ How many pictures were published in each newspaper?

¶ Of these pictures, how many were about the event?

¶ Did some of the pictures appear in more than one newspaper? Why?

¶ How many pictures were from local photographers?

Activity 3

Using the questions listed in the preceding activities, let the students from both groups discuss the similarities and differences in the political cartoons and pictures of the morning and afternoon newspapers and other newspapers.

LESSON 3: COMPARING THE CONTENT

Activity 1

Students should be given the opportunity to compare and contrast the entertainment features of their newspapers. Have students answer the following questions during a general discussion period.

¶ How many comics does your newspaper have? Where are they located?

¶ Compare the comic sections from different newspapers to determine whether there is any difference in the size and number of comics? If there is, what might be some of the reasons?

¶ Locate the TV information in your newspaper. How much space is devoted to TV listings?

¶ Are there any articles about upcoming TV shows? Reviews of the previous night's programs? Is there a TV critic?

¶ Using the index, locate the movie schedule. How many different movies are listed? How many different theaters? Is there a map showing the general location of the movie theaters?

¶ What is the earliest time you could go to a movie? What is the latest time?

Activity 2
Briefly discuss the role of advertising in the newspaper industry. Be sure to explain the difference between retail and classified advertising. Lead a discussion comparing the retail ads and the classified ads found in the newspapers.

Activity 3
Allow students time to discuss the similarities and differences in the information given by each newspaper in the following areas:

Vital statistics (births and deaths)

Weather section

School schedules and news

Community meetings and events

Feature story subjects

Activity 4
Have students find one feature of their newspaper that is not found in most other newspapers. Have students discuss why these features are found in their respective newspapers.

LESSON 4: LOCAL COMPARISON

Activity 1
Have each student compare his or her newspaper to the local newspaper. List the following items on the board and instruct students to use the list to help them write their critiques.

Style

Format

Type of print

Coverage of the event

Editorial content

Variety of information

Activity 2
Arrange the students in groups of five or six. Give each group a large sheet of newsprint or butcher paper, scissors, glue, and pencils. Let each group choose the best features from their newspapers and make a new front page about the event. Allow each group the opportunity to tell the class why they chose these items.

These strategies have been described to help you and your students make use of the newspaper addresses that follow in chapter 7. You are encouraged to think of your own ideas for using these resources to nurture your students toward increasing their knowledge of current affairs while improving learning and thinking skills.

CHAPTER 7

Newspaper Names and Addresses

This chapter provides the names and addresses of newspapers in the United States and several other countries that have newspaper in education programs. The purpose of these references is so students can examine and work with other newspapers to enhance their language and social studies skills and knowledge, using a strategy such as Target Day and the variations on this theme described in chapter 6.

U.S. Newspapers

Alabama

Birmingham News
P.O. Box 2553
Birmingham, AL 35202

Decatur Daily
P.O. Box 2218
Decatur, AL 35602

Times Daily
219 W. Tennessee
Florence, AL 35630

The Huntsville Times
P.O. Box 1487
Huntsville, AL 35807

The Mobile Press
P.O. Box 2488
Mobile, AL 36652

Advertiser-Journal
P.O. Box 1000
Montgomery, AL 36101

The Selma Times-Journal
P.O. Box 611
Selma, AL 36702

The Tuscaloosa News
P.O. Drawer 1
Tuscaloosa, AL 35402

Alaska

Anchorage Daily News
P.O. Box 14-9001
Anchorage, AK 99514-9001

Fairbanks Daily News-Miner
P.O. Box 710
Fairbanks, AK 99707

Ketchikan Daily News
P.O. Box 7900
Ketchikan, AK 99901

Arizona

Casa Grande Dispatch
P.O. Box C-3
Casa Grande, AZ 85222

Arizona Daily Sun
417 W. Santa Fe Ave.
Flagstaff, AZ 86002

Mohave Daily Miner
P.O. Box 3909
Kingman, AZ 86402

**The Arizona Republic/
   The Phoenix Gazette**
P.O. Box 1950
Phoenix, AZ 85001

The Prescott Courier
P.O. Box 312
Prescott, AZ 86302

The Arizona Daily Star
P.O. Box 26807
Tucson, AZ 85726

Tucson Citizen
4850 S. Park Ave.
P.O. Box 26767
Tucson, AZ 85726

The Yuma Daily Sun
P.O. Box 271
Yuma, AZ 85366

Arkansas

El Dorado News-Times
P.O. Box 912
El Dorado, AR 71731

The Jonesboro Sun
518 Carson
Jonesboro, AR 72401

Arkansas Democrat
P.O. Box 2221
Little Rock, AR 72203

Arkansas Gazette
P.O. Box 1821
Little Rock, AR 72203

The Daily Leader
P.O. Box 531
Stuttgart, AR 72160

California

Anaheim Bulletin
P.O. Box 70004
Anaheim, CA 92825

The Register
Disneyland
1313 Harbor Blvd.
Anaheim, CA 92803

The Bakersfield Californian
P.O. Box Bin 440
Bakersfield, CA 93302

The Camarillo Daily News
P.O. Box 107
Camarillo, CA 93011

Enterprise-Record
P.O. Box 9
Chico, CA 95927

Orange Coast Daily Pilot
P.O. Box 1560
Costa Mesa, CA 92628

Imperial Valley Press
P.O. Box 2770
El Centro, CA 92244

The Fresno Bee
1626 East St.
Fresno, CA 93786

USA Today
13962 Nautilus Dr.
Garden Grove, CA 92643

The Dispatch
P.O. Box 22365
Gilroy, CA 95021

The Hanford Sentinel
P.O. Box 9
Hanford, CA 93232

Alameda Newspaper Group
116 W. Winston
Hayward, CA 94540

Copley Newspapers
P.O. Box 1530
La Jolla, CA 92038

Press-Telegram
P.O. Box 230
Long Beach, CA 90801

La Opinion
1436 S. Main St.
Los Angeles, CA 90015

Los Angeles Herald Examiner
1111 S. Hill St.
Suite 200
Los Angeles, CA 90015

Los Angeles Times
Times Mirror Square
Los Angeles, CA 90053

The Modesto Bee
P.O. Box 3928
Modesto, CA 95352

USA Today
150 Alameda del Prado
Novato, CA 94947

The Tribune
P.O. Box 24304
Oakland, CA 94623

Report
P.O. Box 4000
Ontario, CA 91761

The Times Tribune
P.O. Box 300
Palo Alto, CA 94302

Star-News
525 E. Colorado Blvd.
Pasadena, CA 91109

Progress Bulletin
P.O. Box 2708
Pomona, CA 91769

Record Searchlight
1101 Twin View Blvd.
Redding, CA 96003

West County Times
3905 MacDonald Ave.
Richmond, CA 94805

The Press-Enterprise
P.O. Box 792
Riverside, CA 92502

The Sacramento Bee
2100 Q St.
P.O. Box 15779
Sacramento, CA 95852

The Sacramento Union
P.O. Box 2711
Sacramento, CA 95812

Californian
P.O. Box 81091
Salinas, CA 93912

**The San Bernardino
  County Sun**
399 N. D St.
San Bernardino, CA 92401

The San Diego Union
P.O. Box 191
San Diego, CA 92112

San Francisco Chronicle
901 Mission St.
San Francisco, CA 94103

San Francisco Examiner
925 Mission St.
San Francisco, CA 94103

San Jose Mercury News
750 Ridder Park Dr.
San Jose, CA 95190

The County Telegram Tribune
P.O. Box 112
San Luis Obispo, CA 93406

San Mateo Times
1080 S. Amphlett Blvd.
San Mateo, CA 94402

The Orange County Register
P.O. Box 11626
Santa Ana, CA 92711

**Copley Los Angeles
  Newspapers, Inc.**
1920 Colorado Ave.
Santa Monica, CA 90404

The Press Democrat
P.O. Box 569
Santa Rosa, CA 95402

The Enterprise
888 Easy St.
Simi Valley, CA 93065

The Stockton Record
P.O. Box 900
Stockton, CA 95201

News-Chronicle
P.O. Box 3129
Thousand Oaks, CA 91359

Daily Breeze
5215 Torrance Blvd.
Torrance, CA 90509

Tracy Press
P.O. Box 419
Tracy, CA 95378

Advance-Register
P.O. Box 30
Tulare, CA 93275

Vallejo Times-Herald
P.O. Box 3188
Vallejo, CA 94590

Visalia Times-Delta
P.O. Box 31
Visalia, CA 93279

Contra Costa Times
P.O. Box 5088
Walnut Creek, CA 94596

Colorado

Daily Camera
P.O. Box 591
Boulder, CO 80306

**Colorado Springs Gazette
    Telegraph**
P.O. Box 1779
Colorado Springs, CO 80901

The Denver Post
1560 Broadway
Denver, CO 80202

Rocky Mountain News
400 W. Colfax Ave.
Denver, CO 80204

Durango Herald
P.O. Drawer A
Durango, CO 81302

The Daily Sentinel
P.O. Box 668
Grand Junction, CO 81502

**The Lamar Daily News and
    Holly Chieftain**
P.O. Box 1217
Lamar, CO 81052

Daily Times-Call
350 Terry St.
Longmont, CO 80501

**Loveland Daily
    Reporter-Herald**
P.O. Box 59
Loveland, CO 80539

Pueblo Chieftain
P.O. Box 4040
Pueblo, CO 81003

Connecticut

The Bridgeport Post-Telegram
410 State St.
Bridgeport, CT 06604

Bristol Press
99 Main St.
Bristol, CT 06010

News-Times
333 Main St.
Danbury, CT 06810

Greenwich Times
20 E. Elm St.
Greenwich, CT 06830

The Hartford Courant
285 Broad St.
Hartford, CT 06115

The Lakeville Journal
P.O. Box 353
Lakeville, CT 06039

Record-Journal
11 Crown St.
Meriden, CT 06450

The Middletown Press
P.O. Box 471
Middletown, CT 06457

Naugatuck Daily News
195 Water St.
Naugatuck, CT 06770

The Herald
P.O. Box 2050
New Britain, CT 06050

New Haven Register
40 Sargent Dr.
New Haven, CT 06511

The Day
P.O. Box 1231
New London, CT 06320

The Advocate
P.O. Box 9307
Stamford, CT 06904

The Waterbury
   Republican-American
389 Meadow St.
Waterbury, CT 06722

Delaware

The News Journal
P.O. Box 15505
New Castle, DE 19720

District of Columbia

The Mini Page
P.O. Box 24110
Washington, DC 20024

USA Today
P.O. Box 500
Washington, DC 20044

Washington Post
1150 15th St. NW
Washington, DC 20071

The Washington Times
3600 N.Y. Ave. NW
Washington, DC 20002

Florida

The Bradenton Herald
P.O. Box 921
Bradenton, FL 34206

The Clearwater Sun
301 S. Myrtle Ave.
Clearwater, FL 33517

Daytona Beach News-Journal
901 Sixth St.
Daytona Beach, FL 32117

Broward Tribune
P.O. Box 23909
Fort Lauderdale, FL 33307

News
101 N. New River Dr., E
Fort Lauderdale, FL 33301

News-Press
2442 Anderson Ave.
Fort Myers, FL 33901

The Tribune
P.O. Box 69
Fort Pierce, FL 34954

Northwest Florida Daily News
P.O. Box 2949
Ft. Walton Beach, FL 32549

The Gainesville Sun
2700 S.W. 13th St.
Gainesville, FL 32608

The Florida Times-Union
1 Riverside Ave.
Jacksonville, FL 32202

Jacksonville Business Journal
1851 Executive Center Dr.
Suite 227
Jacksonville, FL 32207

Lake City Reporter
P.O. Box 1709
Lake City, FL 32056

Florida Today
P.O. Box 363000
Melbourne, FL 32936

The Miami Herald
1 Herald Plaza
Miami, FL 33132

The Orlando Sentinel
P.O. Box 2833
Orlando, FL 32802

Palatka Daily News
P.O. Box 777
Palatka, FL 32178

The News Herald
P.O. Box 1940
Panama City, FL 32402

Pensacola News Journal
1 News-Journal Plaza
Pensacola, FL 32501

St. Petersburg Times
490 First Ave. S
St. Petersburg, FL 33701

Florida Department of Education
Knott Building
Tallahassee, FL 32301

Tallahassee Democrat
P.O. Box 990
Tallahassee, FL 32302

The Tampa Tribune
P.O. Box 191
Tampa, FL 33601

USA Today
The Corporate Center
Suite 500
6704 Benjamin Rd.
Tampa, FL 33614

The Palm Beach Post
P.O. Box 24700
West Palm Beach, FL 33416

Georgia

The Albany Herald
P.O. Box 48
Albany, GA 31703

Athens Banner Herald/Daily News
P.O. Box 912
Athens, GA 30603

The Atlanta Constitution/ The Atlanta Journal
P.O. Box 4689
Atlanta, GA 30302

Georgia Press Association
1075 Spring St. NW
Atlanta, GA 30309

The Augusta Chronicle-Herald
P.O. Box 1928
Augusta, GA 30903

The Post-Searchlight
P.O. Box 277
Bainbridge, GA 31717

The Times-Georgian
P.O. Box 460
Carrollton, GA 30117

Columbus Ledger-Enquirer
P.O. Box 711
Columbus, GA 31902

The Times
P.O. Box 838
Gainesville, GA 30503

Griffin Daily News
P.O. Drawer M
Griffin, GA 30224

The Coastal Courier
P.O. Box 498
Hinesville, GA 31313

Gwinnett Daily News
P.O. Box 1000
Lawrenceville, GA 30246

Macon Telegraph and News
P.O. Box 4167
Macon, GA 31208

The Madisonian
P.O. Box 191
Madison, GA 30650

The Union-Recorder
P.O. Box 520
Milledgeville, GA 31061

Observer
P.O. Box 889
Moultrie, GA 31776

Rome News-Tribune
P.O. Box 1633
Rome, GA 30162

News/Press
111 W. Bay St.
Savannah, GA 31401

Statesboro Herald
P.O. Box 888
Statesboro, GA 30458

Times-Enterprise
P.O. Box 650
Thomasville, GA 31799

The Tifton Gazette
P.O. Box 708
Tifton, GA 31793

USA Today
1901 Montreal Rd.
Suite 123
Tucker, GA 30084

The Daily Sun
P.O. Box 6129
Warner Robins, GA 31095

Hawaii

**Sunday Star Bulletin and
  Advertiser**
605 Kapiolani Blvd.
Honolulu, HI 96813

Idaho

The Idaho Statesman
P.O. Box 40
Boise, ID 83707

Coeur d'Alene Press
Second and Lakeside
Coeur D'Alene, ID 83814

The Post-Register
333 Northgate Mile
Idaho Falls, ID 83401

Lewiston Morning Tribune
505 C St.
Lewiston, ID 83501

Idaho Press Tribune
P.O. Box 9399
Nampa, ID 83652

Idaho State Journal
305 S. Arthur
Pocatello, ID 83204

Times-News
P.O. Box 548
Twin Falls, ID 83303

Illinois

The Telegraph
P.O. Box 278
Alton, IL 62002

Belleville News-Democrat
P.O. Box 427
Belleville, IL 62222

The Pantagraph
301 W. Washington St.
Bloomington, IL 61701

Southern Illinoisan
710 N. Illinois
Carbondale, IL 62901

News-Gazette
P.O. Box 677
Champaign, IL 61824

Chicago Sun-Times
401 N. Wabash Ave.
Chicago, IL 60611

Chicago Tribune
435 N. Michigan Ave.
Chicago, IL 60611

Southtown Economist
5959 S. Harlem
Chicago, IL 60638

Commercial-News
17 W. North St.
Danville, IL 61833

Herald & Review
P.O. Box 311
Decatur, IL 62525

Herald-News
300 Caterpillar Dr.
Joliet, IL 60436

The Daily Journal
8 Dearborn Square
Kankakee, IL 60901

The Daily Dispatch
1720 Fifth Ave.
Moline, IL 61265

Journal Star
1 News Plaza
Peoria, IL 61643

The Quincy Herald Whig
P.O. Box 909
Quincy, IL 62306

Rockford Register Star
99 E. State St.
Rockford, IL 61104

State Journal-Register
P.O. Box 219
Springfield, IL 62705

Times-Press
115 Oak St.
Streator, IL 61364

Breeze-Courier
P.O. Box 440
Taylorville, IL 62568

The News-Sun
100 W. Madison St.
Waukegan, IL 60085

Indiana

The Anderson Herald-Bulletin
1133 Jackson
Anderson, IN 46015

The Evening Star
P.O. Box 431
Auburn, IN 46706

The Times-Mail
P.O. Box 849
Bedford, IN 47421

The Herald-Times
P.O. Box 909
Bloomington, IN 47402

The Brazil Times
P.O. Box 429
Brazil, IN 47834

The Republic
333 Second St.
Columbus, IN 47201

Connersville News-Examiner
P.O. Box 287
Connersville, IN 47331

Truth
P.O. Box 487
Elkhart, IN 46515

The Call-Leader
P.O. Box 85
Elwood, IN 46036

**The Evansville Courier/
   The Evansville Press**
P.O. Box 268
Evansville, IN 47702

The Journal-Gazette
600 W. Main St.
Ft. Wayne, IN 46802

The News-Sentinel
P.O. Box 102
Fort Wayne, IN 46801

Times
P.O. Box 9
Frankfort, IN 46041

Post-Tribune
1065 Broadway
Gary, IN 46402

The Goshen News
P.O. Box 569
Goshen, IN 46526

Herald-Press
P.O. Box 860
Huntington, IN 46750

The Indianapolis Star/
The Indianapolis News
P.O. Box 145
Indianapolis, IN 46206

The Herald
P.O. Box 31
Jasper, IN 47546

News-Sun
P.O. Box 39
Kendallville, IN 46755

Journal and Courier
217 N. Sixth St.
Lafayette, IN 47901

The Reporter
117 E. Washington St.
Lebanon, IN 46052

Pharos-Tribune
P.O. Box 210
Logansport, IN 46947

The Madison Courier
310 Courier Square
Madison, IN 47250

Chronicle-Tribune
P.O. Box 309
Marion, IN 46952

Martinsville Daily Reporter
60 S. Jefferson St.
Martinsville, IN 46151

The News Dispatch
121 W. Michigan Blvd.
Michigan City, IN 46360

The Muncie Star/Muncie
Evening Press
125 S. High St.
Muncie, IN 47302

The Times
601 45th St.
Munster, IN 46321

Peru Daily Tribune
P.O. Box 87
Peru, IN 46970

Hendricks County Flyer
P.O. Box 6
Plainfield, IN 46168

The Commercial Review
309 W. Main St.
Portland, IN 47371

Palladium-Item
P.O. Box 308
Richmond, IN 47375

Shelbyville News
123 E. Washington St.
Shelbyville, IN 46176

South Bend Tribune
225 W. Colfax Ave.
South Bend, IN 46626

World
114 E. Franklin
Spencer, IN 47460

The News
537 Main St.
Tell City, IN 47586

Tipton Tribune
110 N. Madison St.
Tipton, IN 46072

Vidette-Messenger
1111 Glendale Blvd.
Valparaiso, IN 46383

Vincennes Sun-Commercial
702 Main St.
Vincennes, IN 47591

The News Gazette
224 W. Franklin St.
Winchester, IN 47394

Iowa

The Daily Tribune
317 Fifth St.
Ames, IA 50010

Boone News-Republican
P.O. Box 100
Boone, IA 50036

Cedar Rapids Gazette
500 Third Ave. SE
Cedar Rapids, IA 52406

Quad-City Times
P.O. Box 3828
Davenport, IA 52808

The Des Moines Register
P.O. Box 957
Des Moines, IA 50304

Telegraph Herald
P.O. Box 688
Dubuque, IA 52004

Press-Citizen
P.O. Box 2480
Iowa City, IA 52244

The Times-Republican
135 W. Main St.
Marshalltown, IA 52240

Sioux City Journal
Sixth and Pavonia Sts.
Sioux City, IA 51102

The Daily Reporter
416 First Ave. W
Spencer, IA 51301

Daily Freeman-Journal
720 Second St.
Webster City, IA 50595

Kansas

Traveler
Fifth Ave. and A St.
Arkansas City, KS 67005

The Garden City Telegram
P.O. Box 958
Garden City, KS 67846

The Hutchinson News
P.O. Box 190
Hutchinson, KS 67504

Daily Union
222 W. Sixth St.
Junction City, KS 66441

Southwest Daily Times
P.O. Box 889
Liberal, KS 67905

Mercury
P.O. Box 787
Manhattan, KS 66502

The Newton Kansan
121-125 W. Sixth St.
Newton, KS 67114

The Olathe Daily News
P.O. Box 130
Olathe, KS 66061

Herald
104 S. Cedar St.
Ottawa, KS 66067

Parsons Sun
220 S. 18th St.
Parsons, KS 67357

Pittsburg Morning Sun
701 N. Locust St.
Pittsburg, KS 66762

The Pratt Tribune
P.O. Box 909
Pratt, KS 67124

The Salina Journal
P.O. Box 740
Salina, KS 67402

The Topeka Capital-Journal
616 Jefferson St.
Topeka, KS 66607

Wellington Daily News
P.O. Box 368
Wellington, KS 67152

Wichita Eagle
P.O. Box 820
Wichita, KS 67201

Kentucky

The Daily Independent
226 17th St.
Ashland, KY 41101

Trimble-Banner Democrat
West St.
Bedford, KY 40006

Tribune Courier
P.O. Box 185
Benton, KY 42025

Berea Citizen
P.O. Box 207
Berea, KY 40403

Booneville Sentinel
P.O. Box 43
Booneville, KY 41314

Daily News
P.O. Box 9012
Bowling Green, KY 42102

**Central Kentucky
   News-Journal**
P.O. Box 51
Campbellsville, KY 42719

Cynthiana Democrat
P.O. Box 160
Cynthiana, KY 41031

Advocate-Messenger
330 S. Fourth St.
Danville, KY 40422

Herald-News
P.O. Box 87
Edmonton, KY 42129

The News-Enterprise
408 W. Dixie
Elizabethtown, KY 42701

Franklin Favorite
103 N. High St.
Franklin, KY 42134

Menifee County News
HCR 71 Box 170
Frenchburg, KY 40322

The Harlan Enterprise
P.O. Drawer E
Harlan, KY 40831

Harrodsburg Herald
P.O. Box E
Harrodsburg, KY 40330

Ohio County Times-News
P.O. Box 226
Hartford, KY 42347

Hazard Herald-Voice
P.O. Box 869
Hazard, KY 41702

The Gleaner and Journal
455 Klutey Park Plaza
Henderson, KY 42420

Kentucky New Era
P.O. Box 729
Hopkinsville, KY 42241

Anderson News
P.O. Box 116
Lawrenceburg, KY 40342

Lexington Herald-Leader
100 Midland Ave.
Lexington, KY 40508

The Courier-Journal
525 W. Broadway
Louisville, KY 40202

The Messenger
P.O. Box 529
Madisonville, KY 42431

The Crittenden Press
P.O. Box 191
Marion, KY 42064

Mayfield Messenger
201 N. Eighth St.
Mayfield, KY 42066

Mt. Sterling Advocate
40 S. Bank St.
Mt. Sterling, KY 40353

Murray Ledger and Times
P.O. Box 1040
Murray, KY 42071

Messenger-Inquirer
P.O. Box 1480
Owensboro, KY 42302

Sun
P.O. Box 2300
Paducah, KY 42002

Sentinel-News
P.O. Box 399
Shelbyville, KY 40066

Commonwealth-Journal
P.O. Box 859
Somerset, KY 42502

Wolfe County News
P.O. Box 187
West Liberty, KY 41472

The Winchester Sun
P.O. Box 4300
Winchester, KY 40392

Louisiana

Alexandria Daily Town Talk
1201 Third St.
Alexandria, LA 71301

Enterprise
119 E. Hickory St.
Bastrop, LA 71221

State-Times/Morning Advocate
525 Lafayette St.
Baton Rouge, LA 70802

Courier and Terrebonne Press
P.O. Box 2717
Houma, LA 70361

Advertiser
P.O. Box 3268
Lafayette, LA 70502

Lake Charles American Press
P.O. Box 2893
Lake Charles, LA 70602

News-Star
P.O. Box 1502
Monroe, LA 71210

The Times-Picayune
3800 Howard Ave.
New Orleans, LA 70140

Daily World
P.O. Box 1179
Opelousas, LA 70571

Shreveport Journal/The Times
P.O. Box 31110
Shreveport, LA 71130

Comet
705 W. Fifth St.
Thibodaux, LA 70301

Maine

Kennebec Journal
274 Western Ave.
Augusta, ME 04330

Maine Department of Education
State House Station 23
Augusta, ME 04333

Bangor Daily News
491 Main St.
Bangor, ME 04401

Journal Tribune
P.O. Box 627
Biddeford, ME 04005

Times-Record
Industry Rd.
Brunswick, ME 04011

Lewiston Sun-Journal/Sunday
104 Park St.
Lewiston, ME 04240

**Portland Press-Herald/Evening
   Express**
P.O. Box 1460
Portland, ME 04104

**Central Maine Morning
   Sentinel**
25 Silver St.
Waterville, ME 04901

Maryland

The Capital
P.O. Box 911
Annapolis, MD 21404

The Sun
501 N. Calvert St.
Baltimore, MD 21202

USA Today
1819 Whitehead Rd.
Baltimore, MD 21207

Star-Democrat/Sunday Star
P.O. Box 600
Easton, MD 21601

The Frederick Post/The News
P.O. Box 578
Frederick, MD 21701

The Morning Herald/
The Daily Mail
P.O. Box 439
Hagerstown, MD 21741

Montgomery County Sentinel
P.O. Box 1272
Rockville, MD 20849

Carroll County Times
P.O. Box 346
Westminister, MD 21157

Massachusetts

Beverly Times
Dunham Road
Beverly, MA 01915

The Boston Globe
135 Morrissey Blvd.
Boston, MA 02125

The Christian Science Monitor
One Norway St.
Boston, MA 02115

The Enterprise
P.O. Box 1450
Brockton, MA 02403

The News
309 Central St.
Gardner, MA 01440

The Recorder
14 Hope St.
Greenfield, MA 01301

The Haverhill Gazette
447 W. Lowell Ave.
Haverhill, MA 01832

Transcript-Telegram
120 Whiting Farms Rd.
Holyoke, MA 01040

Cape Cod Times
P.O. Box 550
Hyannis, MA 02601

Lawrence Eagle-Tribune
P.O. Box 100
Lawrence, MA 01842

Sun
P.O. Box 1477
Lowell, MA 01853

Item
P.O. Box 951
Lynn, MA 01903

Fri.-Sat.-Sun.
Enterprise-Sun Newspaper
230 Maple St.
Marlborough, MA 01752

The Standard-Times
555 Pleasant St.
New Bedford, MA 02740

Daily Hampshire Gazette
115 Conz St.
Northampton, MA 01060

The Patriot Ledger
400 Crown Colony Dr.
Quincy, MA 02169

Salem Evening News
155 Washington St.
Salem, MA 01970

Somerville Journal
P.O. Box 312
Somerville, MA 02143

Union-News/Sunday Republican
1860 Main St.
Springfield, MA 01101

Daily Times Chronicle
1 Arrow Drive
Woburn, MA 01801

Telegram and Gazette
P.O. Box 15012
Worcester, MA 01615

Michigan

News
130 Park Place
Alpena, MI 49707

The Ann Arbor News
340 E. Huron St.
Ann Arbor, MI 48104

Battle Creek Enquirer
155 W. Van Buren St.
Battle Creek, MI 49017

Times
311 Fifth St.
Bay City, MI 48708

Cadillac News
P.O. Box 640
Cadillac, MI 49601

Daily Tribune
308 N. Main St.
Cheboygan, MI 49721

Detroit Free Press
321 W. Lafayette Blvd.
Detroit, MI 48231

The Detroit News
615 W. Lafayette Blvd.
Detroit, MI 48226

The Flint Journal
200 E. First St.
Flint, MI 48502

The Grand Rapids Press
155 Michigan St. NW
Grand Rapids, MI 49503

Hillsdale Daily News
33 McCollum St.
Hillsdale, MI 49242

The Holland Sentinel
54 W. Eighth St.
Holland, MI 49423

The Daily News
215 E. Ludington
Iron Mountain, MI 49801

Citizen Patriot
214 S. Jackson St.
Jackson, MI 49201

Kalamazoo Gazette
401 S. Burdick St.
Kalamazoo, MI 49007

Lansing State Journal
120 E. Lenawee St.
Lansing, MI 48933

Daily News
202 N. Rath Ave.
Ludington, MI 49431

Manistee News Advocate
75 Maple St.
Manistee, MI 49660

Sun
215 N. Main St.
Mt. Pleasant, MI 48858

**The Muskegon Chronicle/
  The Sunday Chronicle**
P.O. Box 59
Muskegon, MI 49443

The Argus-Press
201 E. Exchange St.
Owosso, MI 48867

News-Review
319 State St.
Petoskey, MI 49770

The Saginaw News
203 S. Washington Ave.
Saginaw, MI 48607

Evening News
109 Arlington St.
Sault Ste. Marie, MI 49783

Minnesota

The Pioneer
P.O. Box 455
Bemidji, MN 56601

Dispatch
215 S. Sixth St.
Brainerd, MN 56401

Duluth News-Tribune
P.O. Box 169000
Duluth, MN 55816

Sentinel
64 Downtown Plaza
Fairmont, MN 56031

Star Tribune
425 Portland Ave.
Minneapolis, MN 55415

Mississippi

The Panolian
P.O. Box 393
Batesville, MS 38606

The Sun Herald
P.O. Box 4567
Biloxi, MS 39535

Daily Leader
P.O. Box 551
Brookhaven, MS 39601

The Clarksdale Press Register
P.O. Box 1119
Clarksdale, MS 38614

Bolivar Commercial
P.O. Box 1050
Cleveland, MS 38732

Itawamba County Times
P.O. Box 1549
Fulton, MS 38843

Delta Democrat-Times
P.O. Box 1618
Greenville, MS 38702

Greenwood Commonwealth
P.O. Box 8050
Greenwood, MS 38930

The Daily Sentinel Star
P.O. Box 907
Grenada, MS 38901

Hattiesburg American
825 N. Main St.
Hattiesburg, MS 39401

De Soto Times
P.O. Box 100
Hernando, MS 38632

The Clarion-Ledger and News
P.O. Box 40
Jackson, MS 39205

Franklin Advocate
P.O. Box 576
Meadville, MS 39653

Star
814 22nd Ave.
Meridian, MS 39301

The Natchez Democrat
P.O. Box 1447
Natchez, MS 39121

New Albany Gazette
P.O. Box 300
New Albany, MS 38652

The Oxford Eagle
P.O. Box 866
Oxford, MS 38655

Mississippi Press
405 Delmas Ave.
Pascagoula, MS 39567

The Pontotoc Progress
P.O. Box 210
Pontotoc, MS 38863

News
P.O. Drawer 1068
Starkville, MS 39759

**Northeast Mississippi Daily
 Journal**
P.O. Box 909
Tupelo, MS 38802

Vicksburg Evening Post
920 South St.
Vicksburg, MS 39180

Daily Times Leader
227 Court St.
West Point, MS 39773

Missouri

Southeast Missourian
301 Broadway
Cape Girardeau, MO 63701

Columbia Daily Tribune
P.O. Box 798
Columbia, MO 65205

**News Democrat/Jefferson
 County Weekend Journal**
Three Industrial Dr.
Festus, MO 63028

The Fulton Sun
115 E. Fifth St.
Fulton, MO 65251

Hannibal Courier-Post
201 N. Third St.
Hannibal, MO 63401

The Examiner
P.O. Box 458
Independence, MO 64051

The Globe
117 E. Fourth St.
Joplin, MO 64801

The Kansas City Star
1729 Grand Ave.
Kansas City, MO 64108

USA Today
6000 CT St.
Kansas City, MO 64120

Lamar Democrat
P.O. Box 458
Lamar, MO 64759

The Lebanon Daily Record
290 S. Madison St.
Lebanon, MO 65536

Ledger
300 N. Washington
Mexico, MO 65265

The Nevada Daily Mail/
   Nevada Herald
131 S. Cedar
Nevada, MO 64772

Daily American Republic
P.O. Box 7
Poplar Bluff, MO 63901

News
101 W. Seventh St.
Rolla, MO 65401

St. Joseph News-Press/Gazette
Ninth and Edmond Sts.
St. Joseph, MO 64501

Post-Dispatch
900 N. Tucker Blvd.
St. Louis, MO 63101

The Sedalia Democrat
700 S. Massachusetts
Sedalia, MO 65301

Standard
205 S. New Madrid St.
Sikeston, MO 63801

The News-Leader
651 Boonville Ave.
Springfield, MO 65806

Republican-Times
122 E. Eighth St.
Trenton, MO 64683

Washington Missourian
P.O. Box 336
Washington, MO 63090

Daily Fort Gateway Guide
P.O. Box 578
Fort Wood Spur
Waynesville, MO 65583

Montana

The Billings Gazette
P.O. Box 36300
Billings, MT 59107

Bozeman Daily Chronicle
P.O. Box 1188
Bozeman, MT 59771

Montana Standard
25 W. Granite St.
Butte, MT 59701

The Independent-Record
317 Cruse St.
Helena, MT 59601

Miles City Star
13 N. Sixth St.
Miles City, MT 59301

Missoulian
P.O. Box 8029
Missoula, MT 59807

Nebraska

Beatrice Daily Sun
P.O. Box 847
Beatrice, NE 68310

Columbus Telegram
P.O. Box 648
Columbus, NE 68602

Fremont Tribune
P.O. Box 9
Fremont, NE 68025

Grand Island Independent
First and Cedar Sts.
Grand Island, NE 68801

The Hastings Tribune
P.O. Box 788
Hastings, NE 68902

Lincoln Star/Lincoln Journal
P.O. Box 81689
Lincoln, NE 68501

Norfolk Daily News
525 Norfolk Ave.
Norfolk, NE 68701

Omaha World-Herald
World-Herald Square
Omaha, NE 68102

Nevada

Nevada Appeal
200 Bath St.
Carson City, NV 89703

Las Vegas Review-Journal
P.O. Box 70
Las Vegas, NV 89118

Las Vegas Sun
P.O. Box 4275
Las Vegas, NV 89127

New Hampshire

**Carroll County Independent
and Pioneer**
P.O. Box 38
Center Ossipee, NH 03814

Eagle Times
19 Sullivan St.
Claremont, NH 03743

Concord Monitor
Three N. State St.
Concord, NH 03301

The Keene Sentinel
60 West St.
Keene, NH 03431

Union Leader
35 Amherst St.
Manchester, NH 03101

Nashua Telegraph
17 Executive Dr.
Nashua, NH 03051

New Jersey

USA Today
P.O. Box 6600
Bridgewater, NJ 08807

Courier-Post
301 Cuthbert Blvd.
Cherry Hill, NJ 08002

The Record
150 River St.
Hackensack, NJ 07601

Asbury Park Press
P.O. Box 1550
Neptune, NJ 07754

The Central New Jersey Home News
P.O. Box 551
New Brunswick, NJ 08903

The Star-Ledger
Star-Ledger Plaza
Newark, NJ 07101

North Jersey Herald-News
988 Main Ave.
Passaic, NJ 07055

The Press of Atlantic City
1000 W. Washington Ave.
Pleasantville, NJ 08232

The Wall Street Journal
c/o Dow Jones Co. Inc.
P.O. Box 300
Educational Services Bureau
Princeton, NJ 08543

Times
P.O. Box 847
Trenton, NJ 08605

Burlington County Times
Route 130
Willingboro, NJ 08046

News Tribune
One Hoover Way
Woodbridge, NJ 07095

Gloucester County Times
309 S. Broad St.
Woodbury, NJ 08096

New Mexico

Albuquerque Journal/Tribune
7777 Jefferson NE
Albuquerque, NM 87109

Carlsbad Current-Argus
P.O. Box 1629
Carlsbad, NM 88221

Clovis News-Journal
P.O. Box 1689
Clovis, NM 88102

Farmington Daily Times
P.O. Box 450
Farmington, NM 87499

The Independent
P.O. Box 1210
Gallup, NM 87305

Hobbs Daily News-Sun
P.O. Box 860
Hobbs, NM 88241

Sun-News
P.O. Box 1749
Las Cruces, NM 88004

Las Vegas Optic
614 Lincoln
Las Vegas, NM 87701

Roswell Daily Record
P.O. Box 1897
Roswell, NM 88202

The New Mexican
P.O. Box 2048
Santa Fe, NM 87504

The Taos News
P.O. Box U
Taos, NM 87571

New York

The Times-Union
P.O. Box 15000
Albany, NY 12212

The Recorder
One Venner Rd.
Amsterdam, NY 12010

Citizen
25 Dill St.
Auburn, NY 13021

News
P.O. Box 870
Batavia, NY 14021

Press and Sun-Bulletin
P.O. Box 1270
Binghamton, NY 13902

The Buffalo News
1 News Plaza
Buffalo, NY 14203

The Daily Messenger
73 Buffalo St.
Canandaigua, NY 14424

Evening Observer
8-10 E. Second St.
Dunkirk, NY 14048

Star-Gazette
P.O. Box 285
Elmira, NY 14902

The Leader-Herald
8-10 E. Fulton St.
Gloversville, NY 12078

The Ithaca Journal
123-125 W. State St.
Ithaca, NY 14850

The Post-Journal
15 W. Second St.
Jamestown, NY 14701

Union-Sun and Journal
459-491 S. Transit St.
Lockport, NY 14094

Malone Telegram
136 E. Main St.
Malone, NY 12953

Times Herald-Record
40 Mulberry St.
Middletown, NY 10940

New York Daily News
220 E. 42nd St.
New York, NY 10017

New York Newsday
Grand Central Station
P.O. Box 4092
New York, NY 10163

The New York Times
229 W. 43rd St.
New York, NY 10036

Noticias Del Mundo
401 Fifth Ave.
New York, NY 10016

Press-Republican
170 Margaret St.
New York, NY 12901

Gazette
310 Niagara St.
Niagara Falls, NY 14303

USA Today
310 Niagara St.
Niagara Falls, NY 14303

Olean Times-Herald
639 Norton Dr.
Olean, NY 14760

The Daily Star
P.O. Box 250
Oneonta, NY 13820

Press-Republican
170 Margaret St.
Plattsburgh, NY 12901

Poughkeepsie Journal
85 Civic Center Plaza
Poughkeepsie, NY 12601

Democrat and Chronicle
55 Exchange St.
Rochester, NY 14614

Daily Sentinel
P.O. Box 471
Rome, NY 13440

The Saratogian
20 Lake Ave.
Saratoga Springs, NY 12866

Syracuse Herald-Journal
P.O. Box 4915
Syracuse, NY 13221

USA Today
1876 Niagara Blvd.
Tonowanda, NY 14150

Record
501 Broadway
Troy, NY 12180

Observer-Dispatch
221 Oriskany Plaza
Utica, NY 13501

Watertown Daily Times
260 Washington St.
Watertown, NY 13601

**New Rochelle Standard-Star/
   Rockland Journal-News**
1 Gannett Dr.
White Plains, NY 10604

North Carolina

Asheville Times
P.O. Box 2090
Asheville, NC 28802

Chapel Hill Newspaper
505 W. Franklin St.
Chapel Hill, NC 27516

The Charlotte Observer
600 S. Tryon St.
Charlotte, NC 28202

**Durham Morning Herald/The
   Durham Sun**
115 Market St.
Durham, NC 27701

Fayetteville Observer-Times
P.O. Box 849
Fayetteville, NC 28302

The Gaston Gazette
P.O. Box 1538
Gastonia, NC 28053

News-Argus
310 N. Berkeley Blvd.
Goldsboro, NC 27534

Greensboro News and Record
P.O. Box 20848
Greensboro, NC 27402

The Daily Reflector
209 Cotanche St.
Greenville, NC 27858

Henderson Daily Dispatch
304 S. Chestnut St.
Henderson, NC 27536

Daily News
P.O. Box 0196
Jacksonville, NC 28541

Free Press
2103 N. Queen St.
Kinston, NC 28501

The Dispatch
P.O. Box 908
Lexington, NC 27293

The Sun Journal
P.O. Box 1149
New Bern, NC 28563

Observer News-Enterprise
309 N. College Ave.
Newton, NC 28658

The News and Observer
P.O. Box 191
Raleigh, NC 27602

Salisbury Post
131 W. Innes St.
Salisbury, NC 28144

Record and Landmark
220 E. Broad St.
Statesville, NC 28677

The Daily Southerner
504 W. Wilson St.
Tarboro, NC 27886

The Times
512 Turner St.
Thomasville, NC 27360

Washington Daily News
217 N. Market St.
Washington, NC 27889

Wilmington Morning Star
P.O. Box 840
Wilmington, NC 28402

Wilson Daily Times
P.O. Box 2447
Wilson, NC 27894

Winston-Salem Journal
P.O. Box 3159
Winston-Salem, NC 27102

North Dakota

The Bismark Tribune
P.O. Box 1498
Bismarck, ND 58502

The Forum
P.O. Box 2020
Fargo, ND 58107

Grand Forks Herald
P.O. Box 6008
Grand Forks, ND 58206

Daily News
P.O. Box 970
Wahpeton, ND 58074

Ohio

Beacon Journal
44 E. Exchange St.
Akron, OH 44308

The Athens Messenger
Route 33 N and Johnson Rd.
Athens, OH 45701

The Daily Jeffersonian
831 Wheeling Ave.
Cambridge, OH 43725

Free Press-Standard
P.O. Box 37
Carrollton, OH 44615

Gazette
50 W. Main St.
Chillicothe, OH 45601

The Cincinnati Enquirer
617 Vine St.
Cincinnati, OH 45202

Plain Dealer
1801 Superior Ave. NE
Cleveland, OH 44114

The Columbus Dispatch
34 S. Third St.
Columbus, OH 43215

Dayton Daily News
Fourth and Ludlow Sts.
Dayton, OH 45402

Crescent News
Second and Perry Sts.
Defiance, OH 43512

Herald
405 N. Main St.
Delphos, OH 45833

The Evening Review
210 E. Fourth St.
East Liverpool, OH 43920

Chronicle-Telegram
P.O. Box 4010
Elyria, OH 44036

The Courier
P.O. Box 609
Findlay, OH 45839

The News-Messenger
1700 Cedar St.
Fremont, OH 43420

The Journal
1657 Broadway
Lorain, OH 44052

The Evening Independent
P.O. Box 809
Massillon, OH 44648

Middletown Journal
52 S. Broad St.
Middletown, OH 45044

Mount Vernon News
P.O. Box 791
Mount Vernon, OH 43050

The Advocate
25 W. Main St.
Newark, OH 43055

The Sidney Daily News
911 Vandemark Rd.
Sidney, OH 45365

Herald-Star
401 Herald Square
Steubenville, OH 43952

The Toledo Blade
541 Superior St.
Toledo, OH 43660

News
P.O. Box 100
Troy, OH 45373

The Tribune Chronicle
240 Franklin St. SE
Warren, OH 44483

The Daily Record
P.O. Drawer D
Wooster, OH 44691

The Vindicator
Vindicator Square
Youngstown, OH 44503

The Times Recorder
34 S. Fourth St.
Zanesville, OH 43701

Oklahoma

Examiner-Enterprise
P.O. Box 1278
Bartlesville, OK 74005

Claremore Daily Progress
315 W. Will Rogers Blvd.
Claremore, OK 74017

The Duncan Banner
1001 Elm St.
Duncan, OK 73533

The Edmond Evening Sun
123 S. Broadway
Edmond, OK 73034

News and Eagle
227 W. Broadway
Enid, OK 73701

Constitution/Press
P.O. Box 2069
Lawton, OK 73502

News-Record
14 First Ave. NW
Miami, OK 74354

Phoenix and Times-Democrat
214 Wall St.
Muskogee, OK 74401

The Norman Transcript
P.O. Drawer 1058
Norman, OK 73070

Oklahoman
P.O. Box 25125
Oklahoma City, OK 73125

The Shawnee News-Star
215 N. Bell St.
Shawnee, OK 74801

The Tulsa Tribune/Tulsa World
P.O. Box 1770
Tulsa, OK 74102

Oregon

Bulletin
1526 N.W. Hill St.
Bend, OR 97701

The World
350 Commercial St.
Coos Bay, OR 97420

The Register-Guard
975 High St.
Eugene, OR 97401

Herald and News
1301 Esplanade Ave.
Klamath Falls, OR 97601

The Observer
P.O. Box 3170
LaGrande, OR 97850

The Mail Tribune
P.O. Box 1108
Medford, OR 97501

Argus Observer
1160 W. Fourth St.
Ontario, OR 97914

Oregon City Enterprise-Courier
P.O. Box 471
Oregon City, OR 97045

East Oregonian
211 S.E. Buyers St.
Pendleton, OR 97801

The Oregonian
1320 S.W. Broadway
Portland, OR 97201

The Dalles Chronicle
P.O. Box 902
The Dalles, OR 97058

Pennsylvania

The Morning Call
P.O. Box 1260
Allentown, PA 18105

Press Enterprise
3185 Lackawanna Ave.
Bloomsburg, PA 17815

The Patriot-News Co.
P.O. Box 356
Camp Hill, PA 17001

Public Opinion
77 N. Third St.
Chambersburg, PA 17201

**The Daily Intelligencer/
The Record**
333 N. Broad St.
Doylestown, PA 18901

The Express
30 N. Fourth St.
Easton, PA 18042

News/Times/Times-News
Times Sq.
12th and Sassafrass Sts.
Erie, PA 16501

The Gettysburg Times
18 Carlisle St.
Gettysburg, PA 17325

Tribune-Review
Cabin Hill Dr.
Greensburg, PA 15601

The Patriot/The Evening News
P.O. Box 2265
Harrisburg, PA 17105

Gazette
899 Water St.
Indiana, PA 15701

Intelligencer Journal
P.O. Box 1328
Lancaster, PA 17603

The Reporter
307 Derstine Ave.
Lansdale, PA 19446

Bucks County Courier Times
8400 Route 13
Levittown, PA 19057

The Sentinel
Sixth and Summit Dr.
Lewistown, PA 17044

USA Today
35 Great Valley Pkwy.
Malvern, PA 19355

New Castle News
P.O. Box 60
New Castle, PA 16103

**Philadelphia Daily News/
Philadelphia Inquirer**
P.O. Box 8527
Philadelphia, PA 19101

The Evening Phoenix
225 Bridge St.
Phoenixville, PA 19460

Post-Gazette
P.O. Box 566
Pittsburgh, PA 15230

The Mercury
Hoover and King Sts.
Pottstown, PA 19464

Pottsville Republican
111 Mahantongo St.
Pottsville, PA 17901

Reading Eagle/Reading Times
P.O. Box 582
Reading, PA 19603

The Scranton Times
P.O. Box 3311
Scranton, PA 18505

Daily American
334 W. Main St.
Somerset, PA 15501

Centre Daily Times
P.O. Box 89
State College, PA 16804

Pocono Record
511 Lenox St.
Stroudsburg, PA 18360

The Daily Item
200 Market St.
Sunbury, PA 17801

Valley News Dispatch
P.O. Box 311
Tarentum, PA 15084

The Titusville Herald
P.O. Box 328
Titusville, PA 16354

Herald-Standard
8-18 E. Church St.
Uniontown, PA 15401

The Times Leader
15 N. Main St.
Wilkes-Barre, PA 18702

Rhode Island

Journal-Bulletin
75 Fountain St.
Providence, RI 02903

South Carolina

Anderson Independent-Mail
P.O. Box 2507
Anderson, SC 29622

The News and Courier/
The Evening Post
134 Columbus St.
Charleston, SC 29403

The State
P.O. Box 1333
Columbia, SC 29202

The Greenville News/
Greenville Piedmont
P.O. Box 1688
Greenville, SC 29602

The Sun News
P.O. Box 406
Myrtle Beach, SC 29578

Evening Post
6296 Rivers Ave.
Suite 100
North Charleston, SC 29418

The Herald
P.O. Box 11707
Rock Hill, SC 29731

Herald-Journal
P.O. Box 1657
Spartansburg, SC 29304

South Dakota

Aberdeen American News
P.O. Box 4430
Aberdeen, SD 57402

The Brookings Daily Register
P.O. Box 177
Brookings, SD 57006

Huron Daily Plainsman
49 Third St. SE
Huron, SD 57350

The Mobridge Tribune
111 W. Third St.
Mobridge, SD 57601

Rapid City Journal
P.O. Box 450
Rapid City, SD 57709

Argus Leader
P.O. Box 5034
Sioux Falls, SD 57117

Public Opinion
120 Third Ave. NW
Watertown, SD 57201

Tennessee

Times
P.O. Box 1447
Chattanooga, TN 37401

The Leaf-Chronicle
P.O. Box 829
Clarksville, TN 37041

The Daily Herald
1115 S. Main St.
Columbia, TN 38401

Herald-Citizen
P.O. Box 2729
Cookeville, TN 38502

The Greeneville Sun
121 W. Summer St.
Greeneville, TN 37743

The Jackson Sun
P.O. Box 1059
Jackson, TN 38302

Johnson City Press
P.O. Box 1717
Johnson City, TN 37605

Kingsport Times-News
310 E. Sullivan
Kingsport, TN 37660

Knoxville News-Sentinel
P.O. Box 59038
Knoxville, TN 37950

The Lebanon Democrat
402 N. Cumberland St.
Lebanon, TN 37087

The Commercial Appeal
495 Union Ave.
Memphis, TN 38103

Citizen Tribune
P.O. Box 625
Morristown, TN 37815

Nashville Banner/The Tennessean
1100 Broadway St.
Nashville, TN 37203

USA Today
730 Freelands Station Rd.
Nashville, TN 37228

The Oak Ridger
P.O. Box 3446
Oak Ridge, TN 37831

Monroe County Advocate
P.O. Box 389
Sweetwater, TN 37874

Union City Daily Messenger
613 E. Jackson St.
Union City, TN 38261

Texas

Reporter-News
P.O. Box 30
Abilene, TX 79604

Amarillo Globe-Times/Amarillo Daily News
P.O. Box 2091
Amarillo, TX 79105

Athens Daily Review
201 S. Prairieville St.
Athens, TX 75751

Austin American-Statesman
P.O. Box 670
Austin, TX 78767

Beaumont Enterprise
P.O. Box 3071
Beaumont, TX 77704

Bryan-College Station Eagle
P.O. Box 3000
Bryan, TX 77805

Caller-Times
P.O. Box 9136
Corpus Christi, TX 78469

Corsicana Daily Sun
405 E. Collin
Corsicana, TX 75110

The Dallas Morning News
P.O. Box 655237
Dallas, TX 75265

Dallas Times Herald
1101 Pacific Ave.
Dallas, TX 75202

The Denison Herald
331 W. Woodard
Denison, TX 75020

Denton Record-Chronicle
P.O. Box 369
Denton, TX 76202

Herald-Post/Times
401 Mills Ave.
El Paso, TX 79901

Fort Worth Star-Telegram
P.O. Box 1870
Fort Worth, TX 76101

The Galveston Daily News
P.O. Box 628
Galveston, TX 77553

Greenville Herald Banner
2305 King St.
Greenville, TX 75401

Valley Star
P.O. Box 511
Harlingen, TX 78551

Houston Chronicle
801 Texas St.
Houston, TX 77002

Post
4747 Southwest Freeway
Houston, TX 77072

The Huntsville Item
P.O. Box 539
Huntsville, TX 77342

Kerrville Daily Times
P.O. Box 1428
Kerrville, TX 78029

Killeen Daily Herald
1809 Florence Rd.
Killeen, TX 76541

The Laredo News
2301 Saunders St.
Laredo, TX 78041

**Longview Morning
   Journal/News**
320 E. Methvin St.
Longview, TX 75601

Lubbock Avalanche-Journal
P.O. Box 491
Lubbock, TX 79408

The Lufkin Daily News
P.O. Box 1089
Lufkin, TX 75902

Marshall News Messenger
P.O. Box 730
Marshall, TX 75671

The Monitor
P.O. Box 760
McAllen, TX 78502

American
P.O. Box 2952
Odessa, TX 79760

Palestine Herald-Press
P.O. Box 379
Palestine, TX 75802

News
138 Lamar Ave.
Paris, TX 75460

Port Arthur News
P.O. Box 789
Port Arthur, TX 77641

San Angelo Standard-Times
34 W. Harris Ave.
San Angelo, TX 76903

Express-News
P.O. Box 2171
San Antonio, TX 78297

San Antonio Light
P.O. Box 161
San Antonio, TX 78291

The Seguin Gazette-Enterprise
P.O. Box 1200
Seguin, TX 78156

Temple Daily Telegram
P.O. Box 6114
Temple, TX 76503

Texarkana Gazette
P.O. Box 621
Texarkana, TX 75504

**Tyler Morning Telegraph/
   Courier-Times**
P.O. Box 2030
Tyler, TX 75710

Waco Tribune-Herald
P.O. Box 2588
Waco, TX 76702

Times Record News
P.O. Box 120
Wichita Falls, TX 76307

Utah

The Standard-Examiner
P.O. Box 951
Ogden, UT 84402

Deseret News
P.O. Box 1257
Salt Lake City, UT 84110

Tribune
P.O. Box 867
Salt Lake City, UT 84110

Vermont

The Burlington Free Press
191 College St.
Burlington, VT 05401

Rutland Daily Herald
27 Wales St.
Rutland, VT 05701

Virginia

**The Caroline Progress/Caroline
    Express**
P.O. Box 69
Bowling Green, VA 22427

**Herald-Courier/Virginia-
    Tennessean**
320 Morrison Blvd.
Bristol, VA 24201

Virginia Review
343 Monroe Ave.
Covington, VA 24426

Danville Register and Bee
700 Monument St.
Danville, VA 24540

**Gloucester-Matthews
    Gazette-Journal**
P.O. Box J
Gloucester, VA 23061

Daily News-Record
213 S. Liberty St.
Harrisonburg, VA 22801

The Hopewell News
516 E. Randolph Rd.
Hopewell, VA 23860

The News and Daily Advance
P.O. Box 10129
Lynchburg, VA 24506

**The Daily Press/
    The Times-Herald**
P.O. Box 746
Newport News, VA 23607

The Virginian-Pilot/Ledger Star
150 W. Brambleton Ave.
Norfolk, VA 23510

**Richmond Times-Dispatch/
    The Richmond News Leader**
P.O. Box C-32333
Richmond, VA 23261

Roanoke Times and World News
201-209 Campbell Ave. SW
Roanoke, VA 24011

The Journal Newspapers
6883 Commercial Dr.
Springfield, VA 22151

USA Today
7425 Boston Blvd.
Springfield, VA 22153

The Fauquier Times-Democrat
P.O. Box 631
Warrenton, VA 22186

Washington

The Bellingham Herald
1155 N. State St.
Bellingham, WA 98225

The Sun
545 Fifth St.
Bremerton, WA 98310

The Daily Chronicle
321 N. Pearl
Centralia, WA 98531

Daily Record
Fourth and Main Sts.
Ellensburg, WA 98926

The Herald
P.O. Box 930
Everett, WA 98206

Valley Daily News
P.O. Box 130
Kent, WA 98035

The Daily News
P.O. Box 189
Longview, WA 98632

Skagit Valley Herald
1000 E. College Way
Mt. Vernon, WA 98273

The Olympian
P.O. Box 407
Olympia, WA 98507

Peninsula Daily News
305 W. First St.
Port Angeles, WA 98362

The Seattle Times
P.O. Box 70
Seattle, WA 98111

The Spokesman-Review/
   Spokane Chronicle
P.O. Box 2160
Spokane, WA 99210

The Morning News Tribune
P.O. Box 11000
Tacoma, WA 98411

The Columbian
P.O. Box 180
Vancouver, WA 98666

Walla Walla Union-Bulletin
First and Poplar Sts.
Walla Walla, WA 99362

The Wenatchee World
14 N. Mission St.
Wenatchee, WA 98801

Yakima Herald-Republic
P.O. Box 9668
Yakima, WA 98909

West Virginia

Register/Herald
P.O. Boxes P and R
Beckley, WV 25802

Telegraph
928 Bluefield Ave.
Bluefield, WV 24701

Charleston Gazette/Charleston Daily Mail
1001 Virginia St. E
Charleston, WV 25301

The Herald-Dispatch
P.O. Box 2017
Huntington, WV 25720

Journal
207 W. King St.
Martinsburg, WV 25401

Dominion Post
Greer Bldg.
Route 7, Sabraton
Morgantown, WV 26505

The Parkersburg News/Sentinel
519 Juliana St.
Parkersburg, WV 26101

The Parsons Advocate
212 Main St.
Parsons, WV 26287

Weirton Daily Times
114 Lee Ave.
Weirton, WV 26062

Wisconsin

Antigo Daily Journal
612 Superior St.
Antigo, WI 54409

The Post-Crescent
P.O. Box 59
Appleton, WI 54912

The Daily Press
122 W. Third St.
Ashland, WI 54806

Baraboo News Republic
219 First St.
Baraboo, WI 53913

Daily Citizen
805 Park Ave.
Beaver Dam, WI 53916

News
149 State St.
Beloit, WI 53511

Burlington Standard Press
P.O. Box 437
Burlington, WI 53105

Herald-Telegram
321 Frenette Dr.
Chippewa Falls, WI 54729

Leader-Telegram
P.O. Box 570
Eau Claire, WI 54702

The Reporter
33 W. Second St.
Fond du Lac, WI 54935

Jefferson County Union
28 W. Milwaukee Ave.
Fort Atkinson, WI 53538

Green Bay Press-Gazette
P.O. Box 19430
Green Bay, WI 54307

The Janesville Gazette
One S. Parker Dr.
Janesville, WI 53545

Kenosha News
P.O. Box 190
Kenosha, WI 53141

La Crosse Tribune
401 N. Third St.
La Crosse, WI 54601

**Wisconsin State Journal/
The Capital Times**
1901 Fish Hatchery Rd.
Madison, WI 53713

Herald-Times Reporter
902 Franklin
Manitowoc, WI 54220

Marinette Eagle-Star
1809 Dunlap Ave.
Marinette, WI 54143

Marshfield News-Herald
111 W. Third St.
Marshfield, WI 54449

**The Milwaukee Journal/
Milwaukee Sentinel**
333 W. State St.
Milwaukee, WI 53203

Times
1065 Fourth Ave. W
Monroe, WI 53566

Oconomowoc Enterprise
212 E. Wisconsin Ave.
Oconomowoc, WI 53066

Northwestern
P.O. Box 2926
Oshkosh, WI 54903

Ozaukee Press
125 E. Main St.
Port Washington, WI 53074

Daily Register
309 DeWitt St.
Portage, WI 53901

The Journal Times
212 Fourth St.
Racine, WI 53403

Rhinelander Daily News
314 Courtney St.
Rhinelander, WI 54501

Shawano Evening Leader
1464 E. Green Bay St.
Shawano, WI 54166

The Sheboygan Press
P.O. Box 358
Sheboygan, WI 53082

Journal
1200 Third St.
Stevens Point, WI 54481

The Evening Telegram
1226 Ogden Ave.
Superior, WI 54836

Watertown Daily Times
115 W. Main St.
Watertown, WI 53094

Waukesha County Freeman
P.O. Box 7
Waukesha, WI 53187

Wausau Daily Herald
800 Scott St.
Wausau, WI 54401

The Daily Tribune
220 First Ave. S
Wisconsin Rapids, WI 54494

Wyoming

Casper Star-Tribune
170 Star Ln.
Casper, WY 82604

The Sheridan Press
144 Grinnell
Sheridan, WY 82801

Newspapers from Other Countries

Two major resources are helpful when you or your students are selecting newspapers from cities outside the United States, in addition to the newspapers listed below. Both *Editor and Publisher International Yearbook* and *Europa World Yearbook* should be available in your school library or your local public library.

Many teachers will find students in their classrooms who have access to newspapers from around the world. These can be valuable resources because many students who have come here from other countries are pleased to share a part of their cultural heritage with their classmates.

Argentina

Clarín
Piedras 1743
Third Floor
1140 Buenos Aires

Australia

Queensland Newspapers Party Ltd.
P.O. Box 130
Brisbane, Australia 4001

The Examiner Newspaper Party Ltd.
P.O. Box 99A
Launceston, Tasmania 7250

Austria

Ambassade de France
Bureau de l'Action Linguistique
Palais Clam Gallas
Wahringerstrasse 32, A-1090
    WIEN

Belgium

A.P.E.D.A.C.
B-6280 Gerpinnes

Gazet van Antwerpen
2 Katwilgweg
B-2050 Antwerpen

Het Belang van Limburg
10 Herckenrodesingel
B-3500 Hasselt

Le Soir
21 Place de Louvain
B-1000 Bruxelles

Actualquarto Belgique
501/33 Rue Belle Jardiniere
4300 Angleur

Canada

Calgary Herald
P.O. Box 2400
Station M
Calgary, Alberta T2P 0W8

The Edmonton Journal
10006 101st St.
Edmonton, Alberta T5J 2S6

The Medicine Hat News
P.O. Box 10
Medicine Hat, Alberta T1A 7E6

The Kamloops News
106-63 W. Victoria St.
Kamloops, British Columbia
   V2C 6J6

The Citizen
P.O. Box 5700
Prince George, British Columbia
   V2L 5K9

**The Province/The Vancouver
   Sun**
2250 Granville St.
Vancouver, British Columbia
   V6H 3G2

The Sun
2250 Granville St.
Vancouver, British Columbia
   V6H 3G2

Brandon Sun
501 Rosser Ave.
Brandon, Manitoba R7A 5Z6

The Gleaner
P.O. Box 3370
Fredericton, New Brunswick
   E3B 5A2

The Times-Transcript
939 Main St.
P.O. Box 1001
Moncton, New Brunswick E1C 8P3

**The New Brunswick Telegraph-
   Journal/Times-Globe**
P.O. Box 2350
Saint John, New Brunswick
   E2L 3V8

The Evening Telegram
P.O. Box 5970
St. John's, Newfoundland
   A1C 5X7

**The Chronicle Herald/The
   Mail-Star**
P.O. Box 610
Halifax, Nova Scotia B3J 2T2

The Brantford Expositor
53 Dalhousie St.
Brantford, Ontario N3T 5S8

**The Brockville Recorder and
   Times**
23 King St. W
Brockville, Ontario K6V 5T8

Cobourg Daily Star
P.O. Box 400
Cobourg, Ontario K9A 4L1

The Durham Chronicle
P.O. Box 230
Durham, Ontario NOG 1RO

The Daily Mercury
8-14 Macdonell St.
Guelph, Ontario N1H 6P7

The Hamilton Spectator
P.O. Box 300
Hamilton, Ontario L8N 3G3

Whig-Standard
306 King St. E
Kingston, Ontario K7L 4Z7

Kitchener-Waterloo Record
225 Fairway Rd.
Kitchener, Ontario N2G 4E5

The London Free Press
P.O. Box 2280
London, Ontario N6A 4G1

The North Bay Nugget
P.O. Box 570
North Bay, Ontario P1B 8J6

The Ottawa Citizen
P.O. Box 5020
Ottawa, Ontario K2C 3M4

Le Droit
375 Rideau St.
Ottawa, Ontario K1N 5Y7

The Standard
17 Queen St.
St. Catharines, Ontario L2R 5G5

The Sault Star
P.O. Box 460
Sault Ste. Marie, Ontario P6A 5M5

The Simcoe Reformer
P.O. Box 370
Simcoe, Ontario N3Y 4L2

The Beacon Herald
108 Ontario St.
Stratford, Ontario N5A 6T6

Times News/Chronicle Journal
75 S. Cumberland St.
Thunder Bay, Ontario P7B 1A3

The Canadian Press
36 King St. E
Toronto, Ontario M5C 2L9

CDNPA
890 Yonge St.
Suite 1100
Toronto, Ontario M4W 3P4

Thomson Newspapers
65 Queen St. W
Toronto, Ontario M5H 2M5

The Toronto Star
1 Yonge St.
Toronto, Ontario M5E 1E6

The Toronto Sun
333 King St. E
Toronto, Ontario M5A 3X5

Cord Weekly
Wilfrid Laurier University
75 University Ave. West
Waterloo, Ontario N2L 3C5

The Windsor Star
167 Ferry St.
Windsor, Ontario N9A 4M5

**The Guardian/The Evening
   Patriot**
165 Prince St.
Charlottetown, Prince Edward
   Island C1A 4R7

La Voix de l'Est
76 Dufferin St.
Granby, Quebec J2G 9L4

The Gazette
250 St. Antoine St. W
Montreal, Quebec H2Y 3R7

Quebec Dalles
c/o **La Presse**
7 Rue Saint-Jacques
Montreal, Quebec H2Y 1K9

Le Soleil
390 Rue St. Vallier E
Quebec City, Quebec G1K 7J6

The Record
2850 Delorme St.
Sherbrooke, Quebec J1K 1A1

La Tribune
1950 Roy St.
Sherbrooke, Quebec J1K 2X8

Le Nouvelliste
1850 Rue Bellefeuille
Trois Rivieres, Quebec G9A 5J6

The Leader-Post
P.O. Box 2020
Regina, Saskatchewan S4P 3G4

Star-Phoenix
204 Fifth Ave. N
Saskatoon, Saskatchewan S7K 2P1

Denmark

Danske Daglbades Forening
Skindergrade 7
DK-1159 Copenhagen

Mogeltonder
Stroedet 16
DK-6270 Tonder

Finland

**Finnish Newspaper Publishers
   Association**
Kalevankatu 4
SF-00100 Helsinki

France

C.L.E.M.I.
4/6 Passage Louis Philippe
F-75011 Paris

C.D.I.L.
58 Rue des Caillots
F-93100 Montreuil

Rectorat
Place Lucien Paye
F-13621 Aix en Provence Cedex

Le Bien Public
7 Boulevard Chanoine Kir
F-21015 Dijon Cedex

L'Alsace
25 Avenue du Président Kennedy
F-68053 Mulhouse

La Montagne
28 Rue Morel Ladeuil
F-63003 Clermont-Ferrand

Journal du Centre
3 Rue du Chemin de Fer
F-58001 Nevers Cedex

I.U.T.
F-72000 Le Mans

F.A.D.B.E.N.
25 Rue F. Berat
F-76140 Petit Quevilly

Courrier de l'Ouest
Boulevard Albert Blanchoin
BP 728
F-49005 Angers Cedex

A.P.M.E.P.
68 Rue des Gravilliers
F-75003 Paris

Sud-Ouest
8 Rue de Cheverus
F-33003 Bordeaux Cedex

Dépêche du Midi
Sce Marketing
Avenue Jean-Baylet
F-31095 Toulouse

**Ministerre de l'Education
   Nationale**
Service de Presse
110 Rue de Grenelle
F-75700 Paris

O.F.U.P.
70 Allee de la Robertsau
F-67000 Strasbourg

A.R.P.E.J.
17 Place des Etats-Unis
F-75116 Paris

A.F.E.F.
101 Boulevard Raspail
F-75006 Paris

**La Nouvelle République du
   Centre-Ouest**
232 Avenue de Grammont
F-37048 Tours Cedex

Dernières Nouvelles d'Alsace
17/21 Rue de la Nuée Bleue
F-67000 Strasbourg

C.R.E.L.E.F.
30 Rue Megevant
F-25030 Besancon

La Voix du Nord
8 Place de Gaulle
F-59023 Lille Cedex

Le Courrier Picard
14 Rue Alphonse Paillat
F-80010 Amines Cedex

A.D.P. 59
23 Rue Malus
F-59000 Lille

Ouest France
B.P. 586
F-35012 Rennes Cedex

Van Matin
8 Rue Truget
F-83100 Toulon

Le Provencal
248 Avenue Roger Salengro
F-13316 Marseille Cedex 15

Phosphore
3 Rue Bayard
F-75008 Paris

L'Est Republicain
5 bis Avenue Foch
F-54042 Nancy Cedex

La Republique des Pyrenees
6/8 Rue Despourrins
F-64000 Pau

La Dauphine Libere
Les Iles Cordees
F-38113 Veurey Voroize

Le Telegramme de Brest
Rue Antaole le Braz
F-29205 Morlaix Cedex

A.P.E.
100 Rue Reaumur
F-75002 Paris

A.P.H.G.
B.P. 49
F-75060 Paris Cedex 2

A.P.A.P.
9 Rue Vesale
F-75005 Paris

FIEJ
6 Rue du Fanbourg Poisonniere
Paris 75010

Great Britain

Telegraph and Argus
Hall Ings, Bradford, W. Yorks
  BD1 1JR

Leicester Mercury
St. George St.
Leicester LE1 9FQ

Newspaper Society
Bloomsbury House
74-77 Great Russell St.
London, WC16 3PA

India

The Echo
Pennywell Industrial Estate
Sunderland, India SR4 9ER

Ireland

**Directeur Adjoint due Project
  Authentik**
University
Dublin 2

The Irish Times
11/15 d'Olier St.
Dublin 2

Italy

Corriere della Sera
Via Solferino 28
I-20100 Milano

La Repubblica
Piazza Indipendenza 11b
I-00185 Roma

Jamaica

Daily Gleaner
7 North St.
P.O. Box 40
Kingston, Jamaica

Japan

Nihon Shimbun Kyokal
2-2-1, Uchisaiwaicho
Chiyoda-ku, Tokyo, Japan 100

Hokkaido Shimbun
6, 3-chome, Odori-Nishi,
  Chuo-ku
Sapporo, Hokkaido, Japan 060

Malaysia

New Straits Times
31 Jalan Riong
59100 Kuala Lumpur, Malaysia

Mexico

El Diario
González 2409
Apdo 101
88000 Nuevo Laredo, Mexico

El Porvenir
Galeana Sur 344
Apdo 218
64000 Monterrey, Nuevo León,
    Mexico

Netherlands

Stichiting Krant in de Klas
Joh. Vermeerstraat 14
NL-1071 DR Amsterdam

Norway

**Norwegian Newspapers
    Publishers Association**
Norske Advisers Landsorbund
Storgt. 32
N-0184 Oslo 1

Singapore

The Straits Times
390 Kim Seng Rd.
Singapore 0923

Spain

Generalitat de Catalunya
Portaferrissa 1
E-08002 Barcelona

Bartolome Rotger Amengual
Directeur General d'Education
Spain

Miguel Duran Pastor
Educator
Spain

Sweden

Malmotidningarnas Skoltjanst
Box 125
S-201 21 Malmö

Tidningarnas Skoltjanst
Wennerbergsgatan 10
S-105 15 Stockholm

Switzerland

1 Chemin des Primevères
CH-1258 Perly Certoux
Genève

West Indies

**Trinidad Express Newspapers,
    Ltd.**
35 Independence Square
Port of Spain
Trinidad and Tobago

INDEX